SIMPLY VIBRANT

SIMPLY VIBRANT

ALL-DAY VEGETARIAN RECIPES FOR COLORFUL PLANT-BASED COOKING

ANYA KASSOFF
photography by Masha Davydova

ROOST
Boulder
2018

Roost Books
An imprint of Shambhala Publications, Inc.
4720 Walnut Street
Boulder, Colorado 80301
roostbooks.com

9 8 7 6 5 4 3 2 1

First Edition
Printed in the United States of America

♾ This edition is printed on acid-free paper that meets the American National Standards Institute Z39.48 Standard.
♻ Shambhala Publications makes every effort to print on recycled paper. For more information please visit www.shambhala.com.

Distributed in the United States by Penguin Random House LLC
and in Canada by Random House of Canada Ltd

Library of Congress Cataloging-in-Publication Data
Names: Kassoff, Anya, author.
Title: Simply vibrant: all-day vegetarian recipes for colorful plant-based cooking / Anya Kassoff; photography by Masha Davydova.
Description: First edition. | Boulder: Roost, 2018. | Includes index.
Identifiers: LCCN 2016057919 | ISBN 9781611803846 (hardcover: alk. paper)
Subjects: LCSH: Vegetarian cooking. | Seasonal cooking. | LCGFT: Cookbooks.
Classification: LCC TX837 .K2569 2018 | DDC 641.5/636—dc23 LC record available at https://lccn.loc.gov/2016057919

To our mother and grandmother,
Elena Vladimirovna Golub,
for always feeding us well, and
so much more

CONTENTS

Introduction | *1*

EATING WITH THE SEASONS • *5* PANTRY • *7*
EQUIPMENT • *15*

1. MORNING PORRIDGES AND PANCAKES *21*
2. SALADS AND BOWLS *43*
3. WRAPS AND ROLLS *85*
4. SOUPS AND STEWS *115*
5. RISOTTO, PAELLA, AND PILAF *151*
6. NOODLES, PASTA, AND PIZZA *179*
7. FRITTERS AND VEGGIE BURGERS *217*
8. JUST VEGGIES *241*
9. SWEETS FOR EVERY SEASON *263*
10. BASICS AND SAUCES *295*

Acknowledgments | *318*

Preferred Brands | *319*

Index | *320*

INTRODUCTION

MY GRANDFATHER WAS A SHOEMAKER. His name was Aleksei Gerasimovich Golub, and he was born in the North Caucasus before the Russian Revolution of 1917. He worked for the town theater, crafting custom shoes to go with the actors' performance costumes. He was a master of his work, with an entrepreneur's temperament and a way with words, so much so that the town folk nicknamed him *the aristocrat*.

My grandfather carved his own wooden shoe lasts, based on each actor's foot size and shape. The shoes he made ranged from basic leather boots to ones with bows and feathers, depending on the nature of the upcoming play. As a child, I was able to visit him in his giant, sun-drenched studio on the top floor of the theater, which had big windows that offered a spectacular view of the city. There were beastly metal machines for stitching and stretching, stacks of skins, and rows of wooden shoe lasts, all enveloped by the mysteriously pleasant smell of shoe leather. Next door was the costume studio, with rainbows of tulle and taffeta dispensed from the ceiling. I remember feeling quite proud and special when entering the theater through the employee entrance and announcing to the guard that I was there to visit Aleksei Gerasimovich, my grandfather.

He had a particular story that became folklore in our family, from being told time and time again at family gatherings to almost anyone who would listen. My grandfather was a charming man, with such a magnetic air about him that I welcomed his retelling of the story, discovering something new in it every time.

His story was about a stifling summer morning, when the night brought nearly no relief from the heat, and the giant yellow sun was once again crawling up to its almighty position in the sky. My grandfather was making his way through the streets of Blagodatny on his way to work. There was a heavy pressure in his forehead, and the unpleasant taste that lingered on his tongue reminded him of the previous night's very festive events. Aleksei Gerasimovich swore to himself to never celebrate in this manner again, at least not during the work week. Besides this new commitment, the only other thought in his foggy mind was of an overwhelming thirst for a glass of fresh milk, chilled in a cellar. At this point in the story, he loved pointing out how clearly he imagined it—an impressive vessel, the exterior dotted with plump droplets of condensation, filled to the brim with a cold and flavorful, bright-white liquid. The milk would surely ease the hangover and help him cope with the hot day ahead.

Aleksei Gerasimovich was passing the house of a friend, Pyotr Vasilevich, when it occurred to him that his friend kept a cow. If he dropped by, Pyotr Vasilevich, a very hospitable man, would likely offer his guest some milk. The thirst had gotten so overwhelming that Aleksei Gerasimovich turned back, deciding to go ahead and pay his friend a visit.

The head of the household himself, rather awake and jolly, opened the door. Aleksei Gerasimovich remembered being hit with familiar scents of a wholesome breakfast—millet porridge and warm bread. After the usual greetings, excited ones on Pyotr Vasilevich's end and confused ones on my grandfather's, who was finding it difficult to tie together a coherent sentence, Aleksei Gerasimovich was invited to join the family for breakfast. He declined to come in once and then again, trying to make small talk and feeling increasingly more foolish and regretful of putting himself in this situation. Pyotr Vasilevich, at first perplexed by Aleksei Gerasimovich's strange behavior, later sensed that his friend was unwell and, right as my grandfather was leaving, thought it helpful to offer him a glass of fresh milk straight from an iced pail in the cellar. There it was—the ideal offer to complete Aleksei Gerasimovich's questionable morning agenda. My grandfather of course declined the first offer to show courtesy, as was customary, expecting Pyotr Vasilevich to insist. Insist he did, but Aleksei Gerasimovich declined again out of a stubborn, Slavic politeness that often overcame him, determined to accept the third offer. Another offer never came, Pyotr Vasilevich said goodbye, and Aleksei Gerasimovich was once again on his way, with a dry throat and a heart heavy with regret.

This event took place in the USSR during the 1930s, in a village at the foothills of Caucasus. It was a time of collectivization, which was a communist system of combining privately owned farms into joined, government-controlled farming collectives. Owning a cow was considered a luxury, and very few families did, as most cattle was confiscated for the cause. Milk came to be a rare, sought-after product.

My grandfather never explained why he told his story so persistently. Regret was of course his driving force, but for some reason this very small thing haunted him for the rest of his life, and he found that to be quite humorous. Perhaps it stuck with him because of how close he came to satisfying his desire. It was right there, ripe and at his fingertips, but he pulled away instead of simply reaching out and grabbing it.

What I took away from my grandfather's account is that chances are there to be taken and opportunities don't come around every day, so it makes great sense to take hold of them with a strong grip. I think about this moral of missed chance often, and have used it as a guiding force in my own life. It helps me see the big picture, and I often ask myself whether I'm accepting my glass of milk or letting it go. When it comes to my professional life, which today involves cooking, coming up with recipes, and dreaming about food, I've found one very straightforward way of fulfilling the moral of my grandfather's story: cooking with the seasons. Nature presents us with a beautiful assortment of ingredients every spring, summer, autumn, and winter, and welcoming them into our lives might be one of the simplest and most graceful ways to seize an opportunity. So much has already been said on the subject of seasonality, but the bottom line is that it works beautifully, and eating according to the seasons will improve your life. It is common sense, but the kind of common sense that we've been losing to today's way of life that often prizes convenience and speed.

At its core, the idea of cooking seasonally goes hand in hand with practicality. When it comes to seasonal produce, utilizing the most available resources leads to easier, tastier, and more affordable meals. When a vegetable springs up because Earth came to a perfect tilt relative to the sun to allow it to grow, it is guaranteed to be more abundant and flavorful than anything grown with force

Aleksei Gerasimovich and my grandmother, Anna Fyodorovna, on their wedding day in 1928, sixteen and fifteen years old, respectively.

and under lights, no matter how advanced our agriculture becomes. Little can speak of spring better than green peas, their curling shoots reaching up to the warming sun, their newborn orbs tender and emerald. In the summer, there are many choices, but I always think of berries, which capture the sun's glow in their jammy juiciness, studding our gardens with bright and dusky colors. Fall is for squash, all ochre, amber, and golden, still growing above ground but with tougher skin and closer to the bottom, cozied up with the earth. And if I was ever tasked with explaining winter to someone who has never seen it, I would show them a knobby celeriac or a pale parsnip, growing downward and in the dark, away from the frosty air and toward a different source of warmth, blanketed by soil. There are millions of such examples for every season, and even though our minds house memories of them from generations past, sometimes we need a gentle reminder.

My journey as a cook has been parallel to my life overall—as I grow and mature, so does my style in the kitchen. Years of cooking for my family, including two children, and later for an audience (a big bow to all Golubka Kitchen readers), combined with an inherited passion for food, have allowed me to develop a sort of sixth sense for it all. I first discovered the concept of baker's intuition when I set out to bake bread with techniques from the *Tartine Bread* cookbook, using strictly wild yeast to create a sourdough starter. Besides learning much about patience, I discovered that no matter how closely I followed the instructions, my first, second, and even third loaf of bread would not turn out anywhere near perfect. Each loaf did inevitably get fuller and more handsome, and by my fifth try, I started to recognize when things were going astray in the process and was able to catch them, resulting in better bread. This kind of intuitive approach to cooking is what I aim to explore in this book.

I will walk with you through produce aisles and farmers' markets during each of our four seasons, with ideas for using the ingredients in the most flavorful way. I will explore the possibilities of nose-to-tail cooking (albeit only the noses and tails of plants), giving a chance to those unwanted stalks, stems, rinds, and ends. I will take into account the culinary wisdom learned from common everyday recipes cooked around the world, which is echoed in the structure of this book. Each chapter groups together dishes with a similar framework or method—for example, Wraps and Rolls includes everything from enchiladas and gyros to summer rolls and vegetable sushi.

One thing I took away from writing my first cookbook, *The Vibrant Table*, is that formal recipes can often lead to the dead end of making a dish once and then never again. I still consider recipe writing a true art, but a dish that allows its ingredients to be used in other meals carries a special sort of elegance. The most basic example of this kind of reuse is the act of making broth, which produces at least two things—what was boiled and what it was boiled in—both of which can be used for multiple meals. To explore this further, I've scattered some ideas throughout the chapters on the subject of utilizing the parts of produce that are usually thrown away. When writing these recipes, much time was spent on making each one nourishing and approachable, with the use of attainable, whole food components and compact ingredients lists. Ultimately, it's all about putting breakfast, lunch, and dinner on the table with a bit of elegance, and interweaving ideas of food as medicine, food as nourishment, and food as pleasure.

It's worth mentioning that I like to take a lighter, mostly plant-based approach to cooking, avoiding the heavy-handed use of cheese, eggs, flours, and sugar and depending more on fresh herbs and spices. Although most recipes in this book are vegan, I sometimes call for ghee, eggs, or cheese in a few of them, whether for flavor or for texture. In many cases, however, those ingredients are optional and can be replaced with a plant-based alternative. In the end, this plant-centered yet flexible way of choosing ingredients and preparing food makes me feel my best, and I honestly believe that I'm not compromising any flavor. It's my intent and dream that my reader will pick up what looks ripest and most reflective of the weather from their produce vendor and will then be able to find a delicious way to prepare it within the index of this book. I hope that the following recipes will stay with you and become yours through your very own, ever-evolving cook's intuition.

Eating with the Seasons

Many of us are familiar with the situation of bypassing stands of seemingly alien produce at the market or store, simply because we wouldn't know how to cook with it. When I first moved to the United States from Russia, I was in that boat, stuck with buying only the vegetables I was comfortable with, keeping away from delicious things like asparagus, avocados, and leafy greens for years. It is only now that I know how much I was missing.

Plants are at the heart of this book, and their freshness and intensity of flavor can make or break a dish. Here, I present you with an approximate list of produce to take advantage of in any given season. Use it as a tool to awaken inspiration when planning a meal, and refer to the index of this book to find recipes with any of the listed ingredients. Seasonal produce may overlap at the junction of two seasons, thus a fig is as much a late summer fruit as it is an early fall one. Some of the vegetables and fruit listed may be more obvious and frequently used, while others will hopefully make their way to your kitchen for the first time, and perhaps even become new staples. Strive to buy organic produce and support local farmers whenever possible—investing in good ingredients is as important to the flavor of your dishes as it is to the health of our planet and society.

Spring / Summer

- blackberries
- blueberries
- broccoli
- cabbage
- cauliflower
- cherries
- corn
- cucumbers
- fava beans
- fennel
- green beans
- lemons
- lettuce
- limes
- mangoes
- melons
- new potatoes
- papayas
- peaches
- peas
- pineapple
- radishes
- rhubarb
- spinach
- strawberries
- Swiss chard
- watermelon
- zucchini and summer squash

Summer / Fall

- apples
- beets
- bell peppers
- cabbage
- carrots
- celery
- Concord, Thomcord, and other table grapes
- eggplant
- figs
- kale
- kohlrabi
- lettuce
- plums
- spinach
- Swiss chard
- tomatoes

Fall / Winter

- apples
- beets
- Brussels sprouts
- cabbage
- cauliflower
- celery root
- collard greens
- cranberries
- daikon radishes
- fennel
- kumquats
- leeks
- Meyer lemons
- parsnips
- pears
- persimmons
- pomegranates
- rutabagas
- sweet potatoes
- turnips
- winter squash

Winter / Spring

- asparagus
- collard greens
- grapefruits
- leeks
- oranges
- pomelos
- rainbow chard

Pantry

GARLIC

The most commonly used ingredient in my kitchen. I was raised to believe in its myriad, immunity-boosting powers. Nothing can elevate the flavor of a dish as simply and as quickly as garlic, whether raw or cooked.

FRESH GINGER

Not a day goes by in the kitchen without me reaching for this knobby root. From juices and tea, to soups, stews, and desserts—the applications of this warming, healing wonder are endless.

ONIONS

Both yellow and red onions find their way into my cooking daily. Marinated, caramelized, or raw, they have the ability to brighten any dish.

LEMONS AND LIMES

I wholeheartedly agree with the belief that everything is better with lemon, and would feel lost without these mighty little citruses. Freshly squeezed lemon and lime juice alkalizes the body and is an excellent finishing touch to many dishes, helping with brightening and rounding out all of the flavors. I highly recommend using organic lemons or limes, not only for the standard health reasons, but also to avoid bitterness that often occurs in non-organic lemon rind.

SPICES

Spices are another essential flavor component of my everyday dishes. When I lived in Russia, cooking did not involve any spices, with the exception of a little black pepper, but now, I cannot imagine my kitchen without the aroma of freshly ground cumin, cardamom, or nutmeg. Nothing can help build depth and unique flavor more effectively than a correctly chosen spice, especially when it comes to my lighter approach to cooking. Even desserts can be elevated with the subtlest kiss of spice.

I buy most of my spices whole from the bulk section of the local health-food store, since pre-ground spices do not keep fresh for long and quickly become stale. If buying from a bulk spice section, only pick up the amount you need for a particular recipe; this will assure freshness and save you from buying an unnecessary amount. Store spices in glass jars or airtight plastic bags, in a dark, cool place. Below are the spices I use most frequently for whipping up flavorful, whole food–based meals.

Whole: bay leaves, black mustard seeds, black peppercorns, cardamom pods, coriander seeds, cumin seeds, nutmeg, red pepper flakes, star anise, vanilla beans

Pre-ground: smoked Spanish paprika, sweet Hungarian paprika, turmeric, nutmeg, cinnamon

HERBS

When it comes to confidently building a flavor profile in plant-based meals, fresh herbs are in the same line of importance as freshly ground spices. My refrigerator feels empty without a nice bunch of cilantro, and my counter looks lonely without a fragrant bush of basil or mint.

I tend to have seasonal categories for herbs, just as I do with produce, although most of them are available all year round. It makes more sense to include earthy rosemary and sage in fall and winter recipes, while the brightness of dill, mint, and basil fits seamlessly with spring and summer fare.

Fresh herbs: basil, cilantro, dill, mint, flat leaf parsley, rosemary, sage, thyme

GRAINS

Both my husband and my youngest daughter go wild for grains. A bowl of properly seasoned grains with a touch of ghee or olive oil and a simple salad on the side will always satisfy them. Below is a list of my favorites, which make frequent appearances throughout this book. Gluten-free grains are noted with (gf).

Forbidden black rice: At the top on my list of favorite grains (gf)

Bhutanese red rice or ruby red rice: Great for alternative risottos and stews (gf)

Brown rice: Its neutral taste works well next to bold, spicy flavors (gf)

Arborio rice: The rice traditionally used for risotto (gf)

Barley: Pillowy, slightly chewy in texture, wonderful in many dishes, from soups and stews to veggie burgers and risotto

Farro: Toothsome in texture, great in pilafs and veggie bowls

Steel cut oats: A heartier alternative to rolled oats (gf, if marked as such)

Freekeh: Slightly smoky in flavor, works well paired with roasted or marinated vegetables or as a base for a veggie bowl

Millet: Great for porridges, pilafs, and as an alternative for polenta (gf)

Buckwheat: Subtle in taste, works well as a base for risottos and veggie bowls with zesty dressings (gf)

Teff: Rich, nutty, and chocolatey in flavor and with an impressive nutritional profile to boot, my grain of choice for alternative polenta (gf)

Corn grits: Look for organic and non-GMO, a quick polenta base that can even be used to make pizza crust (page 188) (gf)

Rolled oats: Gluten-free and old-fashioned are my rolled oats of choice (gf)

Quinoa: Good in veggie bowls and salads (gf)

BEANS AND LEGUMES

Beans and legumes make for sensible and delicious additions to any vegetarian meal, being great sources of protein and many other nutrients. Every kind is unique and delicious in its own way, especially when cooked properly from scratch (page 296). At times, though, canned beans cannot be beat for their convenience—if using canned beans, try to seek out ones that come in a BPA-free can, preferably cooked with kombu. I grew up only eating heirloom beans—irregular in size, freckled, and creamy when cooked. If you've never tasted heirlooms, they are worth a try and quite a different experience from mainstream beans. Try some of my favorites—Scarlet Runners, Vaquero, Christmas Lima, etc. Here are the beans and legumes used most frequently in my kitchen and throughout this book:

Lentils: Puy or French lentils, green lentils, Beluga lentils, moong dal

Beans: chickpeas, mung beans, black beans, white beans (cannellini, navy, etc.), red kidney beans, heirloom beans

Aquafaba: A fairly recent discovery for me, aquafaba is the viscous water from cooking beans, which can also be taken directly from canned beans. It is basically free, since it utilizes a byproduct that would otherwise be thrown away. It's practically flavorless when mixed with other ingredients and has an amazing ability to act like eggs when whipped, making vegan meringues and marshmallows a possibility. Unlike eggs, aquafaba can also be re-whipped when it deflates. In this book, I use it as an egg replacement for pancake and cake batters. If using aquafaba from canned beans, try to seek out low-sodium ones that come in BPA-free cans. Any type of beans can be used to make aquafaba, but chickpeas are the most commonly used variety.

FATS

Here is a list of healthy fats and oils and that I use in my kitchen with most frequency. Each one has its unique properties and is able to contribute something different to every recipe, whether in terms of flavor, texture, or as a heating agent.

Unrefined extra-virgin coconut oil: Over the past few years, I've switched over to using coconut oil for most of my cooking. A correctly chosen coconut oil works great for sautéing, roasting, and baking—it has a very high smoking point, which makes it an excellent choice for cooking at high temperatures. It also feels light and less "greasy" than other vegetable oils and has the added bonus of behaving like butter in vegan baking. It is incredibly important to select an oil with a truly neutral taste since there are plenty of coconut oils on the market that will overwhelm your dish with unwanted flavor. The virgin variety of coconut oil tends to be significantly pricier than the refined kind, so I sometimes use the two interchangeably, particularly for frying.

Ghee: Simply put, ghee is clarified butter with caramelized milk solids. It has a rich, aromatic flavor and is believed to aid digestion. I use ghee interchangeably with coconut oil, as their properties are similar when it comes to cooking at high temperatures. I prefer to use ghee for Indian-inspired dishes or when I am craving a more substantial meal.

Extra-virgin olive oil: Versatile, flavorful, healthy, and nutritious, a good quality olive oil is an essential finishing oil for salads, dressings, pasta, etc.

Toasted sesame oil: I keep a small bottle of this pungent oil in the refrigerator for sprinkling on steamed vegetables and for adding mostly to Asian-inspired dishes. A little goes a long way.

VINEGARS

Vinegars are essential to building flavor in plant-based cooking. Below is a list of my favorites, which I use for anything from pickling vegetables to adding an acidic element to sauces, stews, and more.

Unpasteurized apple cider vinegar: I use this vinegar almost daily for everything from a splash in my drinking water, to all kinds of dressings and marinades, to facial toner and disinfectant. Look for unfiltered and naturally fermented apple cider vinegar.

Brown rice vinegar: Perfect for seasoning Asian-inspired dishes, mild in flavor. Look for traditionally brewed, naturally fermented brown rice vinegar.

Balsamic vinegar: Great for adding rich, deep notes and a bit of sweetness to any dish.

Red wine vinegar: A vinegar I use occasionally for marinades, dressing, and sauces like chimichurri (see page 315).

ALWAYS IN MY REFRIGERATOR

Below are a few staple ingredients, without which my refrigerator feels empty. Each one is excellent for building flavor in all types of dishes and for creating powerful sauces, and a little of each goes a long way. All of these ingredients are good for you, and made from whole foods like seeds, nuts, beans, and hot peppers.

Mustard: This condiment is an irreplaceable addition to so many dressings and sauces. Whole-grain Dijon mustard is my mustard of choice.

Miso: A good number of recipes in this book utilize this ancient Japanese ingredient, which is a paste made of fermented beans and grains. Miso is a great source of protein and probiotics and a unique, flavorful addition to soups, dressings, and sauces, both savory and sweet. Look for the unpasteurized, naturally fermented variety. My favorites are white (also commonly called sweet or mild) and chickpea miso.

Chili sauce, such as Sriracha: A few tiny drops of good chili sauce can give a flavorful, spicy kick to many dishes and sauces.

Tahini: This rich, creamy sesame paste finds its way into both sweet and savory recipes in this book. I prefer whole sesame tahini, made of unhulled sesame seeds, for maximum health benefits and flavor.

Almond butter: A great thing to spread on toast and add to smoothies, used in this book for making sauces and dressings, and for adding a rich creaminess to desserts, like Sweet Potato Caramel Pecan Pie (page 288).

SEASONINGS

A moderate amount of salt is essential to the seasoning of most dishes in this book and here is a list of some favorites.

Tamari: A naturally fermented and gluten-free soy sauce, which adds depth and salty notes to many sauces, dressings, sautéed vegetables, grains, and soups.

Sea salt: I use unrefined fine-grain and coarse sea salt such as Celtic, Mediterranean, pink Himalayan, and flaky Maldon for finishing.

NUTS AND SEEDS

Nuts like pistachios, walnuts, and pecans, and seeds like sunflower, pumpkin, sesame, and hemp make flavorful additions to salads and desserts. I keep all my nuts and seeds refrigerated to prevent them from going rancid.

Almonds: My first choice for making Nut Milk (page 298).

Cashews: When it comes to plant-based cooking, it seems there is nothing cashews can't do. They make the creamiest sauces and silky smooth creams and puddings, which resemble well-loved, dairy-rich varieties. I mostly buy cashew pieces instead of whole cashews, as they cost less and will most likely get blended into one creamy sauce or another in my kitchen.

Chia seeds: Unique for their ability to swell in liquids and turn into a gel, chia seeds are useful for mimicking eggs in vegan baking. Chia seeds make nourishing puddings when mixed with milk and fruit juices, and are an excellent addition to smoothies, porridges, and granolas. Their nutritional record is impressive, being one of the best plant-based sources of omega-3 fatty acids. Chia seeds are shelf stable and don't need to be refrigerated. You can use flax seeds as an alternative to chia.

SEA VEGETABLES

Many sea vegetables are rich in iodine, which supports thyroid health and is essential to a balanced plant-based diet. They are also used to contribute a unique flavor of the sea to many dishes, especially soups, broth, and sushi rolls.

Kombu: This thick, mineral-rich seaweed enhances the nutritional profile and flavor of any broth and helps make beans easier to digest.

Agar-agar: A traditional Japanese sea vegetable–based thickener, clear and flavorless, much like gelatin. Agar-agar is easy to work with when making pudding and mousse, and it is full of health-promoting nutrients like iron and calcium, a good digestion aid, and helps reduce inflammation.

Nori: Most commonly used for making sushi rolls, but also a great snack. Nori has all the great health benefits of seaweed, but it is the highest in protein of all seaweeds. I use both raw and toasted nori interchangeably for sushi rolls.

Arame: Thin and fine in shape, full of iron, calcium, and iodine, Arame's mild flavor makes it a great addition to soups and salads.

Wakame: Ribbon-like in shape, this is a great addition to Japanese-inspired soups. I usually use wakame flakes, which don't need to be soaked and can be added directly to soups.

OTHER FLAVOR ENHANCERS

These items, although not necessary for cooking from this book, are worth seeking out. Mostly easy to source and inexpensive, they can add a new world of flavor to your cooking.

Dried shiitake mushrooms: These mushrooms are full of important nutrients, such as selenium, iron, and various vitamins. Dried shiitakes have healing properties and have been used extensively in traditional medicine throughout Asia. I use them to add depth and rich umami flavor to dashi, the broth used for miso-based soups. Dried shiitakes are usually sold in the bulk or spice sections of natural food stores, or packaged next to the seaweed.

Lemongrass: Usually sold at Asian markets and many produce stores, this grass-like plant will add the most enticing aroma to Asian cuisine–inspired soups and stews.

Kaffir lime leaves: These leaves are commonly used in Southeast Asian cooking and have the most magical, tropical, and citrusy aroma. They can add powerful flavor to Thai soups and other Asian cuisine–inspired dishes. You can find them frozen or fresh at Asian and Indian markets, as well as some health-food stores.

Tamarind paste: Made from tamarind fruit, which is indigenous to tropical Africa, this paste has a sweet and sour flavor that makes for a great addition to spring roll dipping sauce and pad thai. It is sold at Asian markets and some health-food stores.

SWEETENERS

Below are my natural sweeteners of choice, used in sauces and desserts throughout this book.

Dates: Unpitted Medjool dates keep fresh and moist longer than pitted ones and are an excellent natural sweetener that can also contribute to the creaminess of desserts. Other dried fruits like raisins, prunes, and apricots can be used to contribute a subtle sweetness and juiciness to sweet and savory dishes alike.

Pure maple syrup: My liquid sweetener of choice.

Coconut sugar: When a recipe requires solid sugar, I love utilizing coconut sugar for its subtle sweetness and molasses-like flavor.

Honey: I use raw, unprocessed, local honey as a liquid sweetener in dishes, where its warming flavor is welcome.

FLOURS AND STARCHES

I've made a habit of using sprouted flours almost exclusively in my baking. As the name suggests, sprouted flours are ground from grains that have been sprouted and dried. The process of sprouting does wonders to any grains—removing the phytic acid that inhibits nutrient absorption, releasing vitamins and enzymes, and making the grains easier to digest and highly nutritious. The process also reduces gluten content, making such flours digestible for some people with gluten sensitivities. Sprouted flour improves the taste of baked goods and contributes to a fluffier texture. There are detailed instructions in my first book, *The Vibrant Table*, on making such flour at home. There are now so many sprouted flours on the market that it's become increasingly easier to find them in health-food stores and online.

Sprouted or whole spelt: My flour of choice for pasta, tortillas, most cakes, and pie crusts.

Buckwheat: This is one of my favorite nutritious, gluten-free flours. I like it both in the raw or sprouted form, which has a neutral taste, and in its regular store-bought form, which has more of a toasty, nutty flavor. I love it in Blueberry Buckwheat Pancakes (page 29) and Sweet Potato Caramel Pecan Pie (page 288).

Oat: A great flour for gluten-free baking. I usually grind old-fashioned, gluten-free oats into flour using my high-speed blender or a food processor.

Almond: Rich, moist, and delicious, this is a great addition to gluten-free and regular flour mixes, especially for tart crusts and cakes.

Brown rice: This flour has a neutral taste, which makes it a good base for gluten-free baking. It's an essential ingredient in my Mushroom and Parsnip Fritters (page 233) and Chocolate and Orange Bundt Cake (page 293).

Quinoa: A protein-rich and nutritious flour, great for gluten-free baking.

Tapioca: A necessary starch component in some gluten-free flour mixes, tapioca can be replaced with other starches of choice.

Arrowroot powder: Made from a dried tropical root, this powder has the ability to soothe the digestive system, and it plays the role of a thickener in desserts.

EGGS AND CHEESE

Both eggs and cheese are used sparingly throughout this book and are mostly optional or replaceable. But if you happen to eat either one, many of the dishes can be topped with a soft-boiled farm egg or a sprinkling of good-quality cheese.

Pastured eggs: I occasionally call for eggs in this book as a binder for vegetable fritters and pancakes. I buy mine from a local farm owned by a friend, where the chickens are getting plenty of sunshine and snacking on bugs and grasses, which leads to nutritious, flavorful eggs with bright-orange yolks.

Unpasteurized goat's and sheep's milk cheese: Occasionally used in this book, but mostly completely optional. Goat and sheep's milk cheeses are easier to digest than cow's milk products, and are a rich and flavorful addition to vegetable-centered dishes like riceless risotto (see chapter 5) and Zucchini Fritters (page 221).

Equipment

In addition to a good knife, a couple of reliable pots and pans, a grater, baking trays, and a tart pan, I find it very helpful to have the following tools in my kitchen.

WELL-SEASONED CAST IRON SKILLET (9- TO 10-INCH)

These pans get better with time and are perfect for practically anything, as they heat food evenly, are naturally non-stick, and can safely travel from the stovetop to the oven.

FOOD PROCESSOR (9- TO 11-CUP CAPACITY)

This is something I use every day for shredding vegetables; grinding nuts and oats; making nut or seed butters, veggie burgers, and cake batters; mixing dough for tart and pie crusts; etc.

UPRIGHT BLENDER

I use my high-speed blender every single day for making nut milks, smoothies, sauces, creams, soups, and dressings, and for grinding sprouted grains into flours and chia and flax seeds into meal.

BAMBOO STEAMER

One of the most affordable and elegant kitchen tools, which makes steaming vegetables quick and straightforward.

SPICE GRINDER, MORTAR AND PESTLE, OR COFFEE GRINDER

A good grinding tool is necessary for turning whole spices into powders. Spice and coffee grinders will also work for grinding chia and flax seeds into meal.

PEPPER GRINDER

I use this daily for freshly grinding peppercorns into almost every meal.

MESH STRAINERS

These are great for sifting flours and cocoa powder, draining grains after soaking, straining various purées, etc.

NYLON OR COTTON NUT MILK BAGS

This is my favorite tool for straining pulp when making homemade nut milk (page 298). They are also great for juicing a small amount of beets, ginger, or turmeric by squeezing the shredded vegetables in the bag to extract the juices.

VEGETABLE PEELER

Aside from easily removing vegetable skins, I use my peeler for making tender ribbons of vegetables like carrots and zucchini, which are beautiful in a finished dish and add a variety of texture.

SPIRALIZER OR JULIENNE PEELER

This inexpensive tool opens up a whole new world of plant-based meal possibilities, utilizing vegetables in the form of noodles. See Daikon Radish Pad Thai (page 206), Chilled Thai Coconut Soup with Zucchini and Carrot Noodles (page 120), Cucumber Noodles with Melon Spheres and Herb Vinaigrette (page 187), and Tropical Cru (page 61).

CITRUS JUICER

Any simple hand juicer will satisfy the need for freshly squeezed citrus juice.

MICROPLANE ZESTER

This is the perfect thing for zesting organic lemons or limes, as well as grinding fresh ginger, nutmeg, and hard cheeses like Parmesan.

GAS VS. ELECTRIC STOVE/OVEN

I developed most of the recipes in this book using an electric stove, as that's what I have in my kitchen. Therefore, all the suggested heat levels for sautéing and frying are based on electric heat. If you are fortunate to have a gas stove, you'll most likely have to adjust the heat a little bit. From my experience, you need less heat when cooking over a gas burner.

MORNING PORRIDGES AND PANCAKES

AS THE FIRST MEAL OF THE DAY, breakfast carries with it some responsibility for launching us into the world well-nourished and, more importantly, satisfied. After considering all the forms a breakfast can take, I determined that my favorite morning meals usually come arranged in a bowl or fried in a pan. In this chapter, I offer some ideas on weaving vegetables and fruits into your breakfasts, along with a variety of nourishing grains and spices, for a wholesome and happy beginning.

22
Stewed Rhubarb Amaranth Porridge

25
Asparagus and Leek Pancakes

26
Strawberry and Rhubarb Oven Pancake

29
Blueberry Buckwheat Pancakes

30
Superfood Summer Porridge

33
Coriander Millet Porridge with Rosemary Concord Grape Compote

34
Rosemary Concord Grape Compote

35
Fig and Grape Oven Pancake

36
Teff and Apple Pancakes

39
Barley and Chia Seed Porridge with Candied Kumquats

40
Creamy Steel Cut Oats with Rainbow Chard and Pine Nuts

STEWED RHUBARB AMARANTH PORRIDGE

This porridge is a good breakfast candidate for the early spring, when morning temperatures are still chilly, yet seasonal rhubarb is starting to show its blush at the markets. It's a rich and warming kind of meal, in both its dessert-like quality and the exceptional nourishment provided by amaranth, a special pseudo-grain full of protein and calcium. Amaranth's pleasant, fine texture, popping on your palate like miniature fireworks, pairs well with the bright and tart slices of stewed rhubarb and the luxurious scents of cardamom and vanilla.

The rhubarb can be stewed the night before and left to infuse with the vanilla until breakfast. Later in the season, strawberries will be a good substitute for the rhubarb here; just reduce their stewing time to 5 minutes.

Serves 4 to 6 | SPRING

FOR THE PORRIDGE

1 cup amaranth, soaked in purified water overnight, then rinsed and drained in a fine-mesh strainer

2 cups almond milk or coconut milk

2 tablespoons coconut sugar

½ vanilla bean, split open, seeds scraped

½ teaspoon freshly ground cardamom (from 3 or 4 pods)

½ teaspoon salt

Poppy seeds, for garnish (optional)

FOR THE RHUBARB

1 pound (450 g) fresh rhubarb, sliced into ½- to 1-inch pieces (¾ cup)

½ vanilla bean, split open, seeds scraped

¼ cup pure maple syrup or honey

TO MAKE THE PORRIDGE

In a medium saucepan, combine the amaranth, almond or coconut milk, coconut sugar, vanilla bean seeds and pod, cardamom, and salt. Bring the mixture to a boil, lower the heat, and simmer, covered, for 15 minutes. Remove the vanilla bean pod when ready to serve.

TO PREPARE THE RHUBARB

In a separate saucepan, combine the rhubarb, vanilla bean seeds and pod, and maple syrup or honey. Bring the mixture to a gentle simmer over medium heat and cook for 7 to 10 minutes, until rhubarb is soft. Remove the vanilla bean when ready to serve.

TO SERVE

Mix the rhubarb into the porridge. Add a few splashes of almond or coconut milk and garnish each serving with poppy seeds if using. You can also add a dollop of yogurt, as pictured.

ASPARAGUS AND LEEK PANCAKES

When mixing up the ingredients for these pancakes, you'll notice that the mixture is predominantly made up of green things barely coated with batter, and that is the idea. Sautéed leeks are sweet and melt into the batter, which is then punctuated by frequent pockets of tender asparagus and greens. I love a savory breakfast, and this one, armed with the power of young spring vegetables, will fill you up in a wonderfully nourishing way.

Makes approximately 16 pancakes | SPRING

3 tablespoons neutral coconut oil, divided

1 medium leek, white and pale green parts only, sliced

1 bunch (about 14 ounces/400 g or 16 fat sprigs) asparagus, tough ends removed, sliced

Sea salt and freshly ground black pepper

2 cups watercress or spinach leaves

1 cup (100 g) sprouted or whole-grain spelt flour or buckwheat flour

1½ teaspoons baking powder

1 teaspoon pure maple syrup

¾ cup warm water (1 cup, if using buckwheat flour)

1 Warm 1 tablespoon of the coconut oil in a large pan over medium-high heat. Add the leeks and sauté for 5 minutes.

2 Add the asparagus, salt, and black pepper to taste; continue to sauté for another 5 minutes.

3 Add the watercress or spinach, stir until the leaves have wilted, and remove the pan from the heat. Taste and add salt if needed; let the vegetable mixture cool while you make the batter.

4 Combine the flour, baking powder, and a large pinch of salt in a medium bowl.

5 Add the remaining coconut oil, maple syrup, and warm water to the flour mixture and mix to just combine. Let rest for about 5 minutes, then fold in the vegetables.

6 Wipe clean the pan used to sauté the vegetables and warm over medium heat. Add about 2 heaping tablespoons of batter per pancake to the pan. Form and even out each pancake with the back of a spoon. Cook 3 to 4 pancakes at a time, or as many as will fit in your pan.

7 Cook pancakes for 2 to 3 minutes, or until their edges darken and dry out a bit, and the pancakes are golden brown on one side. Flip and cook on the other side for about 2 minutes, until golden brown. Add coconut oil to the pan if necessary between batches.

8 Serve right away with Cilantro Tahini Sauce (page 303), Avocado Mayo (page 299), Apple-Miso Mayo (page 300), or plain yogurt.

STRAWBERRY AND RHUBARB OVEN PANCAKE

The method of baking pancakes in the oven is a shortcut to preparing the well-loved breakfast staple, but not without its own cozy ceremony. There will still be thick, fragrant batter to mix with jewel-like fruit—the only thing missing will be the need for frying and tending to the pancakes at the stove. Instead, you might linger impatiently near the oven while the pancake is baking, or attend to other important pre-breakfast business, like making a hot beverage or reading the paper. In the end, there is something grandiose about having one big pancake to slice into, not unlike a pie, especially when knowing that it only took a few active minutes to put together. Strawberry and rhubarb make a perfect spring pairing, but feel free to use any seasonal fruit here. The batter in this recipe is vegan; if you need a gluten-free batter, see the Fig and Grape Oven Pancake on page 35.

Makes one 10-inch pancake | SPRING

¾ cup (75 g) sprouted spelt flour or whole spelt flour

1 teaspoon baking powder

½ teaspoon baking soda

Pinch of sea salt

¾ cup almond milk

⅓ cup unsweetened applesauce

1 tablespoon pure maple syrup

1 teaspoon vanilla extract

1 teaspoon freshly squeezed lemon juice

About 1½ cups strawberries, hulled and sliced (measure before slicing)

About ½ pound (225 g) rhubarb, sliced into ½-inch pieces (1½ cups)

1 tablespoon neutral coconut oil

1 tablespoon coconut sugar

½ teaspoon ground cinnamon (optional)

1 Place a 10-inch cast iron skillet or other ovenproof pan on the center rack of the oven and preheat to 400°F (200°C).

2 Combine the flour, baking powder, baking soda, and salt in a large bowl. Add the milk, applesauce, maple syrup, vanilla extract, and lemon juice; stir to combine. Fold in the strawberries and rhubarb, reserving a few pieces of each for garnishing the top of the pancake.

3 Using oven mitts, take the skillet out of the oven. Working quickly, add the oil to the skillet, tilting it to coat the bottom. Pour in the pancake batter and spread it out with a spoon, if necessary. Sprinkle with the reserved strawberries and rhubarb and coconut sugar. Place the skillet back in the oven and bake for 25 to 30 minutes, until the top and edges of the pancake are golden brown.

4 Take the skillet out of the oven and sprinkle the pancake with cinnamon, if using. Let cool slightly. Slice and serve as is or with more fresh strawberries and/or plain yogurt.

BLUEBERRY BUCKWHEAT PANCAKES

My mother taught me the clever trick of adding zucchini to pancake batter to make pancakes more tender, which is what I do in this recipe. Buckwheat flour is incredibly nutritious and gluten free, with toasty and earthy notes of flavor, and it pairs well with juicy summer blueberries. These pancakes are not only gluten free, but also vegan, due to the substitutions of chia meal for eggs and aquafaba, the liquid left over from cooked or canned beans, for milk.

Makes about 13 (3½-inch) pancakes | SPRING • SUMMER

1 cup plain dairy-free or regular yogurt

2 tablespoons chia meal

6 tablespoons aquafaba (liquid reserved from cooked or canned beans, see page 9)

1 tablespoon coconut sugar

1 cup (140 g) buckwheat flour

Pinch of salt

1 teaspoon baking powder

2 small zucchini, shredded (about 2 cups)

1 cup fresh blueberries, plus more for serving

Neutral coconut oil, for frying

Pure maple syrup, honey, or coconut sugar, for serving

1 Combine the yogurt with the chia meal in a medium bowl. Stir to combine thoroughly and leave the mixture to gel for 10 minutes at room temperature.

2 Combine the aquafaba with the coconut sugar in another medium bowl. Whip with a hand mixer for about 1 minute, until the mixture is very fluffy with peaks that are just beginning to hold their shape.

3 Combine the buckwheat flour with the salt and baking powder in another medium bowl. Add the yogurt-chia gel and whipped aquafaba; quickly mix into the batter with a fork.

4 Fold in the shredded zucchini, stir to incorporate, then fold in the blueberries.

5 Warm 1 teaspoon coconut oil in a medium frying pan over medium heat. Measure ¼ cup of batter per pancake and add it to the pan. Spread the batter with the back of a spoon to make pancakes about 3½ inches in diameter. Cook until bubbles appear on the surface, the edges appear dry, and the underside is golden brown, about 3 minutes. Flip and cook for another 2 to 3 minutes, until the other side is golden brown. Transfer the cooked pancakes to a plate and continue with the remaining batter, adding about 1 teaspoon of coconut oil to the pan for every new batch.

6 Serve the pancakes right away with more blueberries or other berries or fruit and/or a drizzle of maple syrup, honey, or a sprinkle of coconut sugar.

SUPERFOOD SUMMER PORRIDGE

One of my favorite raw breakfasts comes from Carol Alt's raw food cookbook—an avocado-based muesli, which impressed me so much when I first discovered it that I made it for months on end. This porridge is a nod to that memorable dish, perfect for the mornings when you want something substantial but it's too hot to cook anything. Superfoods, in short, are types of foods that are particularly dense in nutrients—vitamins, minerals and phytochemicals. Hemp hearts, bee pollen, cacao nibs, goji berries, chia seeds, mulberries, and maca and cacao powders are a few examples, and I like to keep some of them handy for adding to smoothies, breakfast porridges, salads, and desserts. This porridge is loaded with healthy fats from avocado and protein from chia seeds, nuts, and hemp hearts, starting you off right for the day. It's full of sweet juices from summer peaches and has a variety of pleasant textures—from soft to chewy to crunchy.

Serves 2 to 4 | SUMMER

⅓ cup chia seeds

1 cup almond milk, preferably homemade (page 298)

1 ripe but firm avocado, pitted and roughly chopped

2 ripe, sweet peaches, pitted and roughly chopped

½ cup rolled oats

¼ cup raisins

¼ cup raw nuts such as pistachios, walnuts, or pecans

Juice of ½ lemon

2 tablespoons raw honey

2 tablespoons maca root powder (optional)

OPTIONS FOR TOPPINGS

Sliced peaches

Fresh berries

Hemp hearts

Bee pollen

Cacao nibs

1 Place the chia seeds in a clean, dry jar with a tight-fitting lid and pour the almond milk over them. Tighten the lid and shake well until the chia seeds are evenly coated with milk and there are no clumps. Place the jar in the refrigerator for at least 2 hours; you can also do this the night before and leave the chia to gel overnight.

2 Place the avocado, peaches, oats, raisins, nuts, lemon juice, honey, and maca powder, if using, in a food processor and pulse until the mixture forms a chunky purée. Spoon the mixture into a medium bowl and fold in the chilled chia pudding.

3 Distribute the porridge among individual serving bowls and garnish with all or any of the suggested toppings. This porridge is best eaten within a day.

CORIANDER MILLET PORRIDGE WITH ROSEMARY CONCORD GRAPE COMPOTE

This breakfast warms to the core, with stunning color and a balance of savory and sweet flavors. Millet, with its fine texture and pleasantly mild flavor, makes for a hearty, creamy porridge. Turmeric contributes its anti-inflammatory properties and enhances the yellow coloring of the millet, while coriander adds interest and autumnal notes. And to finish it all off, rosemary Concord grape compote is spooned over the porridge, bringing a welcome juiciness and luxurious purple hues.

Serves 4 to 6 | SUMMER • FALL

1 Drain the millet and thoroughly rinse it in a strainer.

2 Toast the coriander seeds in a medium saucepan over medium heat for 1 to 2 minutes, until fragrant. Grind the coriander seeds in a mortar and pestle; set aside.

3 Add the oil and turmeric to the same pan you used for toasting the coriander, return the pan to medium heat, and stir around for a minute. Add the millet, toasted coriander, and salt, and stir to coat.

4 Add the milk and coconut sugar. Increase the heat to medium high and bring the mixture to a boil. Lower the heat and simmer for 25 to 30 minutes, covered, stirring occasionally until the millet is soft and the porridge is of oatmeal consistency. Add more milk if the porridge becomes too dry.

5 Serve with Rosemary Concord Grape Compote (recipe follows) or fresh fruit. Add a dollop of yogurt and garnish with chopped nuts or bee pollen, if desired.

½ cup millet, soaked in purified water overnight

1 tablespoon coriander seeds

1 tablespoon neutral coconut oil or ghee

½ teaspoon ground turmeric

Pinch of sea salt

2 cups almond milk, or 1 cup purified water plus 1 cup almond milk

1 tablespoon coconut sugar

Rosemary Concord Grape Compote, for serving (recipe follows)

Plain dairy-free or regular yogurt, for serving

Chopped nuts or bee pollen, for serving (optional)

Rosemary Concord Grape Compote

Concord, the darling variety of American table grapes, very much resemble the grapes I grew up with—fruity and musky in flavor, full of seeds, and brilliant in color, with skin covered in a waxy, white layer, which contributes to their stunning iridescence. Finding ways to enjoy the irresistible flavor of Concord grapes can be challenging due to their abundance of seeds, but this grape and rosemary compote is one simple solution. Spoon the compote over yogurt, porridge, or savory dishes for a pop of sweet, earthy, and herbal flavors.

About 5 cups | SUMMER • FALL

2 quarts Concord grapes

¼ cup (35 g) coconut sugar or other natural sugar of choice

1 tablespoon arrowroot powder

2 cups Thomcord grapes or other smaller variety of black or red seedless grapes

1 to 2 large sprigs fresh rosemary, bruised with the back of a knife

1 Remove the Concord grapes from their branches. Place them in the bowl of a food processor and process until the skins are broken down thoroughly.

2 Transfer the puréed grapes to a small saucepan. Add the sugar, bring to a boil over medium heat, then lower the heat and simmer for 3 minutes. Strain and discard the seeds and skins.

3 Scoop 1 tablespoon of the grape purée into a small bowl. Add the arrowroot powder and mix to combine.

4 Return the rest of the purée back to the pan. Add the whole seedless grapes and bring the mixture back to a boil. Lower the heat and simmer for another 3 minutes to lightly cook the grapes.

5 Remove the saucepan from the heat and add the arrowroot mixture, stirring constantly until the compote thickens slightly, 1 to 2 minutes. Add the rosemary and let the compote sit at room temperature for 1 hour to infuse. Store the compote in an airtight container in the refrigerator for up to 3 days.

FIG AND GRAPE OVEN PANCAKE

Brand new cast iron skillets are notoriously finicky. It can take a skillet and a cook some time to adjust to each other, and the pan might need to be tamed with a few cooking and seasoning sessions before it performs smoothly, with no sticking or burning. That being said, once you've mastered your cast iron skillet, it can become one of your most essential tools in the kitchen. One of my favorite breakfast dishes to make in my cast iron skillet is oven-baked pancakes.

No fruits evoke the early fall season better than sweet, plump figs and brilliant purple grapes. The two happen to pair together perfectly, especially when roasted and caramelized, like in this pancake. Thomcord grapes are related in origin and flavor to the well-loved Concord grapes, but lacking the seeds. Feel free to use any other seedless grapes available to you. If in need of a vegan pancake recipe, you can find one on page 26. (Pictured on page 20.)

Makes one 10-inch pancake | SUMMER • FALL

¾ cup (75 g) gluten-free flour (all purpose, quinoa, etc.)

3 heaping tablespoons coconut sugar or other sugar of choice, divided

½ teaspoon baking soda

Pinch of sea salt

1 cup plain dairy-free or regular yogurt

¼ cup purified water

1 egg

1 tablespoon freshly squeezed lemon juice

1 teaspoon vanilla extract

1½ cups ripe, quartered fresh figs

1½ cups Thomcord grapes

1 tablespoon neutral coconut oil or ghee

½ teaspoon ground cinnamon (optional)

1 Place a 10-inch cast iron skillet or other ovenproof pan on the center rack of the oven and preheat to 400°F (200°C).

2 Combine the flour, 2 tablespoons of the sugar, the baking soda, and salt in a large mixing bowl. Mix well with a fork.

3 In a medium bowl, whisk together the yogurt, water, egg, lemon juice, and vanilla. Add the liquid ingredients to the bowl with the dry ingredients and quickly stir to combine.

4 Reserve a few fig slices and a small handful of grapes for arranging on top of the pancake. Fold the rest of the fruit into the batter.

5 Carefully remove the skillet from the oven. Add the oil, letting it melt and coat the bottom of the pan. Pour the batter into the pan and arrange the reserved fruit on top. Combine the remaining tablespoon of sugar with the cinnamon, if using, and sprinkle this mixture over the batter. Bake for 25 to 30 minutes, until the pancake is golden brown on top. Remove it from the oven, let it cool a little, then slice and serve.

TEFF AND APPLE PANCAKES

Teff is a highly nutritious Ethiopian gluten-free grain, rich in iron, protein, and calcium. Teff flour is mild and nutty in flavor and makes an excellent base for these airy and light pancakes. Whipped aquafaba fluff gives the pancakes a porous texture that is usually difficult to achieve in pancakes free of eggs and gluten. Consider making these pancakes on chilly autumn mornings, when a bit more substance and nourishment is welcome. Feel free to substitute the apples with other fruits of choice, such as late-summer plums or peaches.

Makes about 12 to 15 small pancakes | FALL • WINTER

½ cup plus 2 tablespoons warm unsweetened almond milk or other plant-based milk

¼ cup melted neutral coconut oil, plus more for frying

1 tablespoon pure maple syrup, plus more for serving

Pinch of salt

1¼ cups (125 g) teff flour

2 teaspoons baking powder

¼ cup aquafaba (liquid reserved from cooked or canned beans, page 9)

½ teaspoon freshly squeezed lemon juice or apple cider vinegar

2 to 3 small apples, cored and thinly sliced

Coconut sugar, for sprinkling

Ground cinnamon, for sprinkling (optional)

Pure maple syrup, honey, and/or plain dairy-free or regular yogurt, for serving

1 Combine the almond milk, the coconut oil, the maple syrup, and salt in a medium bowl and whisk to combine.

2 Sift the teff flour and baking powder into the same bowl. Mix with a wooden spoon to form a smooth batter.

3 Pour the aquafaba into another medium bowl and beat with a hand mixer for 1 minute, until fluffy. Pour in the lemon juice or vinegar without stopping the mixer. Beat until stiff peaks start to form, about 6 minutes.

4 Fold the aquafaba fluff into the teff batter, taking care not to overmix.

5 Warm 1 teaspoon of coconut oil in a large frying pan over medium heat. Spoon about 2 tablespoons of batter per pancake into the pan. Lightly press 2 to 3 apple slices into each pancake and sprinkle with coconut sugar.

6 Reduce the heat slightly and cook the pancakes until they are bubbly throughout and the edges are slightly dried and golden, about 2 minutes. Flip and cook on the other side for about 1 to 2 minutes, until golden.

7 Continue to cook the pancakes in batches, adding 1 teaspoon of coconut oil to the pan for each batch, until all the batter is used up. Sprinkle with cinnamon, if using.

8 Serve with maple syrup, honey, and/or plain yogurt.

BARLEY AND CHIA SEED PORRIDGE WITH CANDIED KUMQUATS

A comforting winter breakfast of hearty barley and nutritious chia porridge, topped with festive, sweet-tart candied kumquats. If you can't find kumquats, stir about 1 cup of any dried fruit of choice into the porridge at the end, cover and let sit for 5 minutes before adding in the soaked chia seeds.

Serves 4 to 6 | FALL • WINTER

FOR THE PORRIDGE

2 tablespoons chia seeds

1 cup plus 6 tablespoons almond milk or coconut milk, divided

3 cups purified water

½ cup pearled barley, rinsed in a strainer

Sea salt

1 tablespoon coconut sugar

1 teaspoon vanilla extract (optional)

1½ teaspoons ghee (optional)

FOR THE CANDIED KUMQUATS

¾ cup honey

½ cup purified water

1 vanilla bean, seeds scraped out

2 pints (about 4 cups) kumquats, sliced

1 Combine the chia seeds and 6 tablespoons of the almond milk or coconut milk in a small bowl and whisk until well mixed to prevent clumping. Set aside.

2 Bring the water to a boil in a medium saucepan. Add the barley and salt, to taste, lower the heat to a strong simmer, and cook for 30 minutes, partially covered. Check and stir periodically to make sure that not all the water has evaporated, and to prevent the barley from sticking to the bottom of the pan.

3 Add the remaining 1 cup of almond milk, the coconut sugar, and the vanilla, if using, to the barley. Bring the mixture back to a slow simmer and cook for another 10 minutes, uncovered and stirring periodically, until the barley is fully cooked and most of the liquid is absorbed. Taste and adjust with more salt as needed. Add the ghee, if using, and stir to incorporate.

4 Stir in the soaked chia seeds and remove the pan from the heat.

5 Distribute among individual bowls, add more milk and/or ghee, if preferred, and top with Candied Kumquats.

TO PREPARE THE KUMQUATS

1 In a medium saucepan over medium heat, combine the honey, water, and vanilla bean seeds and pod. Bring to a gentle boil. Add in the kumquats and bring the mixture back to a boil, then lower the heat and simmer for 10 minutes until syrupy.

2 Remove the pan from the heat and let the kumquats cool in the syrup. Store the candied kumquats in an airtight container in the refrigerator for up to 1 week.

CREAMY STEEL CUT OATS WITH RAINBOW CHARD AND PINE NUTS

This recipe makes a great case for savory breakfasts. Steel cut oats are whole oat groats cut into small pieces, and although they are almost identical in nutrition to rolled oats, they are lower on the glycemic index. Steel cut oats also take longer to cook than their rolled counterparts, but their superior flavor and creamy, but not mushy, texture make it all worth it. In this porridge, chard gives the oats a hearty flavor, a boost of nutrients, and, if you use a rainbow chard variety, a subtle pink blush. And a garnish of toasted pine nuts adds indulgence and a savory finish.

Serves 4 to 6 | WINTER • SPRING

2 tablespoons neutral coconut oil or ghee, divided

1 cup steel cut oats

3 cups hot, purified water

Sea salt

1 cup almond milk or coconut milk

¼ cup raw pine nuts

5 to 7 rainbow chard leaves, leaves and stems separated and chopped

1 Melt 1 tablespoon of the coconut oil or ghee in a medium saucepan over medium heat. Add the oats and toast for a few minutes until they are golden and fragrant.

2 Add the hot water and a pinch of salt to the pan, bring the mixture to a boil, then cover the pan, reduce the heat to low, and simmer for 25 minutes. Stir the oats periodically to prevent them from sticking to the bottom of the pan.

3 Add the almond milk to the pan and simmer, partially covered, for another 15 minutes until creamy. Keep stirring periodically to prevent any sticking.

4 While the oats are cooking, melt the remaining tablespoon of oil in a medium sauté pan over medium-low heat. Add the pine nuts and a pinch of salt and toast the nuts for about 2 minutes, until golden. Remove the nuts from the pan with a slotted spoon and set them aside.

5 Increase the heat to medium under the sauté pan, add the reserved chard stems, and sauté them for about 5 minutes, until soft.

6 When the porridge has finished cooking, stir in the chard leaves and cooked stems. Remove the pan from the heat and let the porridge stand for 5 minutes, allowing the chard to wilt completely.

7 Distribute the porridge among individual bowls and serve immediately, garnished with the toasted pine nuts.

SALADS AND BOWLS

A SALAD CAN MEAN SO MANY THINGS—a bowl of frilly young greens tossed with vinaigrette, toasted stale bread with wedges of meaty tomatoes, succulent eggplant with herbs and garlic, finely chopped potatoes dressed in mayonnaise, or a fully loaded bowl of seasonal fare.

In this chapter you'll find a variety of delicious, seasonally inspired salads and bowls, including quick ones and others that require a bit more mindfulness, hearty ones and light ones, some that are great as sides and others that are full meals on their own, all guided gently by seasons and wisdom from all over the world.

44
Spring Bowl

46
Spring Panzanella with Radishes and Peas

49
Strawberry, Spinach, and Edamame Salad

51
Grilled Pineapple and Avocado Salsa

52
Millet Polenta with Spring Vegetables and Greens

54
Peach and Tomato Panzanella

56
Tipsy Watermelon, Fennel, and Arugula Salad

58
Watermelon Rind Marmalade

59
Summer Bowl

61
Tropical Cru

62
Naked Taco Bowl

65
Late Summer / Early Fall Bowl

66
Warm Salad of Roasted Cauliflower, Grapes, and Forbidden Black Rice

69
Squash and Pomegranate Panzanella with Autumn Herbs

70
Lentil, Pomegranate, and Brussels Sprout Salad

73
Late Autumn / Winter Bowl

75
Lemony Teff Polenta with Tahini, Leeks, and Chickpeas

78
Heirloom Bean, Fennel, and Citrus Salad

80
Steamed Chioggia Beet and Pear Salad

83
Golden Beet and Pomelo Winter Panzanella

1 cup purified water

½ cup buckwheat groats or other whole grains like millet, farro, rice, freekeh, etc.

Sea salt

½ large or 1 small head romaine lettuce, roughly chopped

Other salad greens of choice (optional)

1½ teaspoons neutral coconut oil

Large handful of fresh sugar snap or snow peas, strings removed

1 bunch radishes with tops, tops cut off and reserved, bulbs thinly sliced

1 cup fresh or frozen green peas, thawed if frozen

12 asparagus spears, tough ends removed

Freshly ground black pepper

1 ripe but firm avocado, sliced

Large handful of pea shoots or other microgreens, for garnish

Handful of fresh cilantro, basil, and mint leaves, for garnish (optional)

Handful of raw chopped pistachios, for garnish (optional)

Cilantro Tahini Sauce (page 303), for serving*

* Any Tahini Sauce will work great here (pages 303 to 304, as will any of the Cashew Cream Sauces (pages 301 to 302) or even the Spring Roll Dipping Sauce (page 308)

SPRING BOWL

The great thing about single-bowl meals is that they allow plenty of room for interpretation. Grab some greens, throw in any grains you fancy, include some protein-rich beans or legumes, and top everything off with seasonal vegetables. To finish, there are always fragrant herbs, crunchy nuts or seeds, and sauce to unify and dress it all up. Ingredients can be added and omitted based on what's available, whether fresh at the market, slightly forgotten in the back of the refrigerator, or stocked in the pantry.

This bowl is a tribute to spring—from the crisp and tender asparagus and peas, to the pink baby radishes and young greens. Buckwheat offers a light but nourishing base, while the green tahini sauce provides a welcome creaminess.

Serves 4 | SPRING

1 In a medium saucepan, bring the water to a boil over high heat. Add the buckwheat and a pinch or two of salt. Reduce the heat to low and cook, covered, for about 15 minutes, or until all the water is absorbed and the buckwheat is soft. If using other grains, adjust the cooking method accordingly.

2 Distribute the lettuce and greens among individual bowls. Spoon the cooked grains over the greens.

3 Melt the coconut oil in a medium pan over medium heat. Add the sugar snaps and a pinch of salt, and cook until they are bright green, about 3 minutes. Add the radish tops and green peas and stir until tops are wilted. Divide this mixture among the bowls on top of the grains.

4 Add the asparagus to the pan, season with another pinch of salt and some black pepper, and cook, undisturbed, for 3 minutes. Flip the asparagus and cook for another 3 to 4 minutes, until the spears are soft and bright green. Arrange on top of the peas and radish greens.

5 Top the bowls with the sliced radishes, avocado, pea shoots or microgreens, herbs, and pistachios, if using. Serve with dollops of Cilantro Tahini Sauce.

SPRING PANZANELLA WITH RADISHES AND PEAS

Panzanella is a Tuscan salad, traditionally made with stale, days-old bread, tomatoes, and a few other add-ins like onions and whatnot. I love the idea of the leftovers of a loaf of bread taking on new life. It's a graceful step toward not only another beautiful meal, but also a wasteless kitchen. Panzanella can be made grand with bright, seasonal produce, and in this chapter I've included a version for every season.

Here, crunchy, newborn spring vegetables are tossed with toasted garlic bread and finished with a bright and citrusy dill vinaigrette.

Serves 4 to 6 | SPRING • SUMMER

FOR THE VINAIGRETTE

4 tablespoons freshly squeezed lemon juice

1 teaspoon Dijon mustard

¼ cup chopped fresh dill

¼ cup olive oil

FOR THE PANZANELLA

4 slices whole-grain bread, torn or cut into cubes

Olive oil, for drizzling the bread

2 garlic cloves, minced

Sea salt

1½ teaspoons neutral coconut oil

2 cups sugar snaps or snow peas, strings removed

2 cups fresh or frozen green English peas, thawed if frozen

10 to 15 radishes, thinly sliced

2 to 3 cups mesclun greens or other salad greens of choice

Freshly ground black pepper

Handful of pea shoots (optional)

1 Preheat the oven to 350°F (180°C). Line a rimmed baking sheet with parchment paper.

2 Combine all of the vinaigrette ingredients in a medium bowl and set aside.

3 Arrange the bread on the prepared baking sheet, drizzle it with olive oil, and sprinkle with the garlic and sea salt to taste. Transfer to the oven and toast the bread for 20 minutes, until golden.

4 In the meantime, melt the coconut oil in a medium sauté pan over medium heat. Add the sugar snaps and a pinch of salt and sauté for 3 to 4 minutes, until they are bright green and lightly cooked, but still crispy. Add the peas and another pinch of salt, stir to coat for a minute, and then remove the pan from the heat.

5 Combine the toasted bread, cooked sugar snaps and peas, radishes, and greens in a large bowl. Pour the vinaigrette over top, season with freshly ground black pepper, and toss well. Scatter on the pea shoots, if using, and serve immediately.

STRAWBERRY, SPINACH, AND EDAMAME SALAD

Strawberries and spinach seem to be made for each other, and I can happily eat the two together in a bowl, no dressing necessary. I like to bring spinach and strawberry salad with me in a small cooler bag on long, overseas flights, as airplane food never serves me well. The salad might not sound as resilient for travel as, say, granola bars, but to me it is perfect—simple, light on the stomach, and surprisingly nourishing, especially during times of travel stress and high altitudes. To this day, my eight-year-old daughter believes that strawberry and spinach salad is standard plane fare.

This recipe is a step up from my travel snack, but still made of just a few simple components that complement one another in a very balanced way. There's added protein from bright edamame, cucumber for crunch, plenty of fresh herbs, and a bit of subtle spice from jalapeño.

Serves 4 | SPRING • SUMMER

FOR THE DRESSING

Juice and zest of 1 lime

1 teaspoon pure maple syrup

1 tablespoon olive oil

FOR THE SALAD

About 2 cups strawberries, hulled and sliced

½ to 1 cup shelled fresh edamame, blanched for 3 minutes in boiling water

½ English cucumber, cut into bite-size pieces

4 cups baby spinach, lightly packed

Large handful of fresh cilantro leaves

Large handful of fresh basil leaves, torn

1 small jalapeño, seeded and minced

1 Whisk all the dressing ingredients in a small bowl until well combined. Set aside.

2 Combine all the salad ingredients in a large bowl. Pour the dressing over and toss gently to combine. Serve right away.

GRILLED PINEAPPLE AND AVOCADO SALSA

I have to say that grilled fruit is simply one of the best things you can add to salsa. Ripe pineapple, already heavenly when raw, becomes its sweetest, juiciest, and most tropical self when grilled. In this salsa, spicy jalapeño, sharp red onion, and piney cilantro contrast the pineapple sweetness, and a generous squeeze of lime juice brings everything together. This salsa is ideal for an outdoor party, since it makes a great accompaniment for all sorts of dishes, and it can even be eaten on its own as a salad. I provide instructions for "grilling" the pineapple in the oven, but if you have an outdoor grill, I encourage you to use that instead.

Serves 4 to 6 | SPRING • SUMMER

1 large, ripe pineapple, peeled, halved lengthwise, cored, and cut into ½-inch-thick slices

2 teaspoons coconut sugar, divided

2 ripe but firm avocados, cubed

¼ medium red onion, finely chopped

1 jalapeño, seeded and finely chopped

2 cups fresh cilantro leaves, chopped

1 teaspoon freshly ground cumin (optional)

Juice of 1 large lime

1 Preheat the oven to 450°F (230°C).

2 Arrange the pineapple slices on a grill pan or a parchment paper–lined baking sheet and sprinkle them with 1 teaspoon of the coconut sugar. Roast the pineapple for 15 minutes, then flip the slices, sprinkle with the remaining teaspoon of coconut sugar, and roast for another 10 minutes until caramelized and golden brown in places. Remove the pineapple from the oven and let it cool.

3 Chop the roasted pineapple into medium chunks and place them in a large bowl. Add the avocado, red onion, jalapeño, cilantro, and cumin, if using. Squeeze the lime juice over the salsa and toss gently. Serve immediately.

MILLET POLENTA WITH SPRING VEGETABLES AND GREENS

Millet is a versatile, gluten-free grain, which works surprisingly well as a light substitute for corn grits in any polenta-like dish. Creamy, zesty, and fragrant, this millet polenta serves as the perfect bed for pungent greens and crispy spring vegetables.

Serves 4 to 6 | SPRING • SUMMER

Sea salt

1½ pounds (680 g) spring greens (dandelion greens, mustard greens, arugula, spinach, etc.)

2 cups total of one or any combination of fresh green peas, fava beans, sugar snaps, snow peas, chopped asparagus, and/or chopped Romanesco

2 tablespoons unpasteurized miso paste

1 tablespoon mustard

1 garlic clove, minced

3 tablespoons olive oil, divided, plus more for drizzling

1 cup millet, soaked in purified water overnight

1 tablespoon neutral coconut oil

2 teaspoons cumin seeds

Juice of 1 lemon

6 cups hot Odds and Ends Vegetable Broth (page 313) or water from blanching the vegetables (see recipe steps 1 and 2)

1 tablespoon tamari

1 Bring a large soup pot of well-salted water to a boil over high heat. Meanwhile, trim the tough ends off your greens, if necessary. When the water is boiling, add the spring greens and blanch for 1 to 3 minutes, depending on how tender and young or mature your greens are. For instance, baby spinach and baby arugula need less than a minute, while mature dandelion stems will need about 3 minutes to soften. Using a large slotted spoon, transfer the greens to a colander and rinse them under cold water; set aside to drain.

2 Next, using the same boiling water, blanch the peas or fava beans for 30 seconds; snow peas, sugar snaps, or asparagus for 2 minutes; and Romanesco for 3 minutes. Use a large slotted spoon to transfer the vegetables to a colander and rinse them under cold water to stop the cooking process. If you don't have vegetable broth for cooking polenta, reserve 6 cups of the blanching liquid and keep it hot over medium-low heat.

3 Squeeze the excess water out of the blanched greens and chop them roughly. Chop the sugar snaps, snow peas, asparagus, and/or Romanesco into bite-size pieces; set aside. Place the blanched greens in a food processor and pulse into a rough purée. Add the miso paste, mustard, garlic, a pinch of salt, and 2 tablespoons of olive oil; process until the purée is very smooth. Scoop the purée into a bowl and set it aside. Rinse the bowl of the food processor.

4 Drain and rinse the millet, then place it in the food processor and grind until it is broken down but not completely smooth; this will ensure that your polenta still has some bite to it.

5 Melt the coconut oil in a medium saucepan over medium heat. Add the cumin seeds and stir around for a minute, until fragrant. Add the millet and a pinch of salt, stir to coat, then add the lemon juice and mix until it is absorbed. Add the hot vegetable broth or reserved blanching water. Bring to a boil, stirring constantly, then lower the heat and simmer for 20 minutes or until the mixture looks smooth and creamy. Stir frequently to prevent the polenta from sticking to the pan.

6 Add the remaining tablespoon of olive oil and the tamari to the polenta, stir well, then stir in half of the green purée. Add the remaining green purée and fold it in by stirring just a couple of times to create uneven green pockets within the polenta. Distribute the polenta among individual bowls. Top with the blanched vegetables, drizzle with some more olive oil, and sprinkle with freshly ground black pepper; serve hot.

PEACH AND TOMATO PANZANELLA

In this more traditional take on panzanella, toasted chunks of bread absorb the juices of sun-ripened tomatoes and sweet, blushed peaches; red onion and crunchy cucumber add savory flavor, and a simple, bright dressing ties it all together.

Serves 4 to 6 | SUMMER

FOR THE VINAIGRETTE

1 tablespoon freshly squeezed lime or lemon juice

1½ teaspoons red wine vinegar

1 teaspoon Dijon mustard

¼ cup olive oil

FOR THE SALAD

½ loaf ciabatta bread or other bread of choice, torn into bite-size pieces

1½ teaspoons olive oil

Sea salt

3 ripe peaches, halved and pitted

1 medium red onion, sliced into 8 wedges

1½ teaspoons melted neutral coconut oil or olive oil

2 ripe heirloom tomatoes or approximately 2 cups heirloom cherry tomatoes

1 small English cucumber, sliced

Freshly ground black pepper

Handful of fresh basil leaves

1 Preheat the oven to 350°F (180°C). Line a rimmed baking sheet with parchment paper.

2 Combine all of the vinaigrette ingredients in a medium bowl; set aside.

3 Arrange the bread on the prepared baking sheet, drizzle with olive oil, and sprinkle with sea salt. Transfer to the oven and toast the bread for 20 minutes, until golden.

4 Preheat an outdoor or indoor grill to high or increase the oven temperature to 400°F (200°C). Grill the peaches for 3 to 4 minutes on each side on an outdoor or indoor grill, then grill the onion wedges for 5 to 7 minutes on each side until they are caramelized and tender. Remove the peaches and onion from the grill and set them aside to cool. Alternatively, use the oven. Arrange the peaches on a parchment paper–lined baking sheet, cut-side up, and add the onion wedges. Drizzle with oil, transfer the baking sheet to the oven, and roast for 20 minutes. Remove the baking sheet from the oven and set it aside to cool.

5 Combine the toasted bread, tomatoes, cucumbers, and grilled or roasted peaches and onion wedges in a large bowl. Pour the vinaigrette over top, season to taste with salt and freshly ground black pepper, add the basil, and toss well. Serve immediately.

TIPSY WATERMELON, FENNEL, AND ARUGULA SALAD

I find few things more desirable on a hot summer day than this simple, incredibly hydrating salad. I got the idea from a friend, who ate something similar at one of the Four Seasons restaurants. Sangria is my boozy marinade of choice for the watermelon, but if that's not your cup of tea, you can use kombucha instead with very similar results. Despite being incredibly easy to prepare, this salad looks impressive, making it an elegant starter at a summer gathering.

Serves 6 | SUMMER

FOR THE SALAD

1 medium seedless watermelon, well chilled, rind removed and saved for another use, such as Watermelon Rind Marmalade (recipe follows), flesh cut into thick, uniform "steaks"

About ½ cup cold sangria or kombucha, for drizzling

1 fennel bulb, shaved with a vegetable peeler or mandoline

3 cups baby arugula leaves

Coarse sea salt

FOR THE DRESSING

¼ cup olive oil

1 tablespoon honey

1 teaspoon apple cider vinegar

1 In a large, shallow dish, drizzle the watermelon generously with sangria or kombucha. Cover the dish and let the watermelon marinate in the refrigerator for about 1 hour.

2 Whisk all of the dressing ingredients together in a small bowl; set aside.

3 To serve, top the marinated watermelon with the shaved fennel and arugula. Drizzle with the dressing and finish it off with a sprinkle of coarse sea salt.

Watermelon Rind Marmalade

Watermelon is a daily staple in our house during the summer, so I was happy to find a purpose for all the leftover rinds that would otherwise go to waste. This watermelon rind marmalade is properly jammy and pleasantly chewy in texture, with a subtle watermelon aroma and hints of ginger and clove.

2 pounds (1 kg) watermelon rinds, from about 1 medium watermelon, green outer skin removed, white parts finely chopped

2 cups (400 g) turbinado sugar or other sugar of choice

Juice of 1 lemon or lime

1-inch piece fresh ginger, peeled and sliced

1 pod star anise

5 whole cloves

1 Combine the chopped watermelon rind, sugar, lemon juice, and ginger in a large bowl. Mix to coat, cover the bowl, and let it sit in the refrigerator for at least 4 hours or overnight.

2 Stir the marinated rinds and transfer the mixture to a medium saucepan. Add the star anise and cloves, cover the pan, and bring the mixture to a boil over medium heat. Reduce the heat to a slow simmer and cook for 55 to 60 minutes, partially covered, until the rind pieces are translucent and golden in color. Remove the pan from the heat.

3 Divide the marmalade among clean glass jars; seal and refrigerate for up to 2 weeks.

SUMMER BOWL

This is a perfectly balanced summer meal in a bowl. At the base there is freekeh, an ancient durum wheat that is harvested while still young and then roasted over an open fire so its outer shells burn off while the seeds remain intact. The resulting grain is pleasantly smoky in flavor with a nice bite. To round out the bowl, I've also added garlicky green beans, juicy tomatoes, corn, cruncy ribbons of carrot, and cucumber, punctuated by briny spheres of capers and olives. Leafy greens add plenty of nutrients, and a lemony vinaigrette rounds everything off in the best possible way.

As with any bowl meal, feel free to substitute any favorite grain for freekeh—quinoa, buckwheat, millet, farro, spelt, barley, and rice are all great options. (Pictured on page 42.)

Serves 4 | SUMMER

1 cup freekeh or other grain of choice

Sea salt

1½ teaspoons neutral coconut oil or other vegetable oil

2 handfuls of fresh green beans, strings removed

Freshly ground black pepper

1 tablespoon tamari

2 large garlic cloves, sliced

2 cups baby spinach or other baby salad greens

1 large carrot, shaved into ribbons with a vegetable peeler (or julienned)

Kernels from 1 to 2 ears of corn

2 cups halved cherry tomatoes, or 2 to 3 medium tomatoes, cubed

1 small English cucumber, thinly sliced

Handful of olives (optional)

2 tablespoons capers (optional)

Handful of sprouts or microgreens (optional)

Small handful of fresh basil leaves (optional)

Dill and Lemon Vinaigrette (see Spring Panzanella with Radishes and Peas, page 46)

Hemp seeds or other seeds, or chopped nuts of choice (optional)

1 Combine the freekeh with 2½ cups water and a large pinch of salt in a medium pot. Bring to a boil, lower the heat, and simmer, covered, for 20 to 25 minutes, until the water is absorbed. If using another grain, adjust the cooking method accordingly.

2 Warm the oil in a large frying pan over medium heat. Add the green beans, sprinkle with black pepper to taste, and sauté for about 5 minutes, until they begin to blister in places. Drizzle the beans with the tamari and scatter the garlic slices over top. Cover the pan, reduce the heat to medium low, and let the beans cook for another 2 to 3 minutes until crisp and tender, stirring a couple of times. Remove the pan from the heat.

3 Divide the spinach or greens among individual bowls. Top with freekeh, green beans, carrot ribbons, corn kernels, tomatoes, cucumber slices, olives, capers, sprouts or microgreens, and basil, if using. Drizzle with the dill vinaigrette and garnish with seeds or nuts, if using. Serve right away.

TROPICAL CRU

Summertime awakens cravings for hydrating and tropical flavors, and this simple dish is one of my favorite answers to such appetites. The inspiration here is *Poisson Cru*, a Tahitian-style ceviche, where lime-marinated fish and vegetables are served with a splash of chilled coconut milk. Crunchy jicama and cucumber, sweet corn, papaya, and mango make up the perfect plant-based cru alternative, with just the right balance of sweet, tart, spicy, juicy, and creamy textures and flavor notes.

Serves 6 to 8 | SUMMER

1 small or ½ large jicama, peeled and cut into cubes

Kernels from 1 ear of corn

Juice of 2 limes

½ ripe papaya

1 large ripe mango

1 English cucumber

1 jalapeño

About 1 cup fresh cilantro leaves

1 (13.5-ounce; 398 ml) can light Thai coconut milk, chilled

1 Combine the jicama and corn kernels in a large bowl. Pour the lime juice over top and toss to coat; set aside to marinate while you prepare and cut the remaining fresh ingredients.

2 Peel the papaya and mango and cut them into bite-size pieces. Julienne the cucumber with a vegetable peeler or cut it into bite-size pieces. Seed and mince the jalapeño. Chop the cilantro leaves.

3 When you're finished prepping the fruits and vegetables, add everything to the bowl with the jicama and corn; toss to combine.

4 Shake the coconut milk can thoroughly before opening to mix up the fat and water in case they have separated. Distribute the ceviche among individual bowls and pour the coconut milk over all, about ¼ cup per serving, or to taste. Serve immediately.

NAKED TACO BOWL

This bowl has all the familiar flavors and textures of a good taco—crunch from the bright salsa and purple cabbage, sweetness and spice from the chipotle-roasted sweet potato and cashew cream, buttery chunks of avocado, and piney notes from cilantro. All the components make up a great salad, but they can also be served inside taco shells if you want something more substantial.

Serves 4 to 6 | SUMMER

2 medium sweet potatoes, peeled and cubed

1½ teaspoons neutral coconut oil

Sea salt

Chipotle powder, for sprinkling

1½ cups cooked or canned black beans

Kernels from 1 ear of corn

1 to 2 medium tomatoes, chopped

¼ red onion, finely chopped

1 small jalapeño, seeded and finely chopped

Approximately 1 cup fresh cilantro leaves, plus more for serving

Freshly ground black pepper

Juice of 1 lime, plus more for serving

1 tablespoon olive oil

½ small head cabbage or lettuce, shredded

1 ripe avocado, sliced

Chipotle Cream (page 301), for serving

1 Preheat the oven to 400°F (200°C). Line a rimmed baking sheet with parchment paper.

2 Arrange the sweet potato cubes on the prepared baking sheet. Sprinkle with the coconut oil and salt and chipotle powder to taste. Transfer the baking sheet to the oven and roast for 20 to 30 minutes, until the sweet potatoes are soft.

3 Combine the beans, corn kernels, tomatoes, onion, jalapeño, and cilantro leaves in a medium bowl. Sprinkle with salt and pepper to taste, squeeze the lime juice over top, and drizzle with the olive oil. Toss to combine.

4 Divide the shredded cabbage among individual bowls. Top with roasted sweet potatoes, black bean salsa, and avocado. Serve with more lime juice, cilantro, and Chipotle Cream.

LATE SUMMER / EARLY FALL BOWL

This bowl is a celebration of tomatoes and eggplants, which are commonly at their ripest in late summer and early fall, having absorbed all of the summer's sun. To bring out their deepest flavors, I roast the tomatoes and eggplant, then combine them with kale, pleasantly toothsome farro, soft chickpeas, bright pickled onions, and a finishing touch of lemony tahini sauce—making for a complete meal full of flavor, texture, and nourishment.

Note: If you have some time, slow-roasting is a great technique for preparing incredibly sweet, caramelized tomatoes. Follow the instructions in step two but adjust oven temperature to 350°F (180°C) and roast for 1½ to 2 hours, or until the tomatoes are wrinkled and caramelized.

Serves 4 to 6 | SUMMER • FALL

1 pound (454 g) ripe Roma or cherry tomatoes, cut in half

3½ tablespoons olive oil, divided

Sea salt and freshly ground black pepper

1 medium (about 1½-pound / 700-g) eggplant, cut into 1-inch cubes

2 tablespoons za'atar spice blend

1 cup farro

3 to 4 medium kale leaves, stems discarded, leaves chopped

1 cup cooked or canned chickpeas

Quick-Pickled Onions (page 314)

Tahini Sauce (pages 303 to 304)

Handful of unsalted toasted hazelnuts or other nuts, chopped

1 Position your oven racks in the two most central positions of the oven. Preheat the oven to 400°F (200°C). Line two rimmed baking sheets with parchment paper.

2 Place the tomatoes cut-side up on one of the prepared baking sheets. Drizzle with 1 tablespoon of the olive oil and season with salt and pepper to taste.

3 Place the eggplant cubes in a single layer on the second prepared baking sheet, drizzle with 2 tablespoons of the olive oil and season with the za'atar spice and salt and pepper to taste. Toss to coat.

4 Place both baking sheets in the oven. Roast the tomatoes for about 20 minutes, until they are soft and caramelized. Roast the eggplant for 25 to 30 minutes, tossing halfway through, until it is soft and golden.

5 Meanwhile, cook the farro according to the instructions on the package.

6 In a large bowl, combine the kale with the remaining ½ tablespoon of olive oil and salt and pepper to taste. Massage for about 5 minutes, until the kale is wilted and softened.

7 Distribute the kale among individual bowls, followed by the farro, eggplant, and tomatoes. Scatter the chickpeas and pickled onions over the vegetables. Drizzle with the tahini sauce and sprinkle with hazelnuts.

WARM SALAD OF ROASTED CAULIFLOWER, GRAPES, AND FORBIDDEN BLACK RICE

This is a fall salad favorite—perfect for grape season. Grapes provide a delicious contrast to the subtle spiciness of the miso-tahini dressing, the earthy roasted cauliflower, and the textural forbidden black rice. If you are not familiar with black rice, it is a delicious variety that's a bit more nutritious than regular rice and full of antioxidants, due to its stunning purplish-black color. It has a pleasant bite and more of an aromatic sweetness than paler types of rice. This beautiful salad would make an excellent addition to your holiday table, especially if you garnish it with a sprinkle of fresh pomegranate kernels.

Serves 6 | SUMMER • FALL

FOR THE DRESSING

1 tablespoon sesame tahini

1 tablespoon unpasteurized miso paste

4 tablespoons freshly squeezed lemon juice

3 tablespoons olive oil

1 teaspoon chili sauce (Sriracha)

FOR THE SALAD

1 cup forbidden black rice

Sea salt

1 medium head cauliflower, cut into florets

2 tablespoons melted neutral coconut oil or other vegetable oil

1 garlic clove, minced

1 teaspoon freshly ground cumin

2 cups halved seedless grapes

1 small chili, seeded and minced

Leaves from 1 bunch cilantro

TO MAKE THE DRESSING

Mix together the tahini and miso paste in a small bowl. Add the rest of the ingredients and whisk into a smooth dressing.

TO MAKE THE SALAD

1 Combine the rice, 1¾ cups of water, and a pinch of salt in a medium saucepan over medium-high heat. Bring the water to a boil, then reduce the heat to low, cover the pan, and simmer for 30 minutes or until all the water is absorbed. Remove the pan from the heat and set it aside.

2 Meanwhile, preheat the oven to 400°F (200°C). Line a rimmed baking sheet with parchment paper.

3 Drizzle the cauliflower florets with the coconut oil, sprinkle with the garlic and cumin, and mix to coat using your hands. Arrange the cauliflower on the prepared baking sheet in a single layer. Transfer the baking sheet to the oven and roast the cauliflower for 20 minutes or until it is soft, rotating the tray and turning the florets halfway through. Remove the cauliflower from the oven.

4 Combine the rice, cauliflower, grapes, chili, and cilantro leaves in a large mixing bowl. Pour the dressing over top and toss to coat. Serve immediately, so that the cauliflower and rice are still warm. This salad also tastes great cold; store it in an airtight container in the refrigerator for up to 3 days.

SQUASH AND POMEGRANATE PANZANELLA WITH AUTUMN HERBS

This version of panzanella is undeniably autumnal, with hearty slices of roasted squash, caramelized roasted red onion, juicy pops of pomegranate kernels, and woodsy sage and rosemary, all dressed in a bright balsamic vinaigrette. If you can find a ripe persimmon, usually around at produce stands in the fall and winter, include it here for extra sweetness and juice.

Serves 6 to 8 | FALL • WINTER

FOR THE PANZANELLA

4 to 5 slices crusty, whole-grain bread or any bread you have on hand, torn into bite-size pieces

2 tablespoons melted neutral coconut oil, divided

1 small winter squash, preferably kabocha, kuri, or butternut, seeded and sliced (peeled only if using butternut)

2 large red onions, sliced about ½-inch thick

Leaves from 2 fresh rosemary sprigs, chopped

10 sage leaves

Sea salt and freshly ground black pepper

Kernels from 1 pomegranate

1 ripe Fuyu persimmon, pitted and sliced (optional)

FOR THE VINAIGRETTE

2 tablespoons freshly squeezed lemon juice

1 tablespoon balsamic vinegar

1 tablespoon apple cider vinegar

1 teaspoon Dijon mustard

¼ cup olive oil

1 Preheat the oven to 400°F (200°C). Line a baking sheet with parchment paper.

2 Arrange the bread pieces on the baking sheet in a single layer, drizzle with ½ tablespoon of the coconut oil, and transfer to the oven. Toast the bread for about 10 minutes or until the edges are golden brown. Transfer the toasted bread to a plate and set it aside. Shake any remaining crumbs off the baking sheet.

3 Combine the squash, onion, and herbs on the same baking sheet, and drizzle them with the remaining 1½ tablespoons of coconut oil. Sprinkle with salt and pepper to taste and toss the vegetables with your hands to combine and coat thoroughly. Make sure the vegetables are arranged in a single layer, then transfer the baking sheet to the oven. Roast the vegetables for about 20 to 30 minutes, until the squash is soft when pricked with a knife. Remove the vegetables from the oven.

4 On a large platter, arrange the roasted vegetables and herbs, toasted bread, pomegranate kernels, and persimmon slices, if using.

5 To make the vinaigrette, whisk together the lemon juice, balsamic, apple cider vinegar, and mustard in a small bowl. Add the olive oil and whisk until smooth.

6 Pour the dressing over the panzanella and serve immediately.

LENTIL, POMEGRANATE, AND BRUSSELS SPROUT SALAD

This salad is another holiday table favorite, stunning and festive in appearance, and full of fresh, bright flavors that give much needed contrast to any heartier, celebratory mains. For an unexpected twist, I simply shred the Brussels sprouts and squash and keep them raw. Protein-rich lentils contribute their soft, legume texture to round out the salad, and they absorb the sweet, citrusy, and mustardy notes of the dressing.

Serves 8 to 10 | FALL • WINTER

FOR THE SALAD

1 cup black Beluga or puy/French lentils, soaked in purified water overnight

Sea salt

1 cup shelled fresh edamame or frozen edamame

10 to 15 Brussels sprouts

Kernels from 1 pomegranate

¼ red kuri, kabocha, or butternut squash, peeled, seeded, and shredded (optional)

FOR THE DRESSING

5 tablespoons olive oil

3 tablespoons pure maple syrup

1 tablespoon Dijon mustard

1 tablespoon tamari

Generous squeeze of lemon juice (optional)

Freshly ground black pepper

1 Cover the lentils with water in a medium saucepan over medium-high heat, and bring the water to a boil. Lower the heat and simmer for about 15 minutes, or until the lentils are soft. Add a generous pinch of salt at the end, then drain the lentils and let them cool.

2 Fill a medium bowl with ice water. Bring a large pot of well-salted water to a boil. Add the edamame, blanch it for about 1 minute, then immediately transfer it to the ice bath to stop the cooking. Alternatively, you can just thaw frozen edamame and leave it raw.

3 Trim the Brussels sprouts and shred them in a food processor using a shredding attachment.

4 Whisk together all the dressing ingredients in a medium bowl until smooth.

5 Combine all of the salad ingredients in a large mixing bowl and pour the dressing over top; toss to coat, and serve.

LATE AUTUMN / WINTER BOWL

A meal in a bowl for the colder months, when the sun sets earlier and you can see your breath in the air. To warm the body and give it that extra substance that it craves on frosty days, this nourishing combination includes roasted squash, roots, and mushrooms over protein-rich quinoa and lentils, with a generous helping of sauce. If you aren't able to find a winter squash, try using sweet potatoes as a substitute.

Serves 4 to 6 | FALL • WINTER

1 cup quinoa or other grain of choice

½ small winter squash (preferably kabocha, kuri, or butternut), seeded

2 medium parsnips

2 medium carrots

2 tablespoons melted neutral coconut oil, divided

Leaves from approximately 5 fresh thyme sprigs (optional)

Sea salt and freshly ground black pepper

1 pound (454 g) small crimini mushrooms

1 tablespoon olive oil

2 to 3 garlic cloves, sliced

1 teaspoon smoked Spanish paprika

½ small head green cabbage, shredded (optional)

1 cup cooked French lentils or beans of choice (see page 70)

Cashew Cream (pages 301 to 302) or Tahini Sauce (pages 303 to 304) of your choice, for serving

Handful of fresh parsley leaves, finely chopped

¼ cup chopped walnuts or pecans

Quick-Pickled Onions (page 314) (optional)

1 In a medium saucepan, combine the quinoa with 1¾ cups water and a large pinch of salt. Bring the water to a boil, reduce the heat to low, and cook, covered, for 15 to 20 minutes, until all the liquid has been absorbed. Remove the pan from the heat, let it rest for 5 minutes, then fluff the quinoa with a fork. If using another grain, adjust the cooking method accordingly.

2 While the quinoa cooks, preheat the oven to 425°F (220°C). Line two rimmed baking sheets with parchment paper.

3 Peel and dice the squash, parsnips, and carrots into bite-size pieces. (If using kabocha or kuri squash, there is no need to peel them, as their skin is edible; slice them into wedges for better presentation.) Place the vegetables on one of the prepared baking sheets, add 1 tablespoon of the coconut oil, and toss to coat. Sprinkle with the thyme, if using, and season to taste with salt and pepper.

4 On the second prepared baking sheet, toss the mushrooms with the remaining tablespoon of coconut oil and salt and pepper to taste.

5 Transfer both baking sheets to the oven, side by side if possible. Roast the squash, carrots, and parsnips for 30 minutes or until they are soft and caramelized, stirring and rotating the tray halfway through. Roast the mushrooms for 30 to 35 minutes or until they are golden brown, tossing a few times. Remove the vegetables from the oven and set them aside.

6 While the vegetables are roasting, combine the olive oil with the garlic and smoked paprika in a small bowl. As soon as the mushrooms are done roasting, drizzle them with the garlic-paprika oil, toss well, and place them back in the oven for 2 to 3 minutes for the mushrooms to absorb the oil and the garlic to become fragrant.

7 Divide the cabbage, if using, among individual bowls. Top with the quinoa, lentils, roasted vegetables, and smoky mushrooms. Sprinkle with the tahini or cashew sauce, parsley, nuts, and pickled onions, if using. Serve right away.

LEMONY TEFF POLENTA WITH TAHINI, LEEKS, AND CHICKPEAS

Like millet, teff makes for a more nutritious and interesting alternative to corn grits in polenta-type dishes. This bowl was inspired by a cold winter's day and nourishes with every bite—requiring simple pantry ingredients and just a few readily available items of produce, which are elevated to a new, delicious level by a lemony tahini sauce.

Serves 4 | FALL • WINTER

½ cup dried chickpeas, soaked in purified water overnight

1 medium yellow onion, cut in half lengthwise

3 to 4 garlic cloves, crushed

6 cups purified water

Sea salt

3 tablespoons tahini

Juice of 2 lemons, divided

1 large garlic clove, minced

2 tablespoons olive oil, divided

Dash of cayenne pepper

1½ tablespoons neutral coconut oil or ghee, divided

1 cup teff

1 teaspoon cumin seeds

2 leeks, white and light green parts only, thinly sliced

Freshly ground black pepper

Handful of fresh parsley leaves, for garnish

1 Drain the chickpeas. Place the chickpeas, onion, garlic, and water in a medium soup pot, and bring the mixture to a boil over high heat. If you have any leftover vegetable stems, tops, etc., add them to the water to make the cooking liquid even more flavorful. Reduce the heat and simmer for about 30 minutes or until the chickpeas are completely soft. Add salt to taste during the last 5 to 10 minutes of cooking. Strain the broth, reserving the liquid and the beans separately; discard the rest of the solids. Keep the broth warm if you are making polenta right away. This step can be done a day or two in advance. If made ahead of time, gently reheat the broth on the stove before making the polenta.

2 Combine the tahini, half of the lemon juice, the minced garlic, 1 tablespoon of the olive oil, a pinch of salt, and the cayenne in a small bowl. Mix until smooth and add ¼ cup of the reserved chickpea broth, stirring to form a smooth, runny sauce. Set aside.

3 Melt about ½ tablespoon of the coconut oil or ghee in a medium saucepan over medium heat. Add the teff and stir it around for 1 to 2 minutes, until fragrant. Add the remaining lemon juice and stir until the juice is absorbed, about 1 minute. Add 3 cups of the reserved chickpea broth with a pinch of salt and bring the liquid to a boil. Reduce the heat and simmer, partially covered, for 15 to 20 minutes, until

the mixture looks creamy. Stir often to prevent the teff from sticking to the bottom of the pan. Remove the pan from the heat and stir in the remaining tablespoon of olive oil. Check for salt, adjust if needed, cover, and set aside.

4 While the teff is cooking, melt the remaining tablespoon of coconut oil in a sauté pan over medium heat. Add the cumin seeds and stir them around for about a minute, until fragrant. Add the leeks and salt and black pepper to taste, and sauté for about 7 to 8 minutes, until the leeks are soft. Add the chickpeas, stir to coat, and let them warm through. Add the tahini sauce, stir to combine, and let everything cook together for 2 minutes. Add 1⁄4 cup of the reserved chickpea broth and cook for another 2 minutes, until creamy. Check for salt and pepper and adjust if needed.

5 Distribute the teff polenta among individual bowls, top with the leek and chickpea mixture, and garnish with parsley. Serve hot.

HEIRLOOM BEAN, FENNEL, AND CITRUS SALAD

Here is an elegant salad that showcases all the beautiful citrus fruit the winter season has to offer. I like to seek out different heirloom varieties of beans; besides their striking speckling of color, each type has its own unique flavor. You can use any of your favorite beans in this recipe, but the larger, flatter ones will work especially well.

Serves 2 to 4 | WINTER • SPRING

½ cup heirloom beans like Scarlet Runners, Cranberry, or Christmas Lima, soaked overnight

3 oranges (preferably a mixed variety like blood orange, navel, or kara-kara), divided

¼ medium red onion, thinly sliced

1 grapefruit

3 tablespoons olive oil

1 large or 2 small fennel bulbs, thinly sliced

2 tablespoons capers

1 to 2 cups mixed greens of choice (optional)

Freshly ground black pepper

Handful of fennel fronds, torn

1 Cook the beans according to the instructions on page 296. Drain them over a colander and let them cool.

2 Juice one orange. Put the sliced onion into a medium bowl and pour half of the juice over the slices. Toss to coat the onions and set aside, reserving the remaining juice.

3 Segment one orange and the grapefruit over a medium bowl, collecting all the juice and then combine the reserved orange juice with the mixed juice. Set the fruit segments aside. To the mixed juice, add the olive oil and whisk to combine into a quick salad dressing.

4 In a large bowl, combine the cooked beans, fennel bulbs, capers, and fruit segments. Drain the onions and add them to the salad. Pour the dressing over and toss gently.

5 Slice the remaining orange. Arrange the salad on a platter or a bed of greens of your choice, as pictured. Garnish with the orange slices, black pepper to taste, and the fennel fronds. Serve immediately.

STEAMED CHIOGGIA BEET AND PEAR SALAD

This salad is a beautiful showcase for candy-colored chioggia beets. Toasting nuts, chickpeas, and raisins with salt and seasoned oil is my go-to trick for spicing up any salad with warm, crunchy, and flavorful toppings.

Serves 4 to 6 | WINTER

⅛ small red onion, thinly sliced

1 tablespoon apple cider vinegar

5 small or 3 medium chioggia beets, peeled and thinly sliced, either by hand or on a mandoline

Juice of 1 lemon

Sea salt and freshly ground black pepper

3 tablespoons neutral coconut oil, divided

1 teaspoon smoked Spanish paprika

¾ cup raw walnuts, chopped

1 tablespoon finely chopped fresh ginger

3 large garlic cloves, thinly sliced

1½ cups cooked or canned chickpeas

½ cup raisins

1 ripe pear, cored and sliced

Large handful of salad greens, for serving

1 Place the onion in a small bowl and drizzle the apple cider vinegar over top. Toss to coat and set the bowl aside.

2 Arrange the sliced beets in a steaming basket, place it over a pot of boiling water, and cover. Steam the sliced beets for 5 to 7 minutes, until soft when pricked with a knife. Transfer the steamed beets to a large bowl and squeeze the lemon juice over top. Sprinkle with salt and pepper to taste, and gently toss to coat.

3 Melt the coconut oil in a medium sauté pan over medium heat. Add a pinch of salt, the paprika, and the walnuts, and let the walnuts toast for 5 minutes or until golden. Using a slotted spoon, transfer the walnuts to a plate and set them aside.

4 Add the ginger to the sauté pan and cook for 2 minutes over medium heat. Add the garlic and stir it around for 30 seconds until fragrant. Add the chickpeas and sauté for 2 to 3 minutes, allowing them to soak up the flavors from the oil. Add the raisins and stir them around for a couple of minutes, until plump.

5 Add the pear slices to the bowl with the beets, followed by the chickpeas, raisins, and the drippings from the pan. Add the toasted walnuts and salad greens. Drain the onions and add them to the salad. Gently toss everything to combine and arrange the salad on a large platter or distribute it among bowls to serve.

GOLDEN BEET AND POMELO WINTER PANZANELLA

This seasonal spin on panzanella incorporates some of my favorite winter ingredients. Juicy and slightly bitter pomelo segments, hearty wedges of golden beets, creamy avocado, red onion, and briny olives lend their flavors to a bed of crusty sourdough bread—a delicious salad option to tide you over until the arrival of juicy summer tomatoes.

Serves 4 | WINTER • SPRING

- 3 small or two medium golden beets
- ⅛ small red onion, thinly sliced
- 2½ tablespoons apple cider vinegar, divided
- Approximately 6 slices of crusty, whole-grain sourdough bread, torn into bite-size pieces
- ¼ cup plus 2 tablespoons olive oil, divided
- 2 large garlic cloves, minced
- ½ teaspoon sea salt
- 1 large pomelo, peeled and segmented
- 1 ripe but firm avocado, sliced
- 10 to 15 pitted olives
- 1 teaspoon Dijon mustard

1 Steam, boil, or bake the beets until they are fully cooked, then peel them and slice them into wedges. To steam the beets, slice them in half and arrange them in a steaming basket. Place it over a pot of boiling water and cover. Steam the beets until tender throughout, for about 30 minutes.

2 Preheat the oven to 350°F (180°C).

3 Place the onion in a small bowl and drizzle 1 tablespoon of the apple cider vinegar over top. Set aside.

4 Place the bread on a baking sheet in a single layer, drizzle with 2 tablespoons of the olive oil, and sprinkle with the minced garlic and salt. Transfer the baking sheet to the oven and toast the bread for 20 minutes, until the edges are golden. Remove the bread from the oven and set it aside.

5 Arrange the beet wedges, toasted bread pieces, pomelo segments, avocado slices, and olives on a platter. Drain the onions and scatter them on top.

6 In a small bowl, whisk the remaining 1½ tablespoons of apple cider vinegar together with the Dijon mustard. Add the remaining ¼ cup of olive oil and whisk until smooth. Pour the dressing over the salad and serve immediately.

WRAPS AND ROLLS

WRAPPING A VARIETY of well-considered ingredients into one unifying envelope is a culinary practice that's made its way all around the world—there are tacos, burritos and enchiladas, doubles, calzones, dolmas, gyros, injera, sushi, spring rolls, and summer rolls, to name just a few. I love their convenience, and the creative possibilities are endless—the key is to use a variety of wholesome, seasonal wrappers and fillings and to get creative with your combinations.

87
Sprouted or Whole Spelt Tortillas

88
Summer Rolls with Savoy Cabbage and Sugar Snaps

91
Spring Cabbage Rolls with Mushrooms, Lentils, Rice, and Tomato Sauce

93
Chickpea and Kohlrabi Salad Wraps

96
Roasted Portobello and Eggplant Gyros

99
Smoky Cauliflower and Black Bean Hummus Burritos

101
Roasted Yam and Collard Green Enchiladas

104
Collard Wraps with Chickpea-Avocado Mash, Roasted Carrots, and Spicy Cranberry Relish

107
Couscous-Stuffed Collard Greens in Coconut Curry Sauce

110
Pickled Turnip, Avocado, Barley, and Black Rice Sushi Rolls

112
Silky Barley Water with Ginger and Citrus

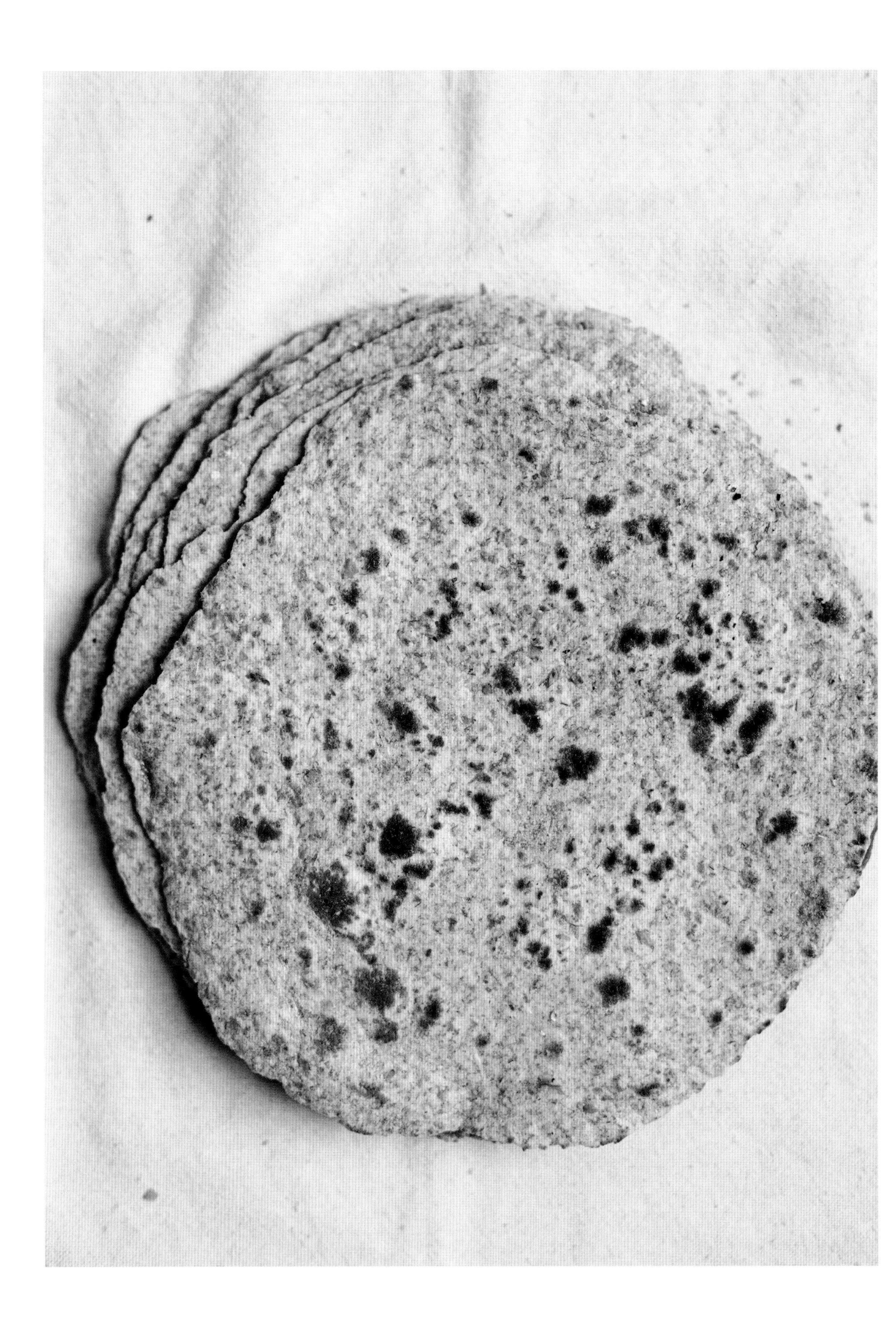

SPROUTED OR WHOLE SPELT TORTILLAS

Homemade tortillas are incredibly simple to prepare and will taste much better than most store-bought wraps.

Makes 16 tortillas

3 cups (300 g) sprouted spelt flour or whole spelt flour

1 teaspoon sea salt

1 teaspoon baking powder

⅓ cup neutral coconut oil, at room temperature, or other neutral vegetable oil

1¼ cups warm purified water

1 Whisk together the flour, salt, and baking powder in a large bowl. Make a well in the center, and pour in the oil and water; mix to combine, gradually incorporating the flour into the oil and water well. Knead into a soft dough. Cover the bowl and let the dough rest for 30 minutes at room temperature.

2 Divide the dough in half and roll each piece into a thick rope. Cut each rope in half, and continue cutting each new piece of dough in half until you have 16 equal-size pieces. Make a ball out of each piece, flatten each with the palm of your hand, and keep them covered.

3 Place a medium skillet over medium-high heat.

4 On a well-floured work surface, roll each piece of dough into a 6- to 7-inch circle. Transfer one circle at a time to the hot pan and cook for about 1 minute on one side, until bubbles appear and just a few pale spots are visible on the underside. Flip and cook for another 30 seconds. Remove the tortilla from the pan and keep it wrapped in a clean kitchen towel.

5 Continue with the rest of the dough circles, stacking the finished tortillas on top of each other and keeping them covered. They are best when used right away. Use them for Roasted Yam and Collard Green Enchiladas (page 101), Smoky Cauliflower and Black Bean Hummus Burritos (page 99), or Roasted Portobello and Eggplant Gyros (page 96), or serve them with Curried Bean and Brussels Sprout Stew (page 133).

SUMMER ROLLS WITH SAVOY CABBAGE AND SUGAR SNAPS

These summer rolls are a fresh, fluffy, and crunchy combination of savoy cabbage, sugar snaps, fresh herbs, and cashews. In combination with the incredibly creamy, sweet-and-sour dipping sauce, they are the perfect spring appetizer or light lunch.

Makes about 15 rolls | SPRING • SUMMER

FOR THE DIPPING SAUCE

2 garlic cloves, crushed into a paste in a mortar and pestle or minced

6 tablespoons almond butter

6 tablespoons freshly squeezed lime juice

2 tablespoons tamari

1½ tablespoons pure maple syrup

¾ teaspoon chili sauce (Sriracha)

FOR THE SUMMER ROLLS

½ small head Savoy cabbage, shredded

2 cups fresh sugar snap peas, strings removed, sliced on the diagonal

½ cup fresh cilantro leaves

Handful of fresh mint leaves, chopped

Handful of fresh basil leaves, torn

About 15 rice paper wrappers

½ cup raw cashews, chopped

1 Mix all of the dipping sauce ingredients in a medium bowl until smooth. Set aside.

2 Place the cabbage, sugar snaps, and herbs in a large bowl; toss to combine.

3 Fill another large bowl with tepid warm water and place a clean, damp kitchen towel nearby. Working with one wrapper at a time, submerge it in the water for a few seconds, just until it is pliable. Make sure not to keep it in the water for too long, as the rice paper will become too fragile.

4 Working quickly, place the soaked wrapper onto the damp towel. Place about 3 tablespoons of the filling in the center of the wrapper. Sprinkle with some chopped cashews. Fold the end of the wrapper closest to you over the filling, then fold in the sides and roll it up tightly. Repeat with the remaining wrappers and filling.

5 Serve immediately with the dipping sauce.

SPRING CABBAGE ROLLS WITH MUSHROOMS, LENTILS, RICE, AND TOMATO SAUCE

These wholesome cabbage rolls can be made all year round, but I especially like preparing them in the spring—using young, fluffy cabbage with green outer leaves that are more tender, flavorful, and easier to roll. I recently learned the amazing trick of fully freezing and thawing a head of cabbage, which immensely improves the leaves' flexibility and ability to separate. As delicious as these rolls are right away, their flavor greatly benefits from a couple of days in the refrigerator. They also freeze well, and seem to be even more savory after defrosting and reheating.

Note: For this recipe, make sure to plan ahead, leaving at least 24 hours for the cabbage to freeze thoroughly and about as much time for thawing.

Serves 6 to 8 | SPRING

1 large head white cabbage, frozen whole for at least 24 hours, then thawed out completely

2 tablespoons neutral coconut oil or olive oil

3 teaspoons cumin seeds, freshly ground

2 teaspoons coriander seeds, freshly ground

½ teaspoon red pepper flakes

1 large red onion, chopped

Sea salt

1 pound (454 g) crimini mushrooms, sliced

1 tablespoon fresh thyme leaves (optional)

Freshly ground black pepper

1 cup brown rice or other rice of choice

½ cup green lentils, preferably soaked in purified water overnight

1 (28-ounce / 794-g) can or box crushed tomatoes, or 2 recipes Universal Tomato Sauce (page 308)

Plain Greek yogurt or sour cream, for serving

1 Bring a large pot of salted water to a boil. Meanwhile, cut a deep, cone-shaped incision in the bottom of the cabbage and take out the core. Set it aside. Carefully separate the cabbage leaves, one by one, taking care to keep them intact. Set aside all the leaves that are too small for wrapping. Submerge the rest of the leaves in the boiling water and cook for 3 minutes. Drain the cabbage in a colander, rinse it under cold water to stop the cooking, and let it sit in the colander to drain some more while you make the filling.

2 Bring 2½ cups of water to a boil in a tea kettle or saucepan.

3 Meanwhile, in a medium pot, warm the coconut or olive oil over medium heat. Add the cumin, coriander, and red pepper flakes, and cook for 1 minute, until fragrant. Add the onion and a pinch of salt, and sauté for 7 to 8 minutes, until the onion is translucent. Add the mushrooms and thyme, if using, along with more salt and pepper to taste. Cook until all the liquid has evaporated and the mushrooms begin to brown, about 8 minutes.

4 Add the rice and the boiling water to the pot. Cover and let the mixture simmer over low heat for 30 minutes. Add the lentils, cover the pot, and continue to simmer for another 15 minutes. Taste the mixture and add more salt as desired.

5 Chop the cabbage core roughly and arrange those pieces, along with all of the smaller, unused leaves, at the bottom of the same pot you used to blanch the cabbage leaves.

6 Working with one blanched cabbage leaf at a time, add about 2 to 3 tablespoons of filling (depending on the size of the leaf) in the center. Fold the lower end over the filling, then fold in the sides and roll it up tightly. Repeat with the rest of the leaves and filling.

7 Arrange the rolls in a snug, single layer on top of the cabbage leaves inside the pot. When you can't fit any more rolls in one layer, cover them with about one third of the crushed tomatoes and continue with the next layer of rolls. Cover with another third of the crushed tomatoes, followed by the rest of the rolls. Finish with the remaining crushed tomatoes.

8 Cover the pot and bring the tomatoes to a boil over high heat. Lower the heat to a strong simmer and cook for 1 hour or until the cabbage is completely cooked and tender. Remove the pot from the heat and let the rolls cool slightly; serve with dollops of plain Greek yogurt or sour cream. The rolls will keep well in an airtight container in the refrigerator for up to 5 days. Reheat them in a pan, covered, over low heat. You can also freeze them for up to 1 month.

CHICKPEA AND KOHLRABI SALAD WRAPS

Olivier salad is probably the most commonly prepared salad in Russia. It's another one of those very satisfying, finely chopped, potato-based and mayo-dressed Soviet salads, which has graced every Russian family's table at one point or another. Although the ingredients in this recipe have very little in common with those of the Olivier (which includes eggs, meat, and potatoes), the overall textural and flavor profiles run along the same lines. My version is very nutritious, with a nice balance of soft and crunchy, smoky and bright, briny and sweet.

I originally built this salad around young, tender kohlrabi (which reminds me of hard-boiled eggs), but you can use jicama or young salad turnips instead with very similar results. If using turnips, cube them and add them to the dish right before serving, as they can turn bitter after sitting in the salad. Feel free to omit a few ingredients if you do not have them on hand—it will still be delicious.

Serves 4 to 6 | SUMMER

FOR THE SALAD

½ cup dried chickpeas, soaked in purified water overnight, or about 1¼ cups cooked or canned chickpeas

1 teaspoon neutral coconut oil

1 cup fresh or frozen green peas, thawed if frozen

Sea salt

2 small or 1 medium kohlrabi, peeled and cut into small cubes

½ medium English cucumber, cut into small cubes

1 to 2 small whole pickles, cut into small cubes

¼ cup black olives, halved or quartered

¼ cup oil-packed sun-dried tomatoes, cut into small pieces

⅛ medium red onion, finely chopped

1 teaspoon smoked Spanish paprika

¼ cup finely chopped fresh dill

2 tablespoons finely chopped fresh parsley

Handful of fresh mint leaves, chopped (optional)

1 tablespoon capers (optional)

Handful of raw walnuts or other nuts, chopped (optional)

Freshly ground black pepper

About 5 tablespoons Apple-Miso Mayo (page 300) or Tahini Miso Sauce (page 304)

TO MAKE THE SALAD

1 If using dried chickpeas, cook them until soft (see page 296). Drain and let them cool.

2 Melt the coconut oil in a medium frying pan over medium-high heat. Add the peas and a pinch of salt, and cook for 1 to 2 minutes, until the peas are bright green. Remove the pan from the heat.

3 In a large bowl, combine the peas, chickpeas, kohlrabi, cucumber, pickles, olives, sun-dried tomatoes, onion, paprika, herbs, capers, and nuts, if using, and season with a pinch of salt and black pepper to taste.

4 Add your sauce of choice and toss to combine. Taste for salt and pepper and adjust if needed.

recipe continues

CHICKPEA AND KOHLRABI SALAD WRAPS, continued

FOR THE WRAPS

4 to 6 medium collard green leaves or other wraps of choice

TO MAKE THE WRAPS

Cut the extending stem off the collard green leaves and shave off the thick part of the remaining stem. Collard green leaves can be blanched using the technique on pages 104–106 for easier handling, or they can be used raw. Spoon about 2 heaping tablespoons of the salad into the center of each leaf, fold the bottom end and then the sides of the leaf over the filling, and roll it up tightly.

ROASTED PORTOBELLO AND EGGPLANT GYROS

This collection of ingredients amazingly resembles a classic gyro from the very first bite. Za'atar-roasted portobellos and eggplant are both meaty and buttery, and pair beautifully with juicy tomatoes, crunchy cucumbers, and the sensational, cashew-based tzatziki sauce. (Pictured on page 84.)

Serves 6 to 8 | SUMMER • FALL

FOR THE TZATZIKI SAUCE

1 cup raw cashews, soaked in purified water for 2 to 4 hours

⅓ cup purified water

1½ tablespoons tamari

1 tablespoon tahini

1 tablespoon freshly squeezed lemon juice

1 garlic clove, chopped

½ English cucumber, shredded or finely diced

¼ cup finely chopped fresh dill

Handful of fresh mint leaves, chopped (optional)

FOR THE GYROS

1 large or 2 small eggplants, halved lengthwise and sliced into ¾-inch-thick half-moons

2 large portobello mushrooms, stemmed and sliced into ¾-inch-thick pieces

2 tablespoons melted neutral coconut oil or olive oil

Sea salt and freshly ground black pepper

2 tablespoons za'atar, divided

Juice of ½ lemon

½ small red onion, thinly sliced

6 to 8 whole wheat wraps or tortillas of your choice

2 medium tomatoes, sliced, or 2 cups cherry tomatoes, halved

¼ to ½ English cucumber, sliced

TO MAKE THE TZATZIKI SAUCE

1 Drain and rinse the cashews. Place them in an upright blender along with the water, tamari, tahini, lemon juice, and garlic. Blend until smooth.

2 Scrape the sauce into a medium bowl, making sure to get all of it from the blender. Mix in the shredded cucumber, dill, and mint, if using. Store the sauce in an airtight container in the refrigerator for up to 3 days.

TO MAKE THE GYROS

1 Preheat the oven to 400°F (200°C). Line a large rimmed baking sheet with parchment paper.

2 Place the eggplant and mushrooms in a large bowl. Drizzle with the oil and sprinkle with salt and pepper to taste. Toss with your hands to coat the vegetables.

3 Arrange the eggplant and mushroom slices on the prepared baking sheet in a single layer. Sprinkle with 1 tablespoon of the za'atar spice. Transfer the baking sheet to the oven and roast the vegetables for 20 minutes, then flip them over, sprinkle with the remaining tablespoon of za'atar, and bake for another 15 minutes until soft and golden brown.

4 In the meantime, pour the lemon juice over the red onion in a small bowl; mix well and let the onion marinate while the eggplant and mushrooms roast.

5 When the eggplant and mushrooms are done, remove them from the oven. Place a few pieces of roasted eggplant and mushroom in the middle of each tortilla and top with a few slices of tomato and cucumber, as well as some marinated red onion. Finish with generous dollops of tzatziki sauce. Wrap and serve.

SMOKY CAULIFLOWER AND BLACK BEAN HUMMUS BURRITOS

The star of this unique take on a traditional burrito is smoky cauliflower, which is caramelized in the pan, then kissed with smoked paprika, maple syrup, and jalapeño. Rounded out with homemade black bean hummus, a few cubes of avocado, and a squeeze of lime, this becomes a warming and substantial meal, with no need for rice. The cauliflower and hummus are also delicious on their own—try the cauliflower as part of a grain and vegetable bowl, a side, or a topping for a salad. Get creative and use the hummus on sandwiches, in bowls, or even as a dip.

Makes 6 to 8 burritos | FALL • WINTER

FOR THE BLACK BEAN HUMMUS

1 cup dried black beans, soaked in purified water overnight

2 bay leaves and/or 2-inch piece kombu (optional)

1 cup torn fresh cilantro leaves and stems

½ ripe but not mushy avocado, peeled and pitted

½ jalapeño, seeded and roughly chopped

2 garlic cloves, roughly chopped

3 tablespoons freshly squeezed lemon juice

1 teaspoon cumin seeds, toasted and freshly ground

Sea salt and freshly ground black pepper

TO MAKE THE BLACK BEAN HUMMUS

1 Drain and rinse the beans and cover them with water in a medium pot. Add the bay leaves and/or kombu, if using, and bring the water to a boil over medium-high heat. Lower the heat to a simmer, partially cover the pot, and cook the beans for about 30 minutes, until they are soft and buttery but not mushy inside. Drain the beans, reserving 2 tablespoons of the cooking liquid for this recipe and storing the rest for future use in a soup or stew, if desired. Let the beans cool and discard the bay leaves or kombu.

2 In a food processor, combine the beans, cilantro, avocado, jalapeño, garlic, lemon juice, ground cumin seeds, and salt and pepper to taste. Process until smooth, adding some of the reserved bean cooking liquid as you go to achieve a smooth consistency. You'll have more hummus than you need for this recipe. Leftover hummus is great as a dip and on tartines or sandwiches; store it in an airtight container in the refrigerator for up to 4 days.

recipe continues

SMOKY CAULIFLOWER AND BLACK BEAN HUMMUS BURRITOS, continued

FOR THE SMOKY CAULIFLOWER

4 tablespoons neutral coconut oil, divided

1 large yellow onion, chopped

Sea salt and freshly ground black pepper

1 large head cauliflower, cut into florets

½ jalapeño or other chili, finely chopped

1 teaspoon smoked Spanish paprika

1 teaspoon pure maple syrup

2 tablespoons freshly squeezed lime or lemon juice

FOR THE BURRITOS

6 to 8 homemade tortillas (page 87) or large store-bought whole-grain tortillas or wraps

2 cups baby spinach, microgreens, or chopped lettuce

Fresh cilantro leaves

½ ripe avocado, cubed (optional)

Juice of 1 lime (optional)

TO PREPARE THE SMOKY CAULIFLOWER

1 Warm 1 tablespoon of the coconut oil in a large frying pan over medium heat. Add the onion, salt, and pepper, and sauté for 10 to 12 minutes, until golden and caramelized. Remove the onion from the pan and set it aside.

2 Return the pan to medium heat and warm the remaining 3 tablespoons of coconut oil. Add the cauliflower to the pan in a single layer, sprinkle with salt and pepper to taste, and cook for 3 to 4 minutes, until lightly browned. Flip the florets and cook on the other side for another 3 to 5 minutes. Continue to cook for a couple more minutes to achieve even caramelization.

3 Add the jalapeño and paprika to the pan with the cauliflower and sauté for 2 to 3 minutes until the cauliflower is golden brown. Drizzle with the maple syrup and lime or lemon juice. Sauté for a minute or two until the liquid reduces into a glaze. Stir in the caramelized onion and remove the pan from the heat.

TO MAKE THE BURRITOS

1 Place one tortilla on a serving plate and spread 2 tablespoons of black bean hummus on top. Add about 2 spoonfuls of smoky cauliflower, followed by a small handful of spinach or other greens. Top with some cilantro, avocado, and lime juice.

2 Fold the lower end of the tortilla over the filling, followed by the sides, and then roll it tightly into a burrito. Repeat with the remaining tortillas and fillings. I prefer to make fresh burritos right before eating, but you can also make these in advance to take with you and enjoy for lunch or at an outing.

ROASTED YAM AND COLLARD GREEN ENCHILADAS

Enchiladas are a messy and cozy affair that I find to be especially fitting for the colder seasons. These are filled with paprika-roasted yams and dark collard greens, and baked in a chunky and slightly spicy red sauce, making for the perfect wintry dinner.

Makes 6 large or 12 small enchiladas | FALL • WINTER

FOR THE FILLING

6 to 8 large collard greens from 1 large bunch, stems removed

Sea salt

2 medium yams or sweet potatoes, peeled and cubed into bite-size pieces

2½ tablespoons melted neutral coconut oil, divided

1 teaspoon smoked Spanish paprika

Freshly ground black pepper

2 large red onions, diced

TO MAKE THE FILLING

1 Preheat the oven to 400°F (200°C). Line a rimmed baking sheet with parchment paper.

2 Place the collard greens in a medium pot, cover them with water, and place the pot over medium-high heat. When the water comes to a boil, lower the heat to a strong simmer, add a pinch of salt, and cook, partially covered, for 30 minutes to 1 hour, until the collard greens are soft but not mushy. Reserve 1 cup of the cooking liquid, then drain the collards and set them aside in a colander.

3 While the collard greens are cooking, place the cubed yams on the prepared baking sheet in a single layer. Drizzle with ½ tablespoon of the coconut oil, sprinkle with the smoked paprika, and season to taste with salt and pepper; mix with your hands to coat the yams in the oil and seasonings, then transfer the baking sheet to the oven and roast the yams for 25 minutes or until they are soft when pricked with a knife. Lower the oven temperature to 350°F (180°C). Make the sauce while the yams roast (see page 103).

4 Once the sauce is done, squeeze any excess liquid out of the cooked collard greens and cut them into bite-size pieces. In a medium sauté pan, melt the remaining 2 tablespoons of coconut oil over medium heat. Add the red onions and a pinch of salt, and sauté for 10 minutes or until the onions are soft and translucent. Reduce the heat to medium low and caramelize the onions for another 15 minutes, stirring occasionally, until they are deep golden brown. Add the chopped collard greens and the rest of the ground cumin from making the

recipe continues

sauce. Increase the heat back to medium and sauté the vegetables for 2 to 3 more minutes, stirring constantly. Remove the pan from the heat.

TO MAKE THE SAUCE

1 Warm a medium saucepan over medium heat. Add the cumin seeds and toast them for 1 to 2 minutes, until fragrant. Remove the pan from the heat and grind the cumin in a mortar and pestle; set aside.

2 Return the saucepan to medium heat, add the oil and onion, and sauté for 7 minutes, until the onion is translucent. Add the garlic and jalapeño, and sauté for another 3 minutes. Add half of the ground cumin along with the smoked paprika, tomatoes, and reserved collard green cooking liquid. Bring the mixture to a simmer and cook for about 10 minutes until the sauce thickens slightly. Taste for salt and adjust if needed.

TO MAKE THE ENCHILADAS

1 Line an 8 x 11-inch (20 x 27-cm) baking dish with parchment paper, extending it up the sides. Spread half of the sauce on the bottom of the dish. Lay out one tortilla at a time on a plate or cutting board. Spoon about 1/4 cup of sweet potato cubes (less for small tortillas) along the diameter of the tortilla, followed by the same amount of collard greens. Sprinkle with about 1 teaspoon of the cheese, if using, leaving some for sprinkling on top. Roll the tortilla tightly and place it in the baking dish, seam-side down. Continue with the rest of the tortillas and fillings, arranging them snugly in a single layer. Spread the remaining sauce on top of the filled tortillas and sprinkle with the remaining cheese, if using. Transfer the baking dish to the oven and bake for 25 to 30 minutes until it is hot throughout.

2 Remove the baking dish from the oven and let it cool slightly. Serve the enchiladas with avocado, lime wedges, and fresh cilantro leaves. Store leftovers in an airtight container in the refrigerator for up to 5 days. Reheat in a sauté pan over low heat.

FOR THE SAUCE

2 teaspoons cumin seeds, divided

1 tablespoon neutral coconut oil

1 medium yellow onion, chopped

3 garlic cloves, sliced

1 jalapeño (seeded if you prefer), finely chopped

1 teaspoon smoked Spanish paprika

1 (28-ounce / 794-g) can or box crushed tomatoes

1 cup cooking liquid from the collard greens

Sea salt

FOR THE ENCHILADAS

6 to 8 homemade tortillas (page 87), or 6 large or 12 small store-bought whole-grain tortillas

½ cup shredded sheep or goat's milk cheese (optional)

1 ripe but firm avocado, diced, for serving

1 lime, cut into wedges, for serving

1 cup fresh cilantro leaves, for serving

COLLARD WRAPS WITH CHICKPEA-AVOCADO MASH, ROASTED CARROTS, AND SPICY CRANBERRY RELISH

I love the idea of collard green wraps and will often throw together some version of these with whichever fresh ingredients I have on hand, mostly for a quick solo lunch. This recipe is more sophisticated with a balanced combination of tasty components. Here, I pair sweet roasted carrots with a hearty chickpea and avocado mash, and I round it all off with the brightness and crunch of tart cranberry relish.

When I'm craving something extra green, I use raw collard leaves as wraps, but most of the time I give them a quick blanch for a more pliable and neutrally flavored shell. The blanched leaves will also keep well for a few days in the refrigerator, if you want to wrap as you go.

Makes 7 to 9 wraps | FALL • WINTER

FOR THE CHICKPEA-AVOCADO MASH

¾ cup dried chickpeas, soaked in purified water overnight

2 bay leaves and/or one 2-inch piece kombu (optional)

A few whole black peppercorns (optional)

Sea salt

1 ripe but not too mushy avocado

Juice of 1 lemon

1 cup loosely packed fresh cilantro leaves, chopped

¼ small red onion, finely chopped

Handful of raw walnuts, toasted and chopped

1 teaspoon cumin seeds, toasted and freshly ground

Freshly ground black pepper

FOR THE ROASTED CARROTS

5 to 7 small to medium carrots, peeled if not organic

1 teaspoon melted neutral coconut oil

Sea salt and freshly ground black pepper

ingredients continue

TO MAKE THE CHICKPEA-AVOCADO MASH

1 Drain and rinse the chickpeas, then place them in a medium saucepan and cover them with plenty of water. Add the bay leaves and/or kombu and black peppercorns, if using, and bring the water to a boil. Lower the heat to a strong simmer and cook, partially covered, for about 30 minutes or until the chickpeas are soft. Add salt to taste during the last 10 minutes of cooking. Use this time to roast the carrots (see page 106). Once the chickpeas are done cooking, drain them well, reserving the cooking liquid for a soup or stew, if desired. Let the chickpeas cool and discard the bay leaves or kombu and black peppercorns.

2 Combine the chickpeas and avocado in a medium bowl and mash them together roughly. Add the lemon juice, cilantro, red onion, walnuts, cumin, salt, and ground black pepper to taste. Stir to combine thoroughly, taste for salt and pepper, and adjust as needed.

COLLARD WRAPS WITH CHICKPEA-AVOCADO MASH, ROASTED CARROTS, AND SPICY CRANBERRY RELISH, continued

FOR THE CRANBERRY RELISH

1 cup fresh or frozen cranberries, thawed if frozen

½ cup seedless grapes

½ jalapeño, seeded (if you prefer) and roughly chopped

Large handful of fresh ciltantro leaves and stems, torn

1 heaping teaspoon chopped fresh ginger

FOR THE WRAPS

7 large or 9 medium collard green leaves

Cashew Cream (page 301 to 302) or Tahini Sauce of your choice (page 303 to 304), for serving, optional

TO ROAST THE CARROTS

1 While the chickpeas are cooking, preheat the oven to 425°F (220°C). Line a rimmed baking sheet with parchment paper.

2 Place the carrots on the prepared baking sheet, drizzle them with the coconut oil, and sprinkle with salt and pepper to taste. Mix to coat using your hands.

3 Transfer the baking sheet to the oven and roast the carrots for 20 to 30 minutes, flipping them once halfway through, until they are soft when pricked with a knife. Remove the baking sheet from the oven and let the carrots cool, then slice them in half crosswise. (If you have thicker carrots, also slice them lengthwise.)

TO MAKE THE CRANBERRY RELISH

Combine the cranberries, grapes, jalapeño, cilantro, and ginger in a food processor. Pulse to chop and combine all the ingredients into a chunky relish.

TO MAKE THE WRAPS

1 Bring a large pot of water to a boil over high heat. Submerge 3 to 4 collard leaves at a time in the boiling water for 30 seconds, holding them by the stems, then immediately remove the leaves from the water and rinse them under cold water to stop the cooking. Repeat with the remaining leaves. Trim the thicker parts of the stems along the length of each leaf.

2 Lay one leaf at a time on a cutting board. Add about two heaping tablespoons of chickpea mash to the center of the leaf, top with 2 to 3 carrot pieces, and finish with about 1 tablespoon of cranberry relish.

3 Fold the lower end of the leaf over the filling, then fold in the sides and roll it up tightly.

4 Repeat with the remaining blanched collard leaves and fillings and serve as is, or with the sauce of your choice. The rolls will keep well in an airtight container in the refrigerator for up to 5 days.

COUSCOUS-STUFFED COLLARD GREENS IN COCONUT CURRY SAUCE

Couscous makes an excellent, neutral, starchy base for absorbing the flavor of creamy, warming coconut curry sauce. Wrapped in sturdy collard green leaves, it is the perfect hearty fare—filling, satisfying, and full of bold taste.

Makes about 12 to 14 rolls | FALL • WINTER

12 to 14 collard green leaves

Sea salt

1 cup Israeli couscous

1 tablespoon neutral coconut oil

⅓ cup pine nuts

1 large yellow onion, chopped

2 to 3 small to medium carrots, peeled if not organic and julienned

3 garlic cloves, sliced

4 teaspoons curry powder, divided

2 tablespoons chopped fresh parsley

1 (13.5-ounce / 398-ml) can unsweetened Thai coconut milk

1 Bring a large pot of water to a boil over high heat. Submerge 3 to 4 collard leaves at a time in the boiling water for 30 seconds, holding them by the stems, then immediately remove the leaves from the water and rinse them under cold water to stop the cooking. Trim the thicker parts of the stems along the length of each leaf. Repeat with the remaining leaves. Set the blanched leaves aside.

2 Bring 1¼ cups of water to a boil in a medium saucepan over high heat. Add a pinch of salt and the couscous, reduce the heat to a simmer, and cook covered for 10 minutes or until the water is absorbed. Remove the pan from the heat and set it aside.

3 Warm the coconut oil in a medium saucepan over medium-low heat, add the pine nuts, and toast for about 2 minutes, until golden. Remove the nuts from the pan with a slotted spoon and set them aside.

4 Increase the heat to medium, add the onion, carrots, and a pinch of salt, and sauté for 7 to 8 minutes, until the onion and carrots are soft. Add the garlic and sauté for another minute, just until fragrant.

5 Add 2 teaspoons of the curry powder, the couscous, pine nuts, and parsley; toss to combine and turn off the heat.

6 Lay one leaf at a time on a cutting board. Add about 2 to 3 heaping tablespoons of couscous to the center,

depending on the size of the leaf. Fold the lower end of the leaf over the filling, then fold in the sides and roll it up tightly.

7 Arrange the rolls in snug layers in the same emptied pot used for blanching the collard leaves. Pour the coconut milk over top and sprinkle with the remaining 2 teaspoons of curry powder and another pinch or two of salt. Bring the liquid to a boil over medium-high heat, then lower the heat to a simmer, cover the pot, and cook for 40 minutes, until the collard green leaves are tender.

8 Remove the pot from the heat and let it cool slightly. Carefully transfer the rolls to a serving plate and spoon some of the curry coconut broth over top. The rolls will keep well in an airtight container in the refrigerator for up to 5 days. Reheat them in a pan, covered, over low heat. You can also freeze them for up to 1 month.

PICKLED TURNIP, AVOCADO, BARLEY, AND BLACK RICE SUSHI ROLLS

Some think that sushi rolls are too difficult or fussy to make at home, but unless you are aiming for perfection, the process is actually quite straightforward. I love to experiment with various vegetable fillings and grains to wrap up in the nori. The first sushi rolls I ever tried upon moving to the United States from Russia were filled with Japanese pickled vegetables, and they made a very strong impression on me—I remember closing my eyes to take in the amazing, new flavor. These rolls are a nod to that first experience, a favorite, wintery version, with electric pink pickled turnips and creamy avocado. For grains, pillowy barley and toothsome black rice are a nice change from traditional sushi rice, offering their own unique textures and mild flavors.

Makes 4 rolls cut into 8 pieces each | FALL • WINTER

2 tablespoons brown rice vinegar, divided

1½ cups cooked forbidden black rice (page 66)

1½ cups cooked pearl barley or another grain of choice, such as quinoa, brown rice, etc.

1 ripe avocado, quartered

Juice of ½ lemon or lime

4 nori sheets, raw or toasted

About 12 pieces Pickled Turnips (page 258)

Tamari or Spring Roll Dipping Sauce (page 308), for serving

Note: To cook barley, combine 1 cup of dried pearl barley with 6 cups of purified water and a pinch of salt in a medium pot. Bring to a boil over high heat, then reduce the heat to a strong simmer and cook, partially covered, for 30 minutes. Test the barley; it should be soft and pleasantly chewy. Continue to cook until ready if necessary. Remove the pot from the heat and drain well. If you are planning to make Silky Barley Water (page 112), increase the amount of cooking water to 10 cups.

1 Drizzle 1 tablespoon of the brown rice vinegar over the black rice in a medium bowl; mix to coat evenly.

2 In a separate bowl, drizzle the remaining tablespoon of brown rice vinegar over the barley; mix to coat evenly.

3 Slice each avocado quarter into three wedges, place them in a small bowl, and squeeze the lemon or lime juice over them to prevent discoloration.

4 Place 1 nori sheet on a sushi mat or cutting board, shiny-side down and lines going horizontally. Measure ¾ cup of black rice or barley and cover the nori with it evenly, leaving a 1-inch border at the side opposite to you, parallel to the horizontal lines of nori. Wet your hands to prevent the rice from sticking to them.

5 Arrange about 3 pickled turnip pieces along the side closest to you, slightly

PICKLED TURNIP, AVOCADO, BARLEY, AND BLACK RICE SUSHI ROLLS, continued

overlapping them. Place 3 avocado wedges on top of the turnips, slightly overlapping them.

6 Lightly moisten the uncovered border of nori with water. Start rolling by folding the end closest to you over the filling, squeezing firmly. Continue rolling firmly all the way to the end—the moistened border will stick and seal the roll. Wrap the sushi mat around the roll and squeeze it gently to shape. If not using a mat, squeeze the roll with your hands to stabilize it. Place the roll seam-side down on a separate plate or surface and repeat with the rest of the nori sheets, black rice or barley, and fillers.

7 Place one roll at a time on a cutting board and slice it in half with a sharp, moistened knife. Cut each piece in half once again, and continue cutting each of the four pieces in half one last time. You should have 8 pieces. Repeat this process with the rest of the rolls. Serve immediately with tamari.

Silky Barley Water with Ginger and Citrus

Drinking barley cooking water is an ancient practice. Barley grain, rich in various vitamins and minerals, passes on many of its benefits to the water it's boiled in. Besides being good for the skin, lowering cholesterol, stimulating metabolism, and helping to stabilize blood glucose levels, it is also a delicious drink, cloudy and pleasantly silky in texture.

Serves 2 to 4

3 cups barley cooking water (see note page 110)

1 cup freshly squeezed orange or grapefruit juice, or the juice of 1 lemon or 2 limes

Honey or pure maple syrup (optional)

½-inch piece fresh ginger, peeled and sliced

Ice (optional)

1 In a bottle or jar, combine the barley water, citrus juice, and honey or maple syrup to taste, if using. Seal the bottle or jar and refrigerate the drink until it is completely chilled.

2 To serve the drink, distribute the ginger slices among individual glasses and muddle or bruise them with a muddler or knife. Add some ice to each glass, if using, and pour the citrus-barley drink into the glasses.

SOUPS AND STEWS

WHEN SETTING OUT TO MAKE SOUP, make a lot. No other dish can offer sustenance for days as gracefully as a big pot of soup. With a little time, it will develop, flourish and come to a new sophistication in flavor. And if you ever find yourself with too much to eat, most soup freezes well, and you will be grateful to have it on a day when time is scarce. This chapter will give you a few soup ideas to prepare during any given season—from a hearty, chunky stew that will comfort and nourish you on a cold day, to a properly chilled, bright gazpacho that will relieve the heat of a summer afternoon.

116
Spring Vegetable Chowder

119
Creamy Coconut Lentils with Broccoli

120
Chilled Thai Coconut Soup with Zucchini and Carrot Noodles

123
Smooth Vegetable Gazpacho with Watermelon Chunks

125
Tomato and Eggplant Green Mung Dahl

127
Spaghetti Squash Ramen with Marinated Tempeh

130
Lentil Tomato Stew with Turnips and Collard Greens

133
Curried Bean and Brussels Sprout Stew with Roasted Kabocha Squash

136
Celery Root Miso Soup

139
Healing Squash and Chickpea Soup

141
Borscht

145
Kitchari Winter Stew

146
A Soup of Odds and Ends

SPRING VEGETABLE CHOWDER

This simple spring chowder gets all of its creaminess from the addition of new potatoes. It is as bright in flavor as it is brilliant in green color from tender peas, green onions, leafy greens, and herbs.

Serves 6 | SPRING

1 tablespoon neutral coconut oil or olive oil

1 teaspoon cumin seeds, freshly ground

½ teaspoon coriander seeds, freshly ground

1 large yellow onion, chopped

Sea salt

3 garlic cloves, minced

2 ribs celery, thinly sliced

2 to 3 small or medium new potatoes, cut into small cubes

Freshly ground black pepper

Juice of ½ lemon

3½ cups vegetable broth or purified water

3 cups fresh or frozen English peas

4 cups young spring greens, such as spinach, dandelion, arugula, watercress, etc.

2 to 3 green onions or chives, thinly sliced, for garnish

Handful of fresh mint leaves, chopped (optional)

1 Heat the oil in a medium soup pot over medium heat. Add the cumin, coriander, onion, and a few pinches of salt; sauté for 5 minutes. Add the garlic, celery, potatoes, a pinch of salt, and black pepper to taste, and cook, stirring, for another 5 minutes until fragrant.

2 Add the lemon juice and let it absorb for 1 minute then pour in the vegetable broth or water. Bring the liquid to a boil, lower the heat to a simmer, and cook, covered, until the potatoes are tender, 10 to 15 minutes.

3 Add the peas and greens to the soup and stir until the greens wilt. Transfer 1½ cups of the soup to a blender and blend until creamy. Return the blended soup to the pot and stir to combine.

4 Taste and adjust the seasonings as necessary. Serve the soup garnished with green onions or chives and fresh mint.

CREAMY COCONUT LENTILS WITH BROCCOLI

This creamy lentil recipe is anything but boring—peppered with bright lime juice and Sriracha, it has some serious zing. The lentils have a velvety quality thanks to the coconut milk, while green florets of broccoli and tender ribbons of carrot provide a fresh, crunchy finish.

Serves 4 | SPRING

1 Warm the oil in a medium saucepan over medium heat. Add the onion and sauté for about 7 minutes, until translucent. Add the garlic, ginger, and salt and pepper to taste, and sauté for 1 to 2 minutes, until just fragrant.

2 Drain and rinse the lentils and add them to the pan along with 1 cup of purified water. Bring the liquid to a boil, lower the heat, and simmer, covered, for 15 to 20 minutes, until the lentils are cooked but not mushy.

3 Scoop 1 cup of the lentils into a blender, trying to catch most of the remaining cooking liquid. Add the coconut milk and blend until smooth. Pour the mixture back into the saucepan with the rest of the lentils. Stir in the tamari, brown rice vinegar, lime juice, and chili sauce, and bring the mixture back to a boil.

4 Add the broccoli florets and simmer for 3 minutes until crisp and tender. Add the carrot and broccoli ribbons, followed by the spinach, if using, and stir the stew to warm everything through and wilt the spinach.

5 Serve right away with an additional squeeze of lime and a garnish of cilantro leaves.

1 tablespoon neutral coconut oil

1 large yellow onion, chopped

2 garlic cloves, sliced

½-inch piece fresh ginger, peeled and finely chopped

Sea salt and freshly ground black pepper

¾ cup green or French lentils, soaked in purified water overnight

1 (13.5-ounce / 398-g) can unsweetened Thai coconut milk

2 tablespoons tamari

2 tablespoons brown rice vinegar

1 tablespoon freshly squeezed lime juice, plus more for serving

½ teaspoon chili sauce (Sriracha)

½ pound (227 g) broccoli, florets and stems reserved separately, stems shaved into ribbons with a vegetable peeler

1 large carrot, peeled if not organic and shaved into ribbons with a vegetable peeler

2 cups baby spinach leaves (optional)

1 cup fresh cilantro leaves, for garnish

1 (14-ounce / 397-g) package firm tofu (optional)

2 (13.5-ounce) cans light Thai coconut milk

1 cup vegetable broth or purified water

1 tablespoon coconut sugar

5 lemongrass stalks, cut into 3-inch pieces, then sliced lengthwise and bruised with the back of a knife

1 shallot, chopped

2-inch piece fresh ginger or galangal, peeled, sliced, and smashed with a knife

1 Thai or other small chili, seeded and sliced

3 to 5 garlic cloves, crushed

10 to 15 kaffir lime leaves, sliced (optional)

1 small or ½ large bunch fresh cilantro, stems and leaves separated

1 cup sliced crimini, white button, or shiitake mushrooms caps

3 tablespoons tamari

2 to 3 limes

1 to 2 small zucchini, spiralized or julienned

1 medium carrot, peeled if not organic and spiralized or julienned

Handful of microgreens (optional)

CHILLED THAI COCONUT SOUP WITH ZUCCHINI AND CARROT NOODLES

Our local raw food restaurant serves a very refreshing, chilled Thai coconut soup with crunchy raw vegetables and fresh coconut water at its base. I elaborated on that idea to create this chilled, aromatic, and creamy broth that serves as the perfect base for mushrooms and zucchini and carrot noodles. It is a bowl of summer delight.

I highly encourage seeking out kaffir lime leaves for their life-changing, aromatic flavor. The leaves can be found fresh or frozen at Asian or Indian markets, they keep very well in the freezer, and they can be used in many soups and stews throughout the year. If you can't find kaffir lime leaves, though, you can make this soup without them—the broth will still be delicious, flavored with aromatic lemongrass and ginger.

Serves 4 to 6 | SUMMER

1 If using tofu, drain and place on a plate. Cover with another plate and place some heavy object on top (a water filled jar is ideal). Leave pressed, letting excess water drain onto the plate for about 30 minutes. Remove the weight and discard any accumulated water. Cut the pressed tofu into bite-size cubes.

2 Meanwhile, combine the coconut milk, broth or water, coconut sugar, lemongrass, shallot, ginger or galangal, chili, garlic, kaffir lime leaves, if using, and cilantro stems in a medium soup pot. Bring the mixture to a boil over medium-high heat, then lower the heat to a simmer, cover the pot, and cook for 15 minutes until infused and fragrant. Remove the pot from heat and let the broth infuse further for 1 hour, then strain it through a fine-mesh sieve and return it to the same soup pot. (If you don't have the time, you can strain it right away.) Discard the solids.

3 Add the mushrooms and tamari to the strained broth, and squeeze in the juice

from 2 of the limes. Bring the broth to a very gentle simmer over medium heat and cook for 2 to 3 minutes, until the mushrooms soften. Remove the pot from the heat, add half of the cilantro leaves, and let the soup cool to room temperature, then refrigerate it for at least 2 hours until the soup is completely chilled.

4 Distribute the veggie noodles and tofu, if using, among individual bowls. Pour the chilled soup over top, then taste the soup and add more lime juice or tamari, if desired. Garnish with the remaining cilantro leaves and microgreens, if using, and serve cold.

Note: This soup can be served hot as well. To do so, add the vegetable noodles and tofu along with the mushrooms in step 3 and cook them just until they are heated through. Remove the pot from the heat and serve immediately.

SMOOTH VEGETABLE GAZPACHO WITH WATERMELON CHUNKS

This incredibly refreshing summer dish is all about contrast. Bursts of juicy and sweet watermelon pieces come as a welcome surprise inside the well-chilled, spicy, and smooth vegetable gazpacho. (Pictured on page 114.)

Serves 4 | SUMMER

Approximately 11 medium heirloom or any ripe summer tomatoes, roughly chopped

1 to 2 English cucumbers, peeled, seeded, and roughly chopped

1 large red bell pepper, seeded and roughly chopped

1 packed cup fresh basil leaves, plus more for serving

1 pimiento cherry pepper, or other hot pepper, seeded and roughly chopped

1 to 2 garlic cloves, peeled (optional)

1 small shallot, peeled (optional)

2 tablespoons red wine vinegar

2 tablespoons olive oil

1 teaspoon sea salt

Freshly ground black pepper, to taste

1 medium ripe seedless watermelon, chilled, flesh cut into bite-size pieces

1 In a blender, combine all of the ingredients except for the watermelon; blend until smooth. You may need to do this in two batches, depending on the size of your blender. Optionally, pass the ingredients through a fine-mesh strainer to achieve a very smooth consistency. Taste and adjust with more salt and pepper as desired. Transfer the gazpacho to an airtight container and refrigerate until it is completely chilled.

2 Distribute the watermelon pieces among individual bowls and pour the gazpacho over them. Serve the soup garnished with fresh basil leaves.

TOMATO AND EGGPLANT GREEN MUNG DAL

Dal is an Indian lentil-based stew, and one of the most aromatic and comforting dishes ever created. It's commonly made with split lentils or moong dal (hence the name), but I use the nutritious whole mung beans in this recipe, as they are more widely available and affordable, and they cook in minutes after an overnight soaking. Eggplant is not a component of traditional dal, but it is a great add-in nevertheless, contributing its buttery texture, while taking on all the flavors and spices of the broth. This stew is quite simple to prepare, and the ingredient list is mostly composed of pantry spices and widely available summer produce. In the end, you will have a big pot of dal that will nourish you throughout the week, and the flavors within will develop and improve with time.

Serves 6 to 8 | SUMMER • FALL

1½ to 2 pounds (680 g to 1 kg) eggplant, sliced into ¾-inch-thick rounds

2 tablespoons melted neutral coconut oil

Sea salt

2 teaspoons coriander seeds

Seeds from 5 cardamom pods

¼ teaspoon black peppercorns

2 tablespoons ghee or neutral coconut oil

2 teaspoons cumin seeds

¼ teaspoon black mustard seeds

1 large yellow onion, chopped

1½-inch piece fresh ginger, peeled and minced

3 garlic cloves, sliced

1½ teaspoons ground turmeric

¼ teaspoon red pepper flakes

4 to 5 medium tomatoes (1½ pounds / 680 g total), chopped

1¼ cups dried mung beans, soaked in purified water overnight

Cooked rice, for serving

Sprouted or Whole Spelt Tortillas (page 87) or other flatbreads, for serving (optional)

Large handful of fresh cilantro leaves

1 teaspoon toasted nigella seeds (optional)

1 Preheat the oven to 400°F (200°C). Line a rimmed baking sheet with parchment paper.

2 Brush the eggplant slices on both sides with the melted coconut oil and arrange them on the prepared baking sheet. Sprinkle them with a couple pinches of salt, then transfer the baking sheet to the oven and roast the eggplant for 20 minutes. Flip each slice and roast for 15 more minutes until it is golden brown and soft. Remove the eggplant from the oven and set it aside.

3 While the eggplant is roasting, grind the coriander, cardamom, and black peppercorns in a dedicated coffee grinder or mortar and pestle; set aside.

4 Melt the ghee or coconut oil in a large pot over medium heat. Add the cumin and mustard seeds and sauté for about 1 minute, until the mustard seeds begin to pop.

5 Add the onion, freshly ground spices, and a pinch of salt, reduce the heat to medium low, and sauté for 7 minutes, until the onion is soft and translucent. Add the ginger and garlic and sauté for 3 more minutes until fragrant. Add the turmeric, red pepper flakes, tomatoes, and a pinch of salt, return the heat to medium, and bring the mixture to a simmer. Cook for 4 minutes, until the tomatoes cook down into a slightly chunky sauce. Meanwhile, bring 6 cups of water to a boil in a tea kettle or saucepan.

6 Drain and rinse the mung beans and add them to the pot along with the boiling water and another pinch of salt. Bring to a simmer and cook for 5 minutes, until the beans are partially cooked.

7 Meanwhile, slice the roasted eggplant into bite-size pieces. Stir the eggplant pieces into the dal at the end of 5 minutes. Simmer for another 5 minutes or until the beans are completely cooked, taste the dal, and add more salt if needed. Remove the pot from the heat.

8 Serve the dal over rice or with homemade tortillas or other flatbread, garnished with fresh cilantro leaves and toasted nigella seeds, if using.

Note: If you prefer to make dal according to Ayurvedic principles, omit the onion and garlic. Sauté 3 sliced celery ribs in place of the onion for 5 minutes. Proceed with the recipe as instructed above.

SPAGHETTI SQUASH RAMEN WITH MARINATED TEMPEH

This entirely plant-based ramen borrows many of its umami flavors from the original Japanese noodle soup. The broth makes an incredibly nutritious soup base, taking its origins from *dashi*—a Japanese broth of soaked kombu and shiitake. A tip I learned from chef Amy Chaplin is to add kombu to any cooking water for extra nutrition—whether for beans, soups, or even grains (as long as the mild seaweed undertone does not interfere with the flavors of your dish). This ramen features spaghetti squash, but feel welcome to use grain-based noodles of choice in place of the squash. Sweet and salty marinated tempeh fills the need for a protein component, and a dotting of glazed, garlicky shiitake slices completes this nourishing bowl of soup.

Serves 6 to 8 | FALL • WINTER

FOR THE MARINATED TEMPEH

1 (8-ounce / 227 g) package tempeh, sliced into ¼-inch-thick pieces

1 tablespoon sesame oil

2 tablespoons melted neutral coconut oil, divided

1 tablespoon tamari

1 tablespoon mirin or brown rice vinegar

1 teaspoon chili sauce (Sriracha)

1 teaspoon pure maple syrup

FOR THE SPAGHETTI SQUASH

1 large spaghetti squash

1 teaspoon neutral coconut oil

Sea salt and freshly ground black pepper

FOR THE BROTH

8 cups purified water

3 garlic cloves, crushed

½-inch piece fresh ginger, peeled if not organic, sliced and crushed

2-inch piece kombu

Fresh shiitake stems, from below

8 to 10 green onions, white parts only (green parts sliced and reserved for serving)

1 chili, seeded and sliced

2 dried shiitake mushrooms (optional)

Juice of 1 lime

TO MARINATE THE TEMPEH

Place the tempeh in a shallow dish. In a small bowl, whisk together the sesame oil, 1 tablespoon of the coconut oil, the tamari, mirin, Sriracha, and maple syrup; pour this mixture over the tempeh. Set the tempeh aside and allow it to marinate while you roast the squash and make the broth.

TO PREPARE THE SQUASH

1 Preheat the oven to 400°F (200°C). Line a rimmed baking sheet with parchment paper.

2 Cut the spaghetti squash in half lengthwise and scrape out the seeds. Rub the remaining tablespoon of coconut oil over the flesh and sprinkle with salt and pepper to taste. Place the squash cut-side down on the prepared baking sheet. Transfer the baking sheet to the oven and roast the squash for about 30 minutes, until it is easily pricked with a knife but not mushy.

TO MAKE THE BROTH

1 In a large soup pot over medium-high heat, combine the water, garlic, ginger, kombu, shiitake stems, white parts of green onions, chili,

SPAGHETTI SQUASH RAMEN WITH MARINATED TEMPEH, continued

FOR THE SHIITAKES

1 teaspoon neutral coconut oil

½ teaspoon sesame oil

1 garlic clove, thinly sliced

1 pound (454 g) fresh shiitake mushrooms, stems removed and reserved, caps sliced

1½ teaspoons tamari

1½ teaspoons brown rice vinegar or mirin

TO ASSEMBLE

¼ cup dried arame or wakame seaweed

3 tablespoons unpasteurized white miso paste

Toasted sesame seeds, for serving (optional)

and dried shiitakes, if using. Bring the mixture to a boil, lower the heat to a simmer, and cook for 20 minutes to infuse the broth. Remove the pot from the heat and stir in the lime juice.

TO COOK THE SHIITAKES

Warm the coconut and sesame oils in a medium frying pan over medium heat. Add the garlic and cook for 1 minute, until fragrant, then add the shiitakes and sauté for 5 more minutes until soft. Add the tamari and brown rice vinegar or mirin and cook for about 1 minute, until the liquid evaporates. Remove the shiitakes and set aside.

TO COOK THE TEMPEH AND ASSEMBLE THE SOUP

1 In the same pan you used for cooking the shiitakes, warm the remaining tablespoon of coconut oil over medium heat. Add the tempeh to the pan in a single layer, keeping the marinade in the dish, and cook for 4 to 5 minutes until golden brown. Flip each piece over and cook on the other side for 2 to 3 minutes, until the tempeh is golden brown on both sides. Drizzle the marinade over the tempeh and add 2 tablespoons of water. Simmer for about 2 minutes, until the liquid evaporates. Flip the tempeh one more time and cook for 1 to 2 more minutes, until both sides are caramelized.

2 Strain the broth through a fine-mesh sieve, reserving the rehydrated dried shiitakes and discarding the rest of the vegetables. Slice the rehydrated shiitakes. Return the broth to the pot over medium-high heat, add the shiitakes and seaweed, heat the broth until it is nearly boiling and remove the pot from the heat.

3 In a small bowl, combine the miso paste with 3 tablespoons of the broth and stir until smooth. Add the miso mixture to the broth; mix to incorporate.

4 Scrape the spaghetti noodles with a fork and distribute them among individual serving bowls. Top each serving with shiitake mushrooms and 2 to 3 tempeh slices. Ladle the hot broth over top, distributing an even amount of seaweed to each bowl. Sprinkle with the reserved green onions and sesame seeds, if using. Serve immediately.

LENTIL TOMATO STEW WITH TURNIPS AND COLLARD GREENS

Smoked Spanish paprika is one of my favorite spices. The spice, which comes from hot peppers that have been smoked dry and then ground, can add just the right amount of deep, savory flavor and medium-level spice to many dishes.

Everyone should have a simple, cold-weather stew in their repertoire, and this is mine. It is made up of common pantry ingredients and familiar produce. The addition of smoked paprika helps elevate the commonplace flavors, giving the tomato-heavy stew some smoky, peppery punches. The active cooking time here is minimal, and the result is the kind of solid, hot stew we crave on cozy, cold autumn evenings.

Serves 6 to 8 | FALL • WINTER

12 to 16 collard green leaves (2 bunches) hard stems removed and discarded, leaves chopped

Sea salt

2 tablespoons neutral coconut oil

1 large yellow onion, chopped

6 garlic cloves, sliced

1 jalapeño, seeded and finely chopped

2 to 3 large carrots, peeled if not organic and diced

1 large or 2 to 3 small turnips, diced into bite-size cubes

1 cup green lentils, soaked in purified water overnight

2 teaspoons cumin seeds, freshly ground

1 teaspoon smoked Spanish paprika

Freshly ground black pepper

2 to 3 bay leaves (optional)

1 (28-ounce / 794 g) can or box crushed tomatoes

1 Cover the collard greens with water in a soup pot over medium-high heat. Bring the water to a boil, add a pinch of salt, lower the heat to a strong simmer, and cook, partially covered, for 30 minutes to 1 hour or until the greens are tender. Drain the collard greens, reserving the cooking liquid for the base of the stew, and set them aside.

2 Warm the coconut oil in the same saucepan over medium heat. Add the onion and sauté for 3 minutes, until the onion is soft and translucent. Add the garlic, jalapeño, carrots, and turnips, stir well, and sauté for 2 more minutes until fragrant.

3 Drain and rinse the lentils and add them to the pan, along with the cumin, smoked paprika, collard greens, and salt and pepper to taste; give everything a stir. Add enough of the reserved collard green cooking liquid to achieve a thick soup consistency, keeping in mind that you will be adding crushed tomatoes later, which will add more liquid. Add the bay leaves, if using. Bring the liquid to a boil, lower the heat to a simmer, and cook for 20 to 30 minutes or until the vegetables and lentils are cooked through.

4 Add the crushed tomatoes, bring the soup back to a simmer, and cook for 10 more minutes, letting all the flavors incorporate. Taste and adjust the seasonings as desired, then serve immediately as is or over rice or any one of your favorite cooked grains.

CURRIED BEAN AND BRUSSELS SPROUT STEW WITH ROASTED KABOCHA SQUASH

This loaded, hearty stew features all of the most nutritious produce the season has to offer, spiced with a curry blend and thickened with rich, creamy coconut milk. Although it does require some initial effort, this one-pot stew is a complete meal that will easily feed you for a week.

All the spices called for in this recipe make up the mixture we know as curry powder. Ever since I made my own homemade curry powder for the first time, I haven't been able to go back to buying it at the store—the flavor far exceeds any pre-made curry I've ever tried. However, feel free to use a store-bought curry to save some time. Since all curries vary greatly in spice and flavor, the exact amount depends on which pre-made blend you buy; start by adding 1 tablespoon and taste as you go.

Serves 6 to 8 | FALL • WINTER

1 cup dried adzuki, kidney, or cannellini beans, soaked in purified water overnight

3 to 4 bay leaves

2 to 3 garlic cloves, crushed

2 to 3 fresh thyme sprigs, leaves separated, stalks reserved for cooking the beans (optional)

Fresh cilantro leaves, for serving (stems reserved for cooking the beans)

Sea salt

1 medium kabocha, kuri, or butternut squash, seeded, cut into bite-size pieces (skin removed only if using butternut)

Freshly ground black pepper

3 tablespoons melted neutral coconut oil, divided

2 teaspoons cumin seeds, freshly ground

Seeds from 5 to 7 cardamom pods, freshly ground

1 tablespoon ground turmeric

Pinch of red pepper flakes

1 tablespoon finely chopped fresh ginger

1 large yellow onion, chopped

¾ cup Bhutanese or ruby red rice, rinsed

Handful of kaffir lime leaves (optional)

ingredients continue

1 Drain and rinse the beans, then place them in a large, heavy-bottomed pot and cover them with at least 14 cups of water. Add the bay leaves, garlic, thyme stalks, and cilantro stems, and bring the liquid to a boil over medium-high heat. Skim off any foam with a slotted spoon and reduce the heat to a strong simmer. Cook for 20 minutes, add a pinch or two of salt, then cook for another 10 minutes or until the beans are tender and buttery inside. Check periodically to make sure that the water is simmering. If the beans are not fully cooked after 30 minutes, continue cooking them until they reach the right consistency—it can take up to an hour or even longer for some beans. Drain the beans, reserving the cooking liquid in a large heatproof bowl for the base of the stew. Discard the bay leaves and all of the stems. Set the beans aside, and do not wash the pot.

2 While the beans are cooking, preheat the oven to 425°F (220°C). Line a rimmed baking sheet with parchment paper.

CURRIED BEAN AND BRUSSELS SPROUT STEW WITH ROASTED KABOCHA SQUASH, continued

1 pound (454 g) halved Brussels sprouts, damaged outer leaves removed, hard ends cut away

1 (13.5-ounce / 398-ml) can unsweetened Thai coconut milk

Zest and juice of 2 limes

4 cups baby spinach or 2 cups chopped kale leaves

3 Place the squash on the prepared baking sheet, add the thyme leaves, salt and pepper to taste, and 1 tablespoon of the coconut oil. Mix to coat using your hands. Spread out the squash in a single layer, transfer it to the oven, and roast for 20 to 30 minutes, stirring at halftime, until the squash is tender when pricked with a knife.

4 In the same pot you used for cooking the beans, warm the remaining 2 tablespoons of coconut oil over medium heat. Add the spices and ginger and stir everything around for 2 minutes, until fragrant. Add the onion and sauté for 7 minutes, until it is soft and translucent.

5 Add the rice, a large pinch of salt, and the kaffir lime leaves, if using; and stir to coat. Add 7 cups of the reserved bean cooking liquid and bring the liquid to a boil. Reduce the heat to a slow simmer, cover the pot, and cook for 20 minutes or until the rice is almost cooked.

6 Increase the heat to medium high and add the Brussels sprouts, cooked beans, and a large pinch of salt. Bring the broth back to a boil, then lower the heat and simmer, covered, for another 10 minutes until the Brussels sprouts and rice are tender.

7 Add the coconut milk, roasted squash, lime zest and juice, and more salt to taste. If using kale, add it at this time as well. Bring the broth back to a gentle boil, lower the heat to a simmer, and cook for 2 minutes.

8 Remove the pot from the heat, taste the broth, and add more salt if needed. Stir in the spinach, if using. Serve hot with fresh cilantro leaves and more freshly squeezed lime juice, if desired.

Coastal Herbs
HARTFORD FARMS
HARTFORD FARMS
PINFLLAS

CELERY ROOT MISO SOUP

Once you have stocked your refrigerator with a jar of miso, a delicious miso soup is only a few minutes away at any given time. It is one of the simplest soups to prepare, requiring little more than miso paste mixed into hot water, with seaweed, tofu, and green onions. I have included celery root in this version for a more substantial, but still very simple, winter soup. Once cooked and blended, its creamy texture and mild, celery-like flavor incorporates seamlessly into an umami miso soup base, with ribbons of tender seaweed and a garnish of crunchy green onion.

Serves 4 | FALL • WINTER

6 to 7 cups purified water

4-inch piece kombu

1 large or 2 medium celery roots, peeled and cut into ½-inch cubes

4 tablespoons unpasteurized miso paste

1 tablespoon tamari

¼ to ⅓ cup wakame or arame seaweed (optional)

4 green onions, thinly sliced

Thinly sliced radishes, for garnish (optional)

1 Combine the water, kombu, and celery root in a medium pot over medium-high heat. Bring the liquid to a boil, lower the heat to a simmer, and cook for 25 to 30 minutes, until the celery root is tender. Remove and discard the kombu.

2 Transfer about half of the celery root and 2 cups of the hot broth into a blender. Add the miso and blend until smooth. Pour this mixture back into the pot with the rest of the broth and celery root. Add the tamari and wakame, if using.

3 Gently reheat the soup, but do not bring it back to a boil. Ladle the hot soup into bowls and garnish with green onions and radish slices; serve immediately.

HEALING SQUASH AND CHICKPEA SOUP

The main component of this soup is the broth—a powerful infusion of all the most healing and warming ingredients: kombu, lemongrass, garlic, ginger, turmeric, and lemon. When I'm under the weather, I like to make this broth on its own, to boost my immunity, soothe the throat, and clear the sinuses. Squash, kale and chickpeas are some of my favorite add-ins, but you can swap in any other vegetables or beans based on your mood and whatever is on hand.

Serves 4 to 6 | FALL • WINTER

1 medium butternut squash, peeled, seeded, and cut into bite-size cubes

Sea salt and freshly ground black pepper

1 tablespoon melted neutral coconut oil

½ cup dried chickpeas, soaked in purified water overnight

4-inch piece kombu

9 cups purified water

2 lemongrass stalks, cut crosswise into thirds, then halved lengthwise and bruised with the back of a knife

3 garlic cloves, sliced

1-inch piece fresh ginger, peeled if not organic and diced

1 teaspoon ground turmeric

1 small chili, seeded and minced

Handful of kaffir lime leaves (optional)

½ medium bunch fresh cilantro, stems and leaves separated

2 lemons

2 to 3 large kale leaves, stems removed and leaves chopped

1 tablespoon tamari

1 Preheat the oven to 400°F (200°C). Line a rimmed baking sheet with parchment paper.

2 Place the squash on the prepared baking sheet, sprinkle with salt and pepper to taste, and drizzle with the coconut oil; toss to coat. Transfer the baking sheet to the oven and roast the squash for 20 to 30 minutes, until it is soft throughout. Remove the squash from the oven and set it aside.

3 In the meantime, drain the chickpeas and place them in a large soup pot along with the kombu and water. Bring the water to a boil over high heat, skim any foam from the surface, then reduce the heat to a simmer and cook for about 30 minutes, until the chickpeas are soft. Add a pinch or two of salt during the last 10 minutes of cooking. When the chickpeas are done cooking, drain them in a colander set over a large, heatproof bowl. Pour the broth back into the same pot; discard the kombu and set the chickpeas aside.

4 Add the lemongrass, garlic, ginger, turmeric, chili, kaffir lime leaves, if using, and cilantro stems to the broth. Bring the mixture to a boil over medium-high heat, then reduce the heat to a slow simmer and cook partially covered for 10 minutes until the broth is infused and fragrant. Remove the pot from heat. Add the juice of 1 lemon, cover the pot, and let the liquid infuse for 30 minutes. Strain the broth through a fine-mesh sieve into a large, heatproof bowl and discard the solids. Pour the broth back into the pot.

5 Add the chickpeas and kale to the broth, bring it to a boil over medium-high heat, then lower the heat to a strong simmer and cook for 5 minutes. Add the roasted squash and bring the broth to a near boil one more time to warm the squash through. Add the juice of the remaining lemon, along with the tamari; taste and adjust the seasoning with more salt as needed.

6 Ladle the soup into individual bowls and garnish with cilantro leaves before serving.

BORSCHT

Borscht is a landmark of Ukrainian and Russian cuisines, and I don't know many Russians who can go too long without this hearty, aromatic soup. Although beet soup is the most popular definition of borscht in the western world, the borscht recipe varies quite a lot throughout different regions of Russia and many Eastern European countries. The borscht most Russians grew up eating consists of a long list of vegetables—all of equal importance—and is based on meat stock, with pieces of meat throughout.

My mother came up with a unique vegetarian version of her beloved staple in an attempt to give us kids lighter, healthier fare. Her way of gently steeping a gigantic amount of various vegetables in their own juices gives this vegetarian borscht irresistible flavor, and it is quite famous in certain circles. I only recently took up the challenge of matching my mother's masterpiece, as I've always been intimidated by her magic touch, and I was surprised when my borscht turned out exactly the same.

Borscht is traditionally made a day in advance so its flavors have time to fully develop. This wisdom is not to be underestimated—the difference in flavor is huge. There is even a popular anecdote, which states that back during the Russian Tzardom, a bowl of fresh borscht at a tavern was sold for ten kopeks, while a bowl of the same soup two days later cost a whole ruble—ten times as much.

Serves 10 | WINTER

1 large or 2 small carrots

2 medium parsnips

1 medium red beet

1 large yellow onion

1 small celery root (optional)

2 green bell peppers

1 small jalapeño

1 tablespoon ghee, neutral coconut oil, or olive oil

Sea salt and freshly ground black pepper

½ medium head green cabbage

4 to 6 yukon gold potatoes, peeled and cut into small cubes

1 (28-ounce / 794-g) can or box crushed tomatoes

7 garlic cloves, minced

¼ cup finely chopped fresh dill, plus more for serving

¼ cup finely chopped fresh parsley, plus more for serving

Sour cream, for serving

1 Peel the carrots, parsnips, beet, onion, and celery root, if using, and remove the seeds from the bell peppers and jalapeño. Roughly chop all the vegetables to fit into the feeding tube of a food processor with a shredding attachment. Shred all the vegetables and transfer the mixture to a large, heavy-bottomed soup pot.

2 Add the ghee or oil to the pot and season to taste with salt and pepper. Turn the heat to medium and let the vegetable juices release and start simmering, then reduce the heat to low, cover the pot, and let the vegetables cook gently in their juices for 30 minutes until all the juices are released and the vegetables are soft.

3 Meanwhile, change the food processor attachment to a slicer. Roughly chop the cabbage to fit into the food processor's feeding tube, and slice it using the attachment. Alternatively, thinly slice the cabbage by hand. Transfer the cabbage to a large bowl and cover it with cold water; set aside.

4 After the shredded vegetables have cooked for 30 minutes, place the potatoes on top and pour in enough water to cover the potatoes completely. Increase the heat to medium, bring the liquid to a boil, then reduce the heat to a simmer and cook, partially covered, for about 10 minutes, until the potatoes are soft.

5 Meanwhile, bring a kettle or medium saucepan of water to a boil. Drain the cabbage and add it to the pot with the potatoes and shredded vegetables. Pour the boiling water over the cabbage, filling the pot but leaving some room for the tomatoes. Add a few big pinches of salt. Simmer for 15 to 20 minutes or until the cabbage is soft, then add the crushed tomatoes and bring the soup back to a boil over medium heat. Taste for salt and adjust if needed. As soon as the soup comes to a boil, remove the pot from the heat and stir in the garlic and herbs.

6 For best results, let the borscht come to room temperature and then refrigerate it overnight so it can develop fully in flavor. When you're ready to serve it, reheat the borscht on the stove. Serve with sour cream and more chopped dill and parsley, if desired.

KITCHARI WINTER STEW

This winter stew recipe was inspired by *kitchari*, a porridge-like, one-pot stew of split mung beans and basmati rice. It is highly regarded in Ayurvedic tradition as one of the most cleansing and easily digestible meals. Using kitchari as my base, I added some root vegetables to take the dish into winter stew territory. I call for red rice in this recipe, but feel free to use any rice you have on hand.

Serves 6 to 8 | WINTER

1 tablespoon ghee or neutral coconut oil

1-inch piece fresh ginger, peeled and minced

2 teaspoons cumin seeds

½ teaspoon black mustard seeds

2 medium potatoes, peeled and diced into bite-size cubes

2 to 3 medium carrots, sliced into bite-size pieces

1½ teaspoons ground turmeric

1 cup Bhutanese or ruby red rice, thoroughly rinsed

Sea salt

7 cups boiling purified water

½ cup yellow split mung dal, preferably soaked in purified water for 3 to 4 hours or thoroughly rinsed

2 cups chopped kale leaves (optional)

Juice of 1 lemon

Toasted nigella seeds (optional)

1 Melt the ghee or oil in a large pot over medium heat. Add the ginger, cumin, and mustard seeds, and sauté for 3 minutes until the mustard seeds begin to pop.

2 Add the potatoes, carrots, turmeric, rice, salt, and boiling water. Bring the mixture to a steady simmer and cook, partially covered, for 10 minutes.

3 Add the mung dal, bring the mixture back to a slow simmer, and cook, covered, for 20 more minutes, until the vegetables and rice are completely cooked. Add the kale, if using, in the last 5 minutes of cooking.

4 Remove the pot from the heat and squeeze the lemon juice over the dal. Taste for salt and adjust if needed. Serve the stew sprinkled with toasted nigella seeds, if using.

Note: This stew may seem too soupy at first, but it will thicken nicely as it sits, and it is especially delicious the next day.

A SOUP OF ODDS AND ENDS

This modest fare is simply a byproduct of something I do frequently when cooking a batch of beans. I save all my veggie scraps—ends, stalks, stems, and whatnot—and use them either in a vegetable broth or in the water for cooking beans. Once the beans are cooked, I have a rich, bean and veggie–flavored broth, which I enjoy as a soup with a few spoonfuls of the cooked beans and some simple add-ins. Since this is just an idea, there is absolutely no need to closely follow the recipe—cook as many beans as you need and feel free to use what you have on hand.

Note: If your scraps include particularly nice and fresh turnip tops or tops from another vegetable that you would like to eat whole, reserve them and stir them into the finished soup, just so they wilt. Separate them from the scraps after straining the broth, and add them to your serving bowl. You can apply the same method to any leafy greens if you feel inclined to add more greens to the soup.

Serves 4 | ALL YEAR ROUND

Approximately 6 cups chopped vegetable scraps (see page 313)

¾ cup dried chickpeas, soaked in purified water overnight

2 garlic cloves, crushed

2 bay leaves

Sea salt

Freshly ground black pepper

Juice of 1 lemon

1 tablespoon tamari (optional)

Chopped fresh parsley and/or dill (optional)

A few slices toasted bread, rubbed with garlic (optional)

1 Combine the veggie scraps, chickpeas, garlic, and bay leaves in a large soup pot, and pour in 12 cups of water. Bring the mixture to a boil over medium heat, reduce the heat to a strong simmer, and cook, partially covered, for 30 minutes. Check the chickpeas: if they are soft, add a pinch or two of salt and cook for another 7 minutes. If they are not yet soft, continue cooking until they reach the right consistency, then add salt to taste.

2 Remove the pot from the heat. Strain the broth through a fine-mesh sieve into a large, heatproof bowl, then pour the strained broth back into the pot. Discard the scraps and add the chickpeas back to the broth. Return the broth to a boil over medium-high heat, then immediately remove it from the heat. Season to taste with black pepper and stir in the lemon juice and tamari, if using.

3 Ladle the hot soup into individual bowls, garnish with parsley and/or dill, and serve with toasted garlic bread, if using.

RISOTTO, PAELLA, AND PILAF

USING UNIVERSALLY LOVED, one-pan rice dishes as a base, this chapter provides you with plenty of flavorful, light, and wholesome twists on the classics. Citrus will replace the wine, healthy plant oils will take the place of butter, and cheese is mostly optional. Despite the seemingly singular subject, you'll find an array of nourishing grains, seasonal vegetables, and techniques, and most of the recipes don't require much elbow grease or any particular experience. If you are looking to avoid grains for any reason, or if you simply want to try something different, there is riceless risotto, which uses chopped vegetables in place of grains to achieve a texture surprisingly similar to the traditional dish.

152
Spring Vegetable Black Rice Pilaf

155
Broccoli Stem Riceless Risotto

157
Cauliflower Riceless Risotto with Spinach and Corn

158
Buckwheat Risotto with Roasted Beets

161
Summer Paella

162
Red Rice and Lacinato Kale Risotto

165
Rutabaga and Brussels Sprout Riceless Risotto

168
Leek and Mushroom Barley Risotto

171
Roasted Root Vegetable Oven Risotto

175
Bukhara Farro Pilaf

SPRING VEGETABLE BLACK RICE PILAF

This quick and easy dish showcases vibrant spring greens against the dramatic, dark purple grains of forbidden black rice. You can improvise and add or substitute any available spring vegetables here—think fava beans, ramps, fiddleheads, snow peas, or sugar snaps.

Serves 6 | SPRING

1½ tablespoons neutral coconut oil or olive oil

½ green chili or jalapeño, seeded and sliced

2 large leeks, white and light green parts only, finely sliced (reserve dark green parts for Odds and Ends Vegetable Broth page 313)

4 garlic cloves, sliced

Sea salt and freshly ground black pepper

Zest and juice of 1 large or 2 small limes

2 cups vegetable broth or purified water

1 cup forbidden black rice

1 bunch asparagus, tough ends removed, sliced diagonally in about 1-inch pieces

2 cups fresh peas or thawed frozen peas

2 to 3 cups chopped spinach leaves or baby spinach

1 Warm the oil in a large, heavy-bottomed saucepan over medium heat. Add the chili or jalapeño and stir it around for 30 seconds. Add the leeks and sauté for 5 minutes until they begin to soften.

2 Add the garlic and salt and black pepper to taste (add more salt here if using water instead of vegetable broth), and sauté for another 2 minutes until the garlic is fragrant. Add the lime juice and cook for another minute until most of the liquid is absorbed.

3 Add the broth or water to the pan, increase the heat to high, and bring it to a boil. Add the rice, scattering it over the broth somewhat evenly. Reduce the heat to a simmer, cover the pot, and cook for 30 minutes or until most of the liquid is absorbed and the rice is tender.

4 Add the asparagus to the pot and stir to incorporate. Cover the pot and let the pilaf cook for 7 minutes until the asparagus is crisp and tender. Add the peas, spinach, lime zest, and a pinch of salt. Stir thoroughly until the spinach wilts, then remove the pot from the heat.

5 Season to taste with more salt and pepper and serve immediately.

BROCCOLI STEM RICELESS RISOTTO

This recipe is a gift to those who feel some guilt when discarding perfectly good broccoli stems after cutting off the florets. Chopped broccoli stems take the place of rice in this creamy spring risotto, making it much more vegetable-packed than the traditional kind.

When shopping for broccoli, try to choose heads with stalks that branch out into thick, long stems. I usually reserve the stems from one broccoli bunch in the refrigerator and then make this risotto once I buy the next bunch, soon after. This recipe is also a great way to use all kinds of spring gems like fava beans, fiddleheads, ramps, and nettles.

Serves 4 to 6 | SPRING

Stems from 4 to 6 broccoli heads, depending on their thickness (about 1¼ pounds / 580 g total)

Florets from 1 large broccoli head, cut into bite-size pieces

Couple handfuls of other spring vegetables, such as peas and chopped asparagus (optional)

Approximately 2 cups baby spinach leaves, divided

Zest and juice of 1 lemon, divided

3½ tablespoons neutral coconut oil or ghee, divided

Sea salt and freshly ground black pepper

1 shallot, chopped

Finely grated Pecorino Romano or Parmesan cheese

Baby greens or microgreens, for garnish (optional)

1 Trim the tough ends from the broccoli stems, and peel off the thick outer layers of skin. You can skip the places where the stems branch into thinner stalks—the skin there is usually tender enough.

2 Chop the peeled stems into medium-size cubes and place them in a food processor. Pulse until the broccoli is in rice-size pieces—you should end up with about 3 cups of broccoli stem "rice." This can also be done by chopping the stems very finely with a good knife.

3 Meanwhile, bring a large pot of well-salted water to a boil and prepare an ice bath for the blanched vegetables. Blanch the broccoli florets for 3 minutes, then, using a large slotted spoon, immediately transfer them to the ice bath to stop the cooking.

4 If using other vegetables, continue to blanch them in the same water according to their type. Blanch asparagus for 2 minutes, and blanch peas for just 30 seconds. Transfer the blanched vegetables to the ice bath, reserving the cooking liquid in the pot.

5 Once the blanched vegetables are cool, drain them thoroughly. Add about half of the broccoli florets to a blender, along with half of the spinach and a few pieces of other blanched spring vegetables, if using. Add half of the lemon juice, 1½ tablespoons of the oil or ghee, a pinch of salt, and black pepper to taste. Add about ⅓ cup of the blanching liquid and start blending, adding more of the liquid if needed to achieve a thin but creamy consistency. Make sure not to make the mixture too runny.

6 Heat the remaining 2 tablespoons of oil or ghee in a large sauté pan or saucepan over medium heat. Add the shallot and sweat it for 3 to 4 minutes, then add the broccoli stem "rice" and a pinch of salt and cook for 8 to 10 minutes, stirring often, until the "rice" is tender but still has a bite to it.

7 Add the blended sauce to the pan, stirring well to combine and adding more of the blanching liquid as needed to achieve a creamy consistency. Add the remaining spinach, and the remaining blanched broccoli florets and other vegetables, if using, and cook until everything is warmed through and the spinach is just wilted. Remove the pan from the heat. Add the cheese, salt and pepper to taste, and the juice of the remaining half lemon. Stir well and serve the risotto garnished with lemon zest, another sprinkle of cheese, and/or microgreens. The risotto will keep refrigerated in an airtight container for up to 2 days. To reheat it, add vegetable broth or water and stir the risotto over low heat until warm.

CAULIFLOWER RICELESS RISOTTO WITH SPINACH AND CORN

This riceless risotto is on high rotation in my kitchen—a breeze to make, quite versatile, and satisfying. Cauliflower "rice" is light and the most visually similar to rice out of all the vegetables in this chapter. If you don't have corn or spinach on hand, practically any other vegetable will do in their place—try peas, asparagus, or any leafy greens. (Pictured on page 150.)

Serves 4 | SUMMER

1 medium head cauliflower

2 tablespoons neutral coconut oil or olive oil

1 yellow onion, chopped

2 garlic cloves, sliced

1 cup fresh or frozen and thawed corn kernels

Sea salt and freshly ground black pepper

Zest and juice of ½ lemon

¼ cup vegetable broth

¼ cup canned unsweetened Thai coconut milk

3 cups baby spinach leaves

Grated Parmesan or crumbled feta cheese (optional)

1 Roughly chop the cauliflower florets. Place them in a food processor and pulse just until they are broken down into rice-size pieces. Take care not to over-process.

2 Warm the oil in a deep, heavy-bottomed pan over medium heat. Add the onion and sauté for about 5 minutes, until translucent. Add the garlic, corn, a large pinch of salt, and black pepper to taste, and sauté for another 2 minutes until the garlic is fragrant.

3 Increase the heat to high and add the cauliflower "rice" and lemon juice. Stir the cauliflower around for a couple of minutes, until the lemon juice is absorbed and evaporated. Bring the heat back down to medium.

4 Add the vegetable broth and coconut milk, and cook for about 8 minutes, until the cauliflower rice is tender but not mushy. Add the spinach and stir until it has wilted completely, then remove the pan from the heat. Add the lemon zest and cheese, if using. Taste for salt, adjust if needed, and serve immediately. The risotto will keep refrigerated in an airtight container for up to 3 days. To reheat it, add more vegetable broth or coconut milk and stir it over low heat until warm.

BUCKWHEAT RISOTTO WITH ROASTED BEETS

This version of risotto is full of vibrant color and light, summery flavors. If you buy a whole bunch of beets with fresh tops, you can use their nutritious greens and stems here as well. Buckwheat is a nutty, gluten-free pseudo-grain, high in protein and other important nutrients. It usually comes in two forms—raw groats (green or untoasted) and toasted (kasha). Make sure to use raw buckwheat groats for this recipe.

Serves 4 to 6 | SUMMER

4 small or 3 medium red beets with their tops, beets peeled and diced into small cubes, tops (optional) separated into stems and leaves

1½ tablespoons melted neutral coconut oil, divided

Sea salt and freshly ground black pepper

1 cup raw buckwheat groats, soaked in purified water for at least 1 hour or overnight

2½ teaspoons sesame oil, divided

1 tablespoon minced fresh ginger

1 cup vegetable broth or purified water, plus more if needed

1 cup canned unsweetened Thai coconut milk, plus more if needed

1½ tablespoons tamari

Juice of 1 lime

2 teaspoons brown rice vinegar or apple cider vinegar

1 teaspoon chili sauce (Sriracha)

Large handful of fresh cilantro and/or basil leaves, for garnish (optional)

1 Preheat the oven to 400°F (200°C). Line a rimmed baking sheet with parchment paper.

2 Toss the beets with 1 tablespoon of the coconut oil, and sprinkle with salt and pepper. Spread the beets on the prepared baking sheet, transfer them to the oven, and roast for 10 minutes. Chop the beet stems into small pieces, add them to the baking sheet with the beets, toss to cover with oil and juices, and rotate the tray. Continue roasting for 10 minutes or until the beets are tender. Remove from the oven and set aside.

3 Drain and rinse the buckwheat. Warm 1½ teaspoons of the sesame oil and the remaining ½ tablespoon of coconut oil in a deep, heavy-bottomed saucepan over medium heat. Add the ginger and stir for a few minutes.

4 Add the buckwheat and a pinch of salt to the pan; stir to coat. Add the vegetable broth or water and bring the mixture to a boil. Lower the heat to a slow simmer, cover the pan, and cook for 10 minutes, until the buckwheat is soft but not mushy. Chop the beet leaves into bite-size pieces.

5 Add the beets, stems, and leaves, coconut milk, tamari, lime juice, vinegar, Sriracha, and the remaining teaspoon of sesame oil to the pan. Bring the heat back up to medium and cook, stirring, for another 3 to 4 minutes to combine the flavors. Add more coconut milk or vegetable broth, if needed, for a creamier consistency.

6 Serve the risotto warm with cilantro and/or basil, if using. To reheat, add more vegetable broth or coconut milk and stir it over low heat until warm.

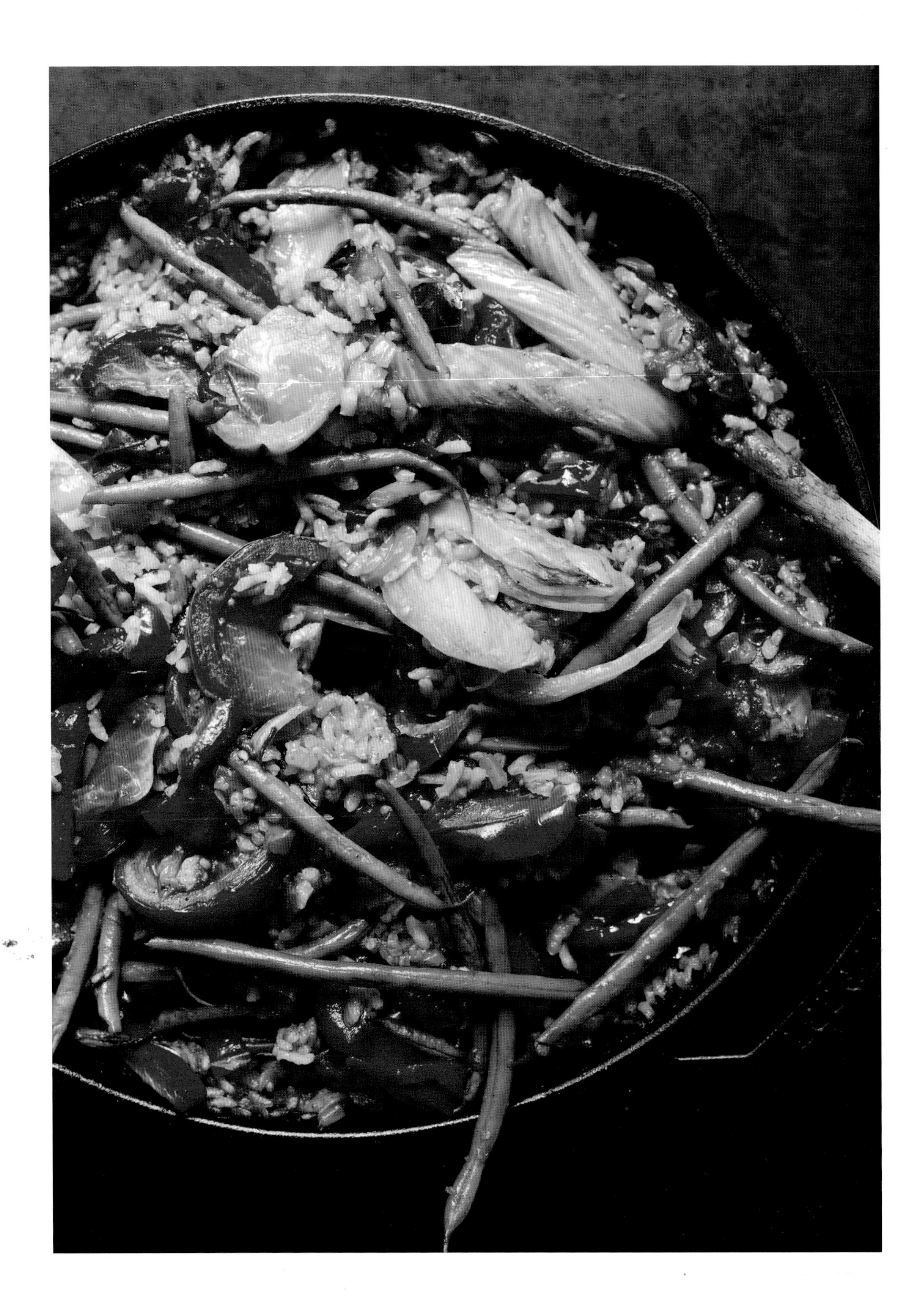

SUMMER PAELLA

This recipe is perfect for a summer party, given its crowd-pleasing ingredient list full of sun-ripened produce. Few of your guests will be able to resist a second helping for its sweet tomatoes, buttery eggplant, caramelized fennel, and tender green beans.

Serves 8 to 10 | SUMMER

2 tablespoons neutral coconut oil or olive oil

1 large yellow onion, chopped

3 garlic cloves, sliced

Sea salt

1 large fennel bulb, cut into 8 wedges

1 medium eggplant, cubed

1 to 2 red bell peppers, seeded and diced

1½ tablespoons tomato paste

1 tablespoon smoked Spanish paprika

Handful of fresh green beans, halved

1½ cups short-grain paella rice or Arborio rice

1 teaspoon saffron threads (optional)

Juice of 1 lemon

2 cups warm vegetable broth

2 medium tomatoes, cut into 8 wedges each

Freshly ground black pepper

Olive oil, for drizzling

1 Preheat the oven to 450°F (230°C).

2 Warm the coconut oil in a large paella pan or cast iron skillet over medium heat. Add the onion, garlic, and a large pinch of salt, and sauté until the onion softens, about 5 minutes.

3 Push the onion to the sides of the pan and add the fennel wedges. Cook the fennel wedges on one side for about 4 minutes, until golden, then flip and cook on the other side for 1 minute. Keep stirring the onions periodically while you cook the fennel, to avoid burning.

4 Add the eggplant, bell pepper, tomato paste, smoked paprika, and another pinch of salt to the pan. Toss to combine and sauté until the eggplant is tender, about 5 minutes.

5 Add the green beans, rice, saffron, if using, a pinch of salt, and the lemon juice. Stir everything around for about 1 minute, until the lemon juice is absorbed.

6 Increase the heat to high. Add enough warm vegetable broth to cover the rice completely. Arrange the tomato slices on top, season with salt and pepper, and drizzle some olive oil over the tomatoes. Bring the mixture to a boil and cook, uncovered, for 2 minutes.

7 Transfer the paella to the oven and bake for 20 minutes, then turn off the oven and let the paella finish cooking, undisturbed, for another 15 minutes until the rice and all the vegetables are tender and cooked through.

8 Serve the paella warm. It will keep refrigerated in an airtight container for up to 4 days. Reheat it over low heat, covered, until warm.

RED RICE AND LACINATO KALE RISOTTO

Bhutanese and ruby red rice, the two varieties of red rice I've encountered the most, work great for this dish and are worth seeking out. Red rice gives newness to this risotto, with its own unique, slightly sweet, aromatic flavor and bite. This is also a chance to eat your kale—a hefty amount of lacinato gives this dish substance and makes it very nourishing. Do not be afraid of having leftovers of this risotto, its flavor greatly benefits from a night or two in the refrigerator.

Serves 6 | SUMMER • FALL

4 cups purified water

4 cups vegetable broth

1½ pounds (680 g) lacinato (Italian) kale, from 1 to 2 bunches

1½ cups Bhutanese or ruby red rice

2 tablespoons neutral coconut oil or olive oil

2 teaspoons freshly ground cumin

Pinch of red pepper flakes

1 large red onion, chopped

2 garlic cloves, minced

Leaves from 5 fresh thyme sprigs

Sea salt and freshly ground black pepper

Juice of 1 large or 2 small limes

Grated Parmesan or crumbled feta (optional)

1 Combine the water and broth in a medium pot, and bring the liquid to a boil over high heat.

2 While the liquid is heating, separate the kale leaves from the stems (save the stems for your next batch of vegetable broth). Add the kale leaves to the boiling liquid, adjust the heat to a strong simmer, and cook for 7 to 10 minutes, until the kale is tender. Using tongs or a large slotted spoon, transfer the kale to a colander and set it over a bowl. Press on the kale to squeeze out any excess liquid, and pour the collected liquid back into the pot.

3 Rinse the rice with cold water, then drain it well and place it in a medium heatproof bowl. Pour in just enough hot broth to cover the rice. Let the rice soak while you work on the next step. Keep the pot with the broth warm over low heat.

4 Warm the oil in a deep, heavy-bottomed pan over medium heat. Add the cumin and red pepper flakes and stir them around until fragrant, about 1 minute. Add the onion and sauté for 7 to 8 minutes, until translucent. Add the garlic, thyme, a pinch of salt, and pepper to taste, and sauté for 2 more minutes until the garlic and thyme are fragrant.

5 Drain the rice in a fine-mesh sieve or colander over the pot with the broth. Add the rice and lime juice to the pan with the sautéed vegetables. Stir until all the liquid is absorbed, then add a ladleful of broth to the pan and let it simmer until the liquid has been absorbed, 3 to 5 minutes.

recipe continues

6 Next, add enough broth to the pan to cover the rice completely. Adjust the heat to a simmer, give the rice a good stir, and partially cover the pan. Continue adding broth by the ladleful to keep the rice covered at all times, and cook for 30 to 40 minutes, stirring often, until the rice is tender but still has some bite to it.

7 Meanwhile, chop the cooked kale into bite-size pieces. Once the rice is cooked to your liking, add the kale to the pan with another ladleful of broth and freshly ground black pepper to taste. Stir to heat everything through. Add the cheese, if using, and taste for salt and pepper. Serve immediately with more cheese sprinkled on top, if desired.

8 The risotto will keep refrigerated in an airtight container for up to 4 days. To reheat leftover risotto, place it in a saucepan and gently warm it up to a creamy consistency with a few tablespoons of vegetable broth.

RUTABAGA AND BRUSSELS SPROUT RICELESS RISOTTO

If you've never tasted rutabaga or cooked with it before, this dish presents the perfect opportunity to give it a try. The process is very simple, and your food processor will turn the root into rice-like pieces in no time. Once cooked, the mild rutabaga gives plenty of bite, serving as an ideal base for this type of risotto. Blanched Brussels sprouts melt in your mouth, while coconut milk makes this dish creamy and luxurious in texture. I have made a habit of keeping a constant supply of pomegranates in my kitchen while they are in season. Not only are they exceptionally delicious and packed with antioxidants, but they can also provide a sophisticated finishing touch to a variety of savory dishes.

Serves 4 | FALL • WINTER

2 medium to large rutabagas

10 to 15 Brussels sprouts, smallest work best

2 tablespoons neutral coconut oil, olive oil, or ghee

1 medium yellow onion, finely chopped

1½ cups vegetable broth

Zest and juice of 2 lemons

Sea salt

1 cup canned unsweetened Thai coconut milk

Freshly ground black pepper

Grated Parmesan, Asiago, or crumbled feta cheese (optional)

Kernels from ½ pomegranate, for serving

1 Peel and roughly chop the rutabagas. Place them in a food processor and pulse just until they are broken down into rice-size pieces. Depending on the size of your food processor, you may need to do this in two batches.

2 Bring a large pot of well-salted water to a boil. Fill a large bowl with ice water and set it nearby. Cut the tough ends off the Brussels sprouts and remove any discolored outer leaves. Cut large sprouts in half lengthwise. Blanch the Brussels sprouts in the boiling water for 5 to 8 minutes, until they are easily pierced with a fork but not mushy. Immediately drain the sprouts and transfer them to the ice water bath to stop the cooking. When the Brussels sprouts are cool, drain them and cut them into quarters.

3 Warm the oil in a deep, heavy-bottomed pan. Add the onions and sauté them over medium heat for about 7 minutes, until translucent.

4 Pour the broth into a small pot and place it over medium-low heat.

5 Add the riced rutabagas to the pan with the onions and sauté for another minute. Add the lemon juice, increase the heat to medium high, and add a generous pinch of salt. Sauté for 2 to 3 minutes, until most of the liquid is evaporated. Add 1 cup of the warm broth to

recipe continues

the pan and sauté for 10 more minutes, stirring often.

6 Add the remaining ½ cup of warm broth to the pan and cook for another 5 minutes, stirring constantly. Add the coconut milk, lemon zest, and freshly ground black pepper to taste, sauté for 2 more minutes, and then add the Brussels sprouts. Cook for 3 more minutes or until the rutabaga “rice” is tender but still has some bite to it. Taste for salt and adjust the seasonings as desired.

7 Serve warm, garnished with a handful of fresh pomegranate kernels. The risotto will keep refrigerated in an airtight container for up to 3 days. To reheat it, add more vegetable broth or coconut milk and stir it over low heat until warm.

LEEK AND MUSHROOM BARLEY RISOTTO

The texture of this risotto closely resembles that of its classic, Arborio-rice counterpart, due to the silky, somewhat creamy texture of pearled barley and the sautéed leeks cooked in broth. The result is an incredibly creamy, perfectly textured dish, brightened with lemony notes and studded with earthy mushrooms.

Serves 6 | FALL • WINTER

4 tablespoons neutral coconut oil or olive oil, divided

1 pound (454 g) crimini mushrooms or a mix of various types of mushrooms, cleaned and sliced

4 garlic cloves, sliced

Sea salt and freshly ground black pepper

4½ cups vegetable broth

2 large leeks, white and light green parts only, sliced

1 cup pearl barley, rinsed under cold water and drained

Zest and juice of 1 lemon

½ teaspoon smoked Spanish paprika

Leaves from 4 fresh thyme sprigs

2 bay leaves (optional)

Grated Parmesan, Asiago, or crumbled feta cheese (optional)

Finely chopped fresh parsley leaves, for garnish (optional)

1 Warm 2 tablespoons of the oil in a medium pot over medium heat. Add the mushrooms, garlic, a pinch of salt, and a few grinds of black pepper, and sauté for about 10 to 15 minutes, until the released liquid evaporates and the mushrooms begin to brown.

2 Pour the broth into the pot with the mushrooms. Increase the heat to high, bring the liquid to a boil, and simmer for a couple of minutes, then remove the pot from the heat. Cover the pot and let the mixture infuse while you work with the leeks.

3 Warm the remaining 2 tablespoons of oil in a deep, heavy-bottomed pan over medium-high heat, add the leeks and a pinch of salt, and sauté for about 8 minutes until the leeks are soft. Meanwhile, measure out 3 cups of the mushroom broth, keeping the mushrooms in their pot.

4 Add the barley to the pan with the leeks and stir to coat for 1 minute. Pour in the lemon juice and stir until absorbed. Add the paprika, thyme, bay leaf, and the 3 cups of reserved mushroom broth. Adjust the heat to a gentle simmer, partially cover the pan to let some steam escape, and cook, stirring occasionally, for 30 minutes. Toward the end of the 30 minutes, use a slotted spoon to remove the mushrooms from their pot, and measure out 1 more cup of the remaining mushroom broth, keeping the last ½ cup of broth in the pot.

5 Add the mushrooms and the reserved cup of mushroom broth to the barley. Continue to cook the barley for about 15 minutes, until it is completely soft. Add the rest of the broth

and the reserved lemon zest to the barley and cook for another couple of minutes until the risotto reaches the right consistency—it should be creamy, yet still a little chewy. Remove the pan from the heat and stir in the cheese, if using. Taste and adjust for salt and pepper. Serve the risotto right away garnished with finely chopped parsley leaves.

6 The risotto will keep refrigerated in an airtight container for up to 4 days. To reheat it, place it in a saucepan and add a few tablespoons of vegetable broth, then cover the pan and and warm it over low heat to achieve a creamy consistency.

ROASTED ROOT VEGETABLE OVEN RISOTTO

This is the only risotto recipe in this chapter that calls for Arborio, the traditional risotto rice. The oven-baked risotto method eliminates the need for constant stirring, allowing the cook to tend to other matters, whether in or away from the kitchen. Various root vegetables bring nourishment, depth, and color to this dish, and the uncommon addition of warming curry spice is especially welcome when the air is crisp.

Serves 6 to 8 | FALL • WINTER

3 medium carrots

2 large or 3 small parsnips

2 medium sweet potatoes or ½ medium winter squash

3 tablespoons melted neutral coconut oil or olive oil, divided

Sea salt and freshly ground black pepper

1 large yellow onion

3 garlic cloves

1 lemon

7 fresh thyme sprigs

7 cups vegetable broth

1½ teaspoons to 1 tablespoon curry powder, depending on how spicy it is

1½ cups Arborio rice

4 cups baby spinach or chopped spinach leaves (optional)

1 Preheat the oven to 425°F (220°C). Line a rimmed baking sheet with parchment paper.

2 Peel and cut the carrots, parsnips, and sweet potatoes or squash into bite-size pieces. Place them on the prepared baking sheet, add 1 tablespoon of the oil, and toss to coat. Sprinkle with salt and pepper, transfer the baking sheet to the oven, and roast the vegetables for 30 minutes, stirring halfway through, until they are soft and caramelized.

3 While the vegetables are roasting, chop the onion into medium-size pieces and mince the garlic. Juice the lemon and separate the thyme leaves from the stems. Pour the broth into a medium saucepan and place it over medium-low heat.

4 When the vegetables are done roasting, remove them from the oven and set them aside. Reduce the oven temperature to 350°F (180°C).

5 Warm the remaining 2 tablespoons of oil in a large Dutch oven or other heavy, ovenproof pot over medium heat. Add the onion and sauté for 5 minutes, until translucent. Add the garlic, thyme leaves, and a big pinch of salt, and sauté for 2 more minutes.

6 Increase the heat to medium high. Add the curry powder, rice, and lemon juice to the pot, and stir until all the liquid is absorbed, 1 to 2 minutes. Remove the pot from the heat and add 5 cups of the warm broth and a pinch of salt. Cover the pot and place it in the oven. Bake the risotto, undisturbed, for 15 minutes.

7 Meanwhile, measure 1½ packed cups of the roasted vegetables and place them in a blender along with the rest of the warm broth. Blend until smooth, pour the mixture into the same pot you used for the broth, and keep it warm over medium-low heat.

8 Take the risotto out of the oven and taste the rice for doneness—it should be cooked with some bite left to it. If the rice seems undercooked, place the pot back in the oven for another 5 minutes. Pour the warm blended vegetable liquid into the risotto and stir vigorously for a couple of minutes. The risotto may seem too soupy at first, but the rice will absorb the liquid as it sits. Add the spinach, if using, and stir until it wilts. Taste for salt and adjust if needed. Add the remaining roasted vegetable pieces and stir to incorporate. Serve immediately.

9 The risotto will keep refrigerated in an airtight container for up to 4 days. To warm up leftover risotto, place it in a saucepan with a few tablespoons of vegetable broth, then cover the pan and and warm it over low heat to achieve a creamy consistency.

BUKHARA FARRO PILAF

Having grown up in southwest Russia, I feel a special affection for pilaf. The flavorful rice dish is a common meal in the Caucasus and into the Middle East and Central Asia. Where I come from, it's common knowledge that the best pilaf is made in Uzbekistan, named after the ancient city of Bukhara. Over time, the authentic Bukhara pilaf recipe has evolved, taking on influences from all over, and many variations exist today. My version features pumpkin and raisins, and if you happen to have saffron and barberries, they would be excellent additions, too. For variety's sake, this recipe calls for farro, an ancient wheat, but feel free to use any type of rice instead.

The way I've been trained to prepare pilaf, a common technique in Russia, is to layer each type of ingredient in a pot, cook them in those layers, completely undisturbed, and then mix them all together just before serving. There is some magic to the process—the layers steam and take on each other's juices and aromas, with no effort required. Opening the pot to a finished, golden, and incredibly aromatic pilaf is always a bit astonishing—it's as if it cooked itself.

Serves 6 | FALL • WINTER

3 tablespoons neutral coconut oil or ghee, or a mix of both

1 tablespoon cumin seeds

3 large yellow onions, thinly sliced

Large pinch plus 2¼ teaspoons sea salt, divided

1 tablespoon ground turmeric

Freshly ground black pepper

1 cup purified water

3 medium carrots, julienned

½ cup raisins

Small handful of barberries (optional)

Small pinch of saffron threads (optional)

ingredients continue

1 Warm the oil in a large, heavy-bottomed pot (a cast iron Dutch oven is ideal) over medium heat. Add the cumin seeds and stir around for a minute, until fragrant.

2 Add the onions, a large pinch of salt, turmeric, and black pepper to taste, and sauté until the onions are slightly golden, 7 to 10 minutes. Pour the purified water over the onions. Add the carrots, scattering them in a single layer. Bring the water to a simmer, reduce the heat to low, and cook, covered, for about 7 minutes or until the carrots are soft.

3 Meanwhile, boil 2 cups of water in a small pot or kettle, and keep it hot for the next step.

4 Increase the heat to medium. Scatter the raisins, barberries, and saffron, if using, in an even layer over the carrots in the pot, followed by the pumpkin. Top with the farro, arranging it in an even layer. Carefully pour the boiling water over the farro, taking care not to disturb the layers. Sprinkle on the remaining 2¼ teaspoons of salt and bring the pilaf mixture to a simmer. Cover the pot, reduce the heat to low, and

1 small pumpkin or other winter squash, peeled, seeded, and cut into ½-inch cubes

1½ cups farro or rice, soaked in 4 cups purified water for 8 to 12 hours

cook undisturbed for 30 minutes.

5 Open the lid, place a kitchen towel over the pot, and place the lid on top of it. Turn off the heat and let the pilaf sit undisturbed for 15 more minutes until the farro and vegetables are completely cooked. Gently toss to mix the layers, and serve hot.

6 The pilaf will keep refrigerated in an airtight container for up to 4 days. Reheat it over low heat, covered, until warm.

NOODLES, PASTA, AND PIZZA

PASTA AND PIZZA are some of the most comforting foods—a hearty bowl of savory noodles and the chewy crunch of the perfect pizza crust are perennial favorites. In this chapter, I offer you some ideas on updating those traditional dishes with the addition of seasonal vegetables and other nourishing ingredients. You will find foundational techniques for making your own basic eggless pasta, flatbread crusts, and dumplings, as well as some twists on the classics, like noodles and pizza crusts made out of vegetables. There are some timesavers too, centered around things like a store-bought package of soba noodles or pizza crust made of polenta. Whether you are motivated by a strong carb craving or looking for a pizza or pasta that is lighter but still satisfying, you will find it among the recipes in this chapter.

180
Basic Sprouted or Whole Spelt Eggless Pasta

182
Roasted Radish Flatbread

185
Blistered Tomato and Green Bean Fettuccine in Smoky Sauce

187
Cucumber Noodles with Melon Spheres and Herb Vinaigrette

188
Polenta Crust Pizza with Romesco and Tomatoes

191
Early Fall Soba Noodles with Broiled Figs, Kabocha Squash, and Kale

192
Spaghetti Squash Noodles with Eggplant-Lentil Meatballs

195
Marinated Roasted Bell Pepper Kamut Spiral Pasta

199
Roasted Eggplant and Bell Pepper Pizza with Gluten-Free Sweet Potato Crust

201
White Bean and Sweet Potato Dumplings

206
Daikon Radish Pad Thai

209
Portobello Bolognese Pasta

210
Spelt Fettuccine with Melted Rainbow Chard

213
Leek, Fennel, and Chard Pizza with Gluten-Free Onion Crust

BASIC SPROUTED OR WHOLE SPELT EGGLESS PASTA

Contrary to common belief, preparing homemade pasta does not take great effort, and the result is incredibly rewarding in flavor. This pasta recipe is very simple and requires no eggs.

Serves 4 to 6; makes about 24 ounces (650 g) fresh pasta or 1 pound (450 g) dried pasta

3 cups (300 g) whole or sprouted spelt flour, plus more for dusting the surface

1 teaspoon sea salt

2 tablespoons melted neutral coconut oil or olive oil

1 cup purified warm water

1 Mix the flour and salt together in a large bowl with a fork. Make a well in the center and pour in the oil and water. Begin to mix with a fork, slowly incorporating the flour into the well of oil and water. When all the flour is mixed in, transfer the dough to a floured surface and knead it for 10 minutes, until smooth and elastic. Form a ball with the dough and tightly wrap it in plastic wrap. Let the dough rest for 30 minutes at room temperature.

2 Place the dough back on the well-floured work surface and knead it for another 10 minutes until even more springy. Cut the dough into 4 equal-size pieces and keep them covered with a damp kitchen towel while you roll out the pasta.

3 Keep your working surface well-floured. Roll one piece of dough at a time into a paper-thin sheet. Cut the rolled-out dough into the desired pasta shape with a pizza cutter or sharp knife. Generously dust the cut pasta with flour and gently toss to coat. At this point, the pasta is ready to be cooked or dried. Continue to roll out and cut the rest of the dough.

4 To cook the pasta, bring a large pot of well-salted water to a boil. Add the pasta and cook for 30 seconds to 2 minutes, depending on its thickness. Test for doneness as you go, taking care not to overcook the pasta.

5 To dry the pasta, hang each strand of pasta on a coat hanger, back of a chair, or drying rack, keeping some space between each pasta strand. Leave out to dry for 8 hours or until completely dry. Dried pasta will keep in an airtight paper bag in a cool, dry place at room temperature for up to 1 month.

ROASTED RADISH FLATBREAD

Most people think of radishes as something to eat raw in a salad, but sautéing or roasting these spring roots transforms them into the most tender, sweet, and silky spheres, free of characteristic sharpness. Spring market radishes tend to come with impressive, sizable green tops, which are perfectly suited for dishes like this flatbread. The easy flatbread dough recipe I provide here is my go-to when I'm craving a quick, pizza-like meal, and it works with all kinds of toppings.

Makes two 10- to 12-inch flatbreads | SPRING • SUMMER

FOR THE DOUGH

2 cups (200 g) sprouted spelt flour or whole spelt flour, plus more for dusting the surface

½ teaspoon sea salt

2 tablespoons melted neutral coconut oil

½ teaspoon baking soda

1 tablespoon apple cider vinegar

¾ cup purified warm water

FOR THE TOPPINGS

1½ tablespoons neutral coconut oil, at room temperature, divided, plus more for greasing

1 small or ½ large red onion, thinly sliced

Sea salt

Freshly ground black pepper

13 to 15 small to medium radishes with tops

2 garlic cloves, minced

1½ teaspoons balsamic vinegar

Handful of baby greens (optional)

TO MAKE THE DOUGH

1 Place the flour in a medium mixing bowl and make a well in the center. Add the salt, coconut oil, and baking soda. Pour the apple cider vinegar over the baking soda and let it bubble.

2 Gradually pour the warm water into the well, mixing constantly with a fork until all of the flour is mixed into the wet ingredients. Transfer the dough to a well-floured work surface and knead it with your hands for 3 to 5 minutes. The dough should be very soft and slightly sticky. Cover the dough with a damp kitchen towel and let it rest for 20 minutes.

TO ASSEMBLE AND BAKE THE FLATBREADS

1 Preheat the oven to 395°F (200°C). Line a large baking sheet with parchment paper, and grease the parchment with coconut oil.

2 Divide the dough in half and flatten each piece with the palm of your hand. On a flour-dusted work surface, roll each piece of dough into a thin, 10- to 12-inch round. Carefully transfer both rounds to the prepared baking sheet. Alternatively, you can place both rounds directly on the prepared baking sheet and spread them into crusts, one at a time, by gently pressing and pushing the dough from the center outward with your hands.

3 In a medium bowl, combine the onion slices with ½ tablespoon of the coconut oil, a large pinch of salt, and black pepper to taste; toss to coat. Spread the onions on top of the rounds of dough, transfer them to

the oven, and bake for 15 minutes.

4 In the meantime, cut the tops from the radishes, chop them roughly and set them aside. Slice the radishes into halves or quarters, depending on their size.

5 Heat the remaining tablespoon of coconut oil in a large saucepan over medium heat. Add the radishes, cut-side down, and cook for 4 minutes undisturbed, then stir and sauté for 3 more minutes or until the radishes are translucent and soft, but not mushy. Add the radish tops and garlic to the pan and sauté for 1 more minute. Add the balsamic vinegar, stir to coat, and remove the pan from the heat.

6 Remove the flatbreads from the oven, top them with the radishes and greens, if using, and bake for 5 more minutes until all the vegetables are fully cooked and golden in places and the crust is dry. Remove the flatbreads from the oven, let them cool slightly, garnish with baby greens, if using, then slice and serve.

BLISTERED TOMATO AND GREEN BEAN FETTUCCINE IN SMOKY SAUCE

This is a fun twist on a classic blistered tomato pasta dish. The addition of green beans and broccoli makes it more vegetable-oriented, and the creamy, brilliant-orange, paprika-spiked sauce brings notes of piquancy and smoke. (Pictured on page 178.)

Serves 4 to 6 | SUMMER

FOR THE SAUCE

2 tablespoons Dijon mustard

1 tablespoon smoked Spanish paprika

Juice of 1 lemon

2 tablespoons olive oil

2 garlic cloves, minced

½ teaspoon chili sauce (Sriracha)

FOR THE PASTA

1 tablespoon neutral coconut oil or olive oil, divided

2 large handfuls of fresh green beans, strings removed

1 small or ½ large head broccoli, cut into florets

Tamari

Freshly ground black pepper

1 pound (454 g) cherry tomatoes

4 garlic cloves, sliced

1 (12-ounce / 340-g) package whole wheat fettuccine or ½ recipe Basic Sprouted or Whole Spelt Eggless Pasta (page 180), cut into fettuccine noodles

2 tablespoons chopped fresh parsley

Handful of fresh basil leaves, torn

TO MAKE THE SAUCE

Combine all the ingredients in a small bowl and whisk until smooth.

TO MAKE THE PASTA

1 Warm ½ tablespoon of the oil in a large cast iron or heavy-bottomed saucepan over medium heat. Add the green beans and broccoli and sauté until they are bright green and blistered in places, 7 to 8 minutes. Add a splash of tamari to the pan, sprinkle with black pepper to taste, and move the vegetables to one side of the pan.

2 Increase the heat to medium high. Add the remaining ½ tablespoon of coconut oil and the tomatoes. Let the tomatoes cook undisturbed for about 1 minute, then toss them and cook, tossing periodically, for about 4 minutes, until the tomato skins are wrinkled and blistered in places. Add a splash of tamari and the garlic, mix in the green beans and broccoli, and remove the pan from the heat.

3 In the meantime, cook the pasta according to the instructions on the package or on page 180. Drain well and add the cooked pasta to the pan with the vegetables, then pour in the sauce and toss to combine. Serve immediately, garnished with parsley and fresh basil leaves.

CUCUMBER NOODLES WITH MELON SPHERES AND HERB VINAIGRETTE

This dish is hydration in a bowl—the perfect meal to enjoy after a long and hot summer day. I got the brilliant idea of combining julienned cucumber "noodles" with salted and spiced watermelon from Laura Wright's blog, *The First Mess*. Laura created the most memorable summer dish of salted watermelon steaks topped with cucumber noodles, and after I tried it the first time, I proceeded to prepare it for several dinners in a row. I have elaborated on the idea here, including different types of melons served in the shape of juicy spheres that burst with every bite.

If you don't have a melon baller, simply cube the melons into uniform, bite-size pieces.

Serves 4 | SUMMER

2 English cucumbers, cut into noodles with a julienne peeler or spiralizer

Large handful of fresh basil leaves, torn, divided, plus more for garnish

Large handful of fresh mint leaves, torn, divided, plus more for garnish

Juice of 1 large lime, divided

1 tablespoon pure maple syrup or honey, divided

1½ teaspoons tamari, divided

2 tablespoons olive oil, divided

1 small or ½ large melon, such as cantaloupe or honeydew, or a mix of both

¼ medium watermelon

Sea salt

1 teaspoon sweet Hungarian paprika (optional)

Handful of raw chopped pistachios, for garnish (optional)

1 In a large mixing bowl, gently toss the cucumber noodles with half of each of the basil, mint, lime juice, maple syrup, tamari, and olive oil.

2 Using a melon baller, scoop spheres out of the melon and watermelon and add them to the cucumber noodles.

3 Squeeze the remaining lime juice over the fruit, followed by the rest of maple syrup, tamari, and olive oil. Add the rest of the herbs and toss gently to combine.

4 Distribute the noodles and fruit among serving plates or bowls and sprinkle with the salt and sweet paprika, if using. Garnish with chopped pistachios, if using, and more herbs. Serve right away.

POLENTA CRUST PIZZA WITH ROMESCO AND TOMATOES

Since polenta and sauce is a very popular dinner in our house, I like to experiment and see how else I can use corn grits in our weekday meals. As it turns out, traditional corn grit polenta also makes for an easy, gluten-free pizza crust—with golden, crisp edges, a warm, soft center, and a bit of its pleasant, fine-grain texture shining through. Feel free to customize the toppings according to what you have on hand (see Universal Tomato Sauce, page 308, for instance).

Makes one 10-inch pizza | SUMMER • FALL

FOR THE POLENTA CRUST

3 cups vegetable broth

Sea salt and freshly ground black pepper

1 teaspoon garlic powder (optional)

1 cup corn grits

2 tablespoons neutral coconut oil or olive oil, divided

FOR THE TOPPINGS

¾ cup Romesco Sauce (page 307)

2 to 3 medium tomatoes, sliced, or 1 cup cherry tomatoes, halved

Sea salt and freshly ground black pepper

Olive oil, for drizzling

Large handful of baby spinach (optional)

Handful of fresh basil leaves

TO MAKE THE CRUST

1 Bring the vegetable broth to a boil in a medium saucepan over high heat. Season to taste with salt and pepper and add the garlic powder, if using. Slowly pour in the corn grits, stirring constantly with a long-handled spoon to prevent the hot polenta from splashing on you. Reduce the heat to low and cook for 5 minutes, stirring frequently to prevent clumping, until the polenta has thickened. When the polenta is done cooking, stir in 1½ tablespoons of the oil.

2 Grease a 10-inch (25-cm) cast iron skillet with the remaining ½ tablespoon of oil. Spoon the cooked polenta into the pan, spreading it out in an even layer with a spatula to form the pizza crust. Refrigerate the polenta for 30 minutes to let it set.

3 Preheat the oven to 450°F (230°C). Bake the crust for 20 minutes or until firm and dry.

TO MAKE THE PIZZA

1 Place an oven rack in a position closest to the broiler. Remove the polenta crust from the oven and preheat the broiler on the low setting.

2 Spoon the romesco onto the crust, spreading it evenly. Arrange the tomato slices on top, sprinkle with salt and black pepper to taste, and drizzle lightly with olive oil.

3 Transfer the skillet to the oven and broil for 10 minutes or until the tomatoes are soft and caramelized.

4 Remove the pizza from the oven and let cool slightly, then top it with the spinach, if using, and basil. Serve.

EARLY FALL SOBA NOODLES WITH BROILED FIGS, KABOCHA SQUASH, AND KALE

This quick soba noodle dish celebrates the abundance of figs, squash, and kale in early fall, finished off with a piney kiss of sage and a sprinkling of pistachios.

Serves 4 | SUMMER • FALL

Sea salt

3 cups peeled and cubed kabocha squash, other winter squash, or sweet potato

3 to 5 kale leaves, stems removed, leaves roughly chopped

3 fresh thyme sprigs (optional)

8 ounces (227 g) soba noodles

8 fresh ripe figs, halved lengthwise

1 tablespoon chopped fresh sage leaves, plus a few whole leaves, divided

¼ cup raw chopped pistachios or other nuts

2½ tablespoons ghee or olive oil

Freshly ground black pepper

Crumbled soft goat cheese or goat or sheep's milk feta, for serving (optional)

1 Bring a large pot of well-salted water to a boil. Add the squash, kale, and thyme, if using, and bring the water back to a boil. Reduce the heat to a strong simmer and cook for 8 to 10 minutes, partially covered, until the squash is soft when pricked with a knife. Using a slotted spoon, transfer the vegetables to a bowl and set them aside. Discard the thyme sprigs.

2 Bring the cooking water back to a boil, add the soba noodles, and cook for 5 minutes or 1 to 2 minutes less than instructed on the package; the noodles will continue cooking later in the pan. Drain the noodles, reserving about ½ cup of the cooking liquid. Rinse the noodles briefly under cold water.

3 Meanwhile, place an oven rack in a position closest to the broiler and preheat the broiler. Line a rimmed baking sheet with parchment paper.

4 Place the figs cut-side up on the prepared baking sheet. Broil for 4 to 5 minutes. Remove the baking sheet from the oven, sprinkle the figs with the chopped sage and pistachios, then place the baking sheet back under the broiler for 1 to 2 minutes, until the figs are caramelized and golden brown at the edges.

5 Meanwhile, warm the ghee and whole sage leaves in a large saucepan over medium-low heat. Add the squash and kale to the pan and gently stir to coat. Add the soba noodles, increase the heat to medium, then add the reserved cooking liquid and salt and black pepper to taste; cook for 2 to 3 minutes, stirring gently to coat until the liquid is fully incorporated.

6 Distribute the noodles and vegetables among individual bowls, top each with figs, and sprinkle with more pistachios and the cheese, if using.

SPAGHETTI SQUASH NOODLES WITH EGGPLANT-LENTIL MEATBALLS

Spaghetti squash is a truly miraculous vegetable with a unique ability to turn into succulent noodles when roasted in the oven. During the fall, dinner at our house is often a bowl of spaghetti squash topped with whatever seasonal fare and sauce we can come up with.

This dish is a play on the classic spaghetti and meatballs, though much more plant-centric. Eggplant, already quite meaty in nature, provides an excellent base for vegetarian meatballs, especially when accompanied by protein-rich lentils and ground cumin. I like to serve this bowl garnished with chimichurri, but any pesto would work here as well.

Serves 6 to 8 | SUMMER • FALL

FOR THE SQUASH NOODLES AND EGGPLANT

1 large spaghetti squash, halved lengthwise, seeds removed

1½ tablespoons melted neutral coconut oil

Sea salt and freshly ground black pepper

3 small or 2 medium eggplants (1½ pounds / 680 g total), sliced into ½-inch-thick rounds

FOR THE MEATBALLS

Sea salt

1 tablespoon melted neutral coconut oil

1 teaspoon cumin seeds, ground

Small pinch of red pepper flakes

1 large leek, white and light green parts only, thinly sliced

¾ cup green or French lentils, cooked according to directions on page 70

ingredients continue

TO ROAST THE SPAGHETTI SQUASH AND EGGPLANT

1 Position both racks in the center of the oven. Preheat the oven to 400°F (200°C). Line two rimmed baking sheets with parchment paper.

2 Rub the cut sides of the spaghetti squash with ½ tablespoon of the coconut oil, and sprinkle with salt and pepper to taste. Place the squash cut-side down on one of the prepared baking sheets.

3 Arrange the eggplant slices on the other prepared baking sheet. Drizzle 1 tablespoon of the coconut oil over the eggplant slices, sprinkle with salt, and mix to coat with your hands. Arrange slices in a single layer.

4 Place both trays in the oven, one on each rack. Roast the spaghetti squash for about 30 minutes or until it is tender but not mushy when pricked with a knife. Take care not to overcook the squash, so that you have nicely formed "noodles." Roast the eggplant for 20 minutes, then flip the slices and roast for 15 more minutes, until they are soft and golden. Remove both trays from the oven and set them aside.

TO MAKE THE MEATBALLS

1 Lower the oven temperature to 375°F (190 C).

2 Warm the coconut oil in a large sauté pan over medium heat. Add the cumin and red pepper flakes and stir them

Juice of 1 lemon

2 cups baby spinach, lightly packed

1 garlic clove, minced

Freshly ground black pepper

¼ cup crumbled feta cheese (optional)

FOR SERVING

Carrot Top Chimichurri (page 315)

around for 1 minute. Add the leek and a pinch of salt and sauté for 8 to 10 minutes, until the leek is soft. Add the cooked lentils and the lemon juice, increase the heat to medium high, and cook for about 3 minutes, until the liquid evaporates. Add the spinach and stir for 1 to 2 minutes or until it has wilted. Remove the pan from the heat.

3 Combine the roasted eggplant slices, lentil-leek sauté, garlic, and black pepper to taste in a food processor. Pulse until all the ingredients are equally incorporated, taking care not to over-process; the mixture should be chunky. Transfer the mixture to a medium bowl and fold in the feta, if using. Taste for salt and adjust if needed.

4 Use the same baking sheet and parchment paper used for roasting the eggplant. With your hands, shape the eggplant-lentil mixture into meatballs about 1-inch in diameter and arrange them on the baking sheet. Transfer the meatballs to the oven and bake them for 25 to 30 minutes, until they are browned and firm. The meatballs will firm up further after they cool down. Remove the meatballs from the oven.

TO SERVE

1 Scrape the spaghetti squash noodles from the baked squash with a fork and distribute them among individual serving bowls. Arrange the desired amount of meatballs on top, and serve garnished with the chimichurri sauce.

2 Refrigerate the meatballs and squash in separate airtight containers for up to 4 days. Reheat the spaghetti squash in a sauté pan over medium-low heat with olive oil or ghee. Reheat the meatballs in the oven at 350°F (180°C) for about 10 minutes, or until warmed through—they are also delicious cold.

MARINATED ROASTED BELL PEPPER KAMUT SPIRAL PASTA

This is an incredibly crowd-pleasing pasta dish. The key here lies in marination—after combining all the ingredients, you set the salad aside to marinate in the juices from the roasted bell pepper, the sautéed garlic, and the dressing for an hour or so before serving. The flavors will develop even more after a few days in the refrigerator.

Kamut is the trademarked name for Khorasan wheat, an ancient wheat grain that has more nutritional content than conventional wheat and is reported to awaken less problems in those with mild gluten sensitivities. Kamut pasta has a nice, hearty texture and is worth a try, but you can use any good whole wheat or even gluten-free pasta instead.

Serves 6 to 8 | SUMMER • FALL

FOR THE DRESSING

2 tablespoons freshly squeezed lemon juice

1 tablespoon apple cider vinegar

1 tablespoon balsamic vinegar

1½ teaspoons tamari

¼ cup olive oil

FOR THE SALAD

5 red bell peppers or mixed red and yellow bell peppers

8 ounces (227 g) whole Kamut pasta spirals or whole wheat pasta spirals

Sea salt

½ cup pitted black olives, halved

⅓ cup oil-packed sun dried tomatoes, chopped

1 tablespoon neutral coconut oil

¼ cup almonds, sliced

4 large garlic cloves, sliced

4 cups baby spinach, lightly packed

1 teaspoon tamari

1 Whisk together all the dressing ingredients in a small bowl until smooth; set aside.

2 Place an oven rack in a position closest to the broiler and preheat the broiler to high. Arrange the bell peppers on a rimmed baking sheet and place them under the broiler. Char the peppers, turning them every 1 to 2 minutes, until their skins are blackened on all sides. Take caution not to burn yourself and use oven mitts. Remove the peppers from the oven and transfer them to a large heatproof bowl. Cover the bowl with plastic wrap and set aside to cool. Once the peppers are cool enough to touch, remove their skins and seeds and slice the peppers into bite-size pieces. This step can be done a few days in advance, keeping the peppers refrigerated in an airtight container.

3 Bring a large pot of water to a boil. Add the pasta and a pinch or two of salt, and cook to al dente according to the package directions, taking care to not overcook. Drain the pasta and transfer it to a large bowl.

recipe continues

4 Add the peppers, olives, and sun-dried tomatoes to the bowl with the pasta.

5 Warm the coconut oil in a large sauté pan over medium-low heat. Add the almonds and toast for 3 minutes, then add the garlic and stir it around for another 30 seconds until the almonds are toasted and the garlic is fragrant. Add the spinach and tamari, and stir until the spinach is wilted. Add the spinach mixture and any leftover cooking oil to the bowl with the pasta.

6 Pour the dressing over the salad and toss thoroughly to combine. Cover the bowl and let it marinate for 1 hour at room temperature. Serve the salad at room temperature or cold. The flavor will improve further the next day, after sitting in the refrigerator overnight.

ROASTED EGGPLANT AND BELL PEPPER PIZZA WITH GLUTEN-FREE SWEET POTATO CRUST

I love experimenting with vegetable-based pizza crusts, as the prospects are always exciting and the possibilities are endless. This is my go-to gluten-free, sweet potato pizza crust, which I shape and bake in a cast iron skillet. You can never go wrong with an eggplant and bell pepper topping for a pizza. Both vegetables have admirable qualities of their own—the eggplant is meaty and savory, and the bell pepper is juicy and sweet—and they come together beautifully on this vibrant, orange crust.

Makes one 10-inch pizza | SUMMER • FALL

FOR THE TOPPINGS

1 medium eggplant, sliced into ½-inch rounds

1 red bell pepper, sliced into quarters, seeds removed

2 tablespoons melted neutral coconut oil, divided

Sea salt and freshly ground black pepper

Cloves from 1 head garlic, unpeeled

1 teaspoon sweet Hungarian paprika

Carrot Top Chimichurri (page 315), for serving

ingredients continue

TO PREPARE THE TOPPINGS

1 Preheat the oven to 400°F (200°C). Line a rimmed baking sheet with parchment paper.

2 Arrange the eggplant and pepper slices on the prepared baking sheet. Drizzle the vegetables with 1 tablespoon of the oil, sprinkle with salt and pepper to taste, and mix with your hands to coat. Spread the vegetables out in a single layer, transfer them to the oven, and roast for 20 minutes. Flip the vegetables, arrange the garlic cloves in between the vegetable pieces, and roast for another 15 minutes until the eggplant is golden and soft and the pepper and garlic are tender when pricked with a knife. You can bake the sweet potato for the crust at the same time (see instructions on the next page).

3 Remove the baking sheet from the oven, and keep the oven on. Peel the roasted garlic and place it in a small bowl. Mash the garlic with a fork, add the remaining tablespoon of oil, a small pinch of salt, and a couple grinds of black pepper, and mix thoroughly. Set aside. Slice the pepper into thin strips.

ROASTED EGGPLANT AND BELL PEPPER PIZZA WITH GLUTEN-FREE SWEET POTATO CRUST, continued

FOR THE CRUST

1 medium sweet potato

1 garlic clove, minced

Sea salt and freshly ground black pepper

1 cup (100 g) plus 1 tablespoon oat flour or buckwheat flour, or other flour of choice

1 teaspoon baking powder

1 teaspoon apple cider vinegar

1 tablespoon neutral coconut oil, divided, plus more for oiling your hands

TO MAKE THE CRUST AND BAKE THE PIZZA

1 Prick the sweet potato with a fork several times and bake it at the same time as the eggplant and pepper slices for about 40 minutes or until it is soft throughout. Let it cool and peel it. Alternatively, you can slice and steam or boil the sweet potato. Mash the cooked sweet potato flesh and measure out 1 cup, reserving any excess for another dish.

2 Combine the mashed sweet potato, minced garlic, salt, pepper, flour, baking powder, apple cider vinegar, and ½ tablespoon of the coconut oil in a food processor. Pulse to combine, scraping the walls of the bowl if needed. You should end up with a soft and sticky dough.

3 Coat the bottom of a 10-inch cast iron skillet with the remaining ½ tablespoon of oil. Scrape the dough into the skillet and use a wet spoon and oiled hands to spread it out in an even layer. Push some of the dough slightly up the sides of the pan to create a border. Place the skillet in the oven and bake for 15 to 20 minutes, until the edges of the crust are slightly browned.

4 Carefully remove the skillet from the oven. Spread the mashed garlic over the crust with a fork. Arrange the eggplant and pepper slices on top and sprinkle with the paprika. Return the skillet to the oven and bake for another 10 minutes until the crust is golden at the edges and the vegetables are heated through. Remove the skillet from the oven, let it cool slightly, and slide the pizza onto a cutting board. Slice and serve the pizza topped with chimichurri.

WHITE BEAN AND SWEET POTATO DUMPLINGS

I'm going to take advantage of a dumpling recipe to tell an anecdote, which has become something of a hilarious legend in our family. The Soviet Union during the 1980s was a patriarchal society, where most women cooked every meal from scratch and most men did not step foot in the kitchen. My mother's female coworker, very much from this kind of family, had to go out of town to take care of urgent business, leaving her husband alone to fend for himself. Worried that her husband might starve to death, she stocked a freezer full of home-cooked foods, including his favorite *vareniki* (Russian potato-filled dumplings). She gave her husband very detailed instructions on how to cook the vareniki, explaining that once they are floating atop the boiling water in the pot, they are ready to be eaten. When the time came to boil the dumplings, our hero followed all his wife's instructions and waited for them to float. He waited a while, something close to an hour, turning up the heat more and more and failing to realize that all the dumplings had stuck to the bottom of the pot, since he had never been instructed to give them the obvious, good stir!

Now that you've learned to always stir your boiling dumplings, consider making these ones, stuffed with white bean and sweet potato mash and flavored with chipotle spice, onion, and garlic—a combination that I cannot say enough about. The dough here is a very simple, go-to dumpling dough, delicate but with a bit of that rustic bite from spelt—a perfect envelope for the soft and hearty, root and bean filling.

Note: I propose my preferred way of shaping the dumplings in this recipe. Alternatively, you can use a ravioli stamp. You can also divide the dough in half and roll out one portion at a time into a ⅛-inch-thick sheet. Then cut out uniform skins using the rim of a glass or a round cookie cutter. Re-shape, re-roll, and re-cut the scraps until you use all of the dough. Be sure to keep the skins covered so they don't dry out during the assembly process. If you use any of these alternative shaping methods, you may end up with a smaller amount of dumplings.

Makes about 50 dumplings | FALL • WINTER

FOR THE DOUGH

1½ cups (150 g) whole or sprouted spelt flour, plus more for rolling

½ teaspoon sea salt

2 tablespoons melted neutral coconut oil or olive oil

½ cup plus 1 tablespoon boiling water

ingredients continue

TO MAKE THE DOUGH

1 Combine flour and salt in a large mixing bowl. Add the oil and work it in with your hands until the oil is incorporated well and the mixture resembles sand.

2 Slowly add the boiling water to the bowl, stirring constantly until just combined. Scrape the dough onto a floured work surface and knead it until it is soft and elastic. Return the dough to the bowl, cover it with a damp kitchen towel or wrap tightly with plastic wrap, and let it rest while you prepare the filling.

FOR THE FILLING

½ cup dried cannellini beans, soaked in purified water overnight

2 bay leaves and/or one 2-inch piece of kombu (optional)

2 to 3 garlic cloves, crushed (optional)

2 tablespoons neutral coconut oil

1 large red onion, chopped

Sea salt

3 garlic cloves, minced

½ teaspoon chipotle powder

2 cups baby spinach leaves

Juice of 1 lime

1 small sweet potato, baked and peeled (see page 289)

Freshly ground black pepper

ingredients continue

TO MAKE THE FILLING

1 Drain and rinse the beans. Place the beans in a medium pot and cover them with plenty of water. Add the bay leaves, kombu, and crushed garlic cloves, if using. Bring the mixture to a boil over medium-high heat, then reduce the heat to a strong simmer and cook for about 30 minutes, or until the beans are soft but not mushy. Drain the beans in a colander set over a large heatproof bowl; reserve the cooking liquid. Discard the kombu and bay leaves.

2 Warm the coconut oil in a large sauté pan over medium heat. Add the onion and, sauté for 8 to 10 minutes or until it begins to brown. Reduce the heat to medium low, add a pinch or two of salt, and sauté for another 10 to 12 minutes, until the onion is caramelized. Add the minced garlic and chipotle powder in the last 3 minutes of cooking. Increase the heat back to medium and add the spinach and lime juice. Stir until the spinach is wilted and the lime juice is absorbed, 1 to 2 minutes.

3 In a food processor, combine the beans, sweet potato, sautéed vegetables, and salt and black pepper to taste. Process until the mixture is smooth and well combined.

TO MAKE THE DUMPLINGS

1 Dust your work surface with flour. Divide the dough into 4 equal pieces. Working with one piece at a time, roll the dough between your hands into an evenly sized rope, about ½ inch in diameter. Keep the other pieces of dough covered.

2 Cut the rope into small pieces, each about ½ inch wide; you should end up with 12 to 13 pieces per rope. Roll each piece in flour and press it into a round disk with the palm of your hand. Using a rolling pin, roll each disc into a dumpling skin about ⅛ inch thick.

3 Place 1 heaping teaspoon of the filling in the center of each dumpling skin. Fold and pinch the edges together to enclose the filling, making sure to secure the seal. The traditional Russian pinched seal (pictured) is optional. If you are not pinching out

FOR SERVING

Melted ghee or neutral coconut oil, or other mild-tasting oil

Pesto sauce, Carrot Top Chimichurri (page 315), plain Greek yogurt, or sour cream

your seals, make sure that your dough sticks together well so your dumplings do not fall apart as they cook. Keep all the small pieces of dough covered with a towel while you assemble each batch of dumplings. Lay the finished dumplings on a well-floured cutting board or a parchment paper–lined baking sheet. Repeat this process with the rest of the dough and filling. Cook the dumplings right away or place the cutting board or baking sheet into the refrigerator and cook them within a day. Or, freeze the dumplings on a tray and transfer them to freezer bags once hardened. They will keep in the freezer for up to 1 month.

4 To cook the dumplings, bring a large pot of well-salted water to a boil. Add all the dumplings and stir gently to prevent them from sticking to the bottom of the pot. Boil for 3 to 4 minutes or until the dumplings float to the surface.

5 Using a slotted spoon, transfer the dumplings to a bowl or platter and toss them gently with melted ghee or oil to prevent them from sticking together. Serve the dumplings hot with pesto, chimichurri, plain Greek yogurt, or the traditional Russian way—with sour cream.

ROGERS A1 PLUS

DAIKON RADISH PAD THAI

All of the beloved flavors and textures of Pad Thai are preserved in this dish, but as a bonus it's made entirely out of vegetables and packed with greens and fresh herbs. Daikon radish, when julienned and cooked in boiling water, becomes surprisingly rice noodle–like in texture, with a neutral flavor and ghostly white color.

Serves 4 | FALL • WINTER

FOR THE DRESSING

1 tablespoon plus 1 teaspoon smooth peanut butter or almond butter

1 tablespoon plus 1 teaspoon pure maple syrup

Juice of 1 large or 2 small limes

1 tablespoon tamari

1 tablespoon tamarind paste or tamarind sour soup base* (optional)

FOR THE PAD THAI

1 large (1-pound / 454-g) daikon radish

1 tablespoon neutral coconut oil

1 medium red onion, finely chopped

2 garlic cloves, minced

1-inch piece fresh ginger, peeled and finely chopped

2 to 3 large kale leaves, chopped or torn into bite-size pieces

Sea salt

1 (14-ounce / 397-g) package firm tofu, pressed to get rid of excess liquid (see page 120), and cubed

2 cups mung bean sprouts

½ cup toasted unsalted cashews, roughly chopped

1 cup fresh basil leaves, torn

Handful of fresh mint leaves, chopped (optional)

1 cup fresh cilantro leaves

TO MAKE THE DRESSING

Combine the nut butter and maple syrup in a medium bowl and mix with a spoon until smooth. Add the lime juice, tamari, and tamarind paste, if using; whisk until smooth and set aside.

TO MAKE THE PAD THAI

1 Bring a large pot of well-salted water to a boil over medium-high heat. Peel and cut the daikon radish into noodles with a vegetable peeler or spiralizer, or by hand with a sharp knife. Add the daikon to the boiling water and cook for 2 minutes. Drain the "noodles," rinse them with cold water, and set aside.

2 Warm the coconut oil in a large pan over medium-high heat. Add the onion and sauté for 5 minutes, until it becomes translucent and begins to brown. Add the garlic, ginger, kale, and salt to taste, reduce the heat to medium, and continue to sauté for another 5 minutes until the kale is wilted and the garlic and ginger are fragrant.

3 Add the daikon noodles, tofu, sprouts, and dressing to to the pan, toss to combine, and let the mixture warm through. Remove the pan from the heat, add the cashews and herbs, and toss well. Serve immediately.

*Tamarind paste and tamarind sour soup base are usually available at Asian markets and many health food stores.

PORTOBELLO BOLOGNESE PASTA

It's hard to imagine a better ingredient than portobello mushrooms for making an inspired, plant-based version of Bolognese. Portobellos, big-capped and plump, have it all in terms of savory meatiness. To achieve a full-bodied flavor associated with the hearty pasta dish, this recipe uses balsamic-soaked prunes, which add a dark, rich dimension.

Serves 6 to 8 | WINTER

5 tablespoons balsamic vinegar

5 large prunes, chopped

2 tablespoons neutral coconut oil or olive oil

1 large yellow onion, chopped

2 medium carrots, peeled and diced

Sea salt

1½ pounds (680 g) portobello mushrooms, stemmed and cut into bite-size cubes

5 garlic cloves, sliced

1 small chili, seeded and finely chopped

Leaves from 3 to 4 fresh thyme sprigs

2 tablespoons minced fresh rosemary

Freshly ground black pepper

½ cup freshly squeezed lemon juice

1 tablespoon tomato paste

2 tablespoons tamari

1 (14-ounce / 397-g) can or box diced tomatoes

1 (14-ounce / 397-g) package whole wheat (or other whole-grain) spaghetti

Handful of fresh parsley leaves, minced

Handful of fresh basil leaves, torn (optional)

Grated Parmesan, for garnish (optional)

1 Pour the vinegar over the prunes in a small bowl and set them aside to soak.

2 Warm the oil in a large sauté pan over medium heat. Add the onion and carrots, season with salt to taste, and sauté for 10 minutes, until the onion is translucent and slightly golden.

3 Add the mushrooms to the onions and sauté until all their juices evaporate, 8 to 10 minutes. Add the garlic, chili, thyme, rosemary, and black pepper to taste, and cook for 2 to 3 more minutes.

4 Increase the heat to medium high. Add the balsamic vinegar from the bowl with the prunes, along with the lemon juice, tomato paste, and tamari; toss to combine. Add the prunes to the pan. Cook for a few more minutes, stirring often, until the liquid is almost completely evaporated.

5 Add the tomatoes to the pan and reduce the heat to a slow simmer. Cover and cook for 30 to 40 minutes, stirring occasionally, until thickened. Taste for salt and pepper and adjust if necessary. Remove the pan from the heat.

6 While the sauce is cooking, bring a large pot of well-salted water to a boil. Add the spaghetti and cook it to al dente according to the directions on the package. Drain the pasta, reserving ¼ cup of the cooking water.

7 Return the pasta to the pot, add the mushroom Bolognese and reserved pasta cooking water, and toss to combine. Divide the pasta among individual bowls and serve immediately, garnished with herbs and grated Parmesan, if using.

SPELT FETTUCCINE WITH MELTED RAINBOW CHARD

This is a simple showcase for rainbow chard—a nutritious leafy green variety with stunning, brightly colored stems. Chard stems frequently get discarded in favor of the leaves, but I cannot stand to see them thrown away, and like to include them in my cooking as much as possible. All the stems require is a bit more cooking time to become tender. I like making this dish with my homemade fettuccine, but any good-quality store-bought pasta will do well here.

Serves 2 | WINTER • SPRING

½ teaspoon sea salt, plus more for salting the cooking water

5 large rainbow chard leaves, leaves and stems separated, leaves torn or roughly chopped and stems chopped into bite-size pieces

3 tablespoons neutral coconut oil or olive oil

¼ cup pine nuts

4 garlic cloves, thinly sliced

Freshly ground black pepper

½ recipe Basic Sprouted or Whole Spelt Eggless Pasta (page 180), cut into fettuccine noodles, or store-bought fettuccine of choice

Shaved Parmesan or crumbled feta cheese (optional)

1 Bring a large pot of well-salted water to a boil over medium-high heat. Add the chard stems and blanch them for 2 minutes. Using a large slotted spoon, transfer the stems to a colander and rinse them under cold water to stop the cooking. Set aside. Cover the pot and keep the water simmering over low heat.

2 Warm the oil in a large saucepan over medium-low heat. Add the pine nuts and the ½ teaspoon of salt. Toast the nuts for 2 minutes or until golden. Using a slotted spoon, transfer the nuts to a plate; set aside.

3 Add the garlic to the saucepan and sauté for 30 seconds or until fragrant. Add the blanched chard stems, chard leaves, and black pepper to taste, increase the heat to medium, and sauté until the chard leaves are wilted.

4 Meanwhile, increase the heat to high under the pot with the blanching water and bring the water to a boil. Add the pasta and cook it according to the instructions on page 180 or on the package. Taste for doneness. Drain the pasta, reserving a couple tablespoons of the cooking liquid.

5 Add the cooked pasta and reserved cooking water to the pan with the chard; toss to combine and coat the pasta. Remove the pan from the heat.

6 Serve the pasta right away with the toasted pine nuts, freshly ground black pepper to taste, and cheese, if using.

LEEK, FENNEL, AND CHARD PIZZA WITH GLUTEN-FREE ONION CRUST

Here is another light and flavorful, vegetable-based, gluten-free pizza crust option, topped with a mountain of greens, caramelized fennel, and leeks. The addition of shredded onion makes for a special pizza dough; the onions become sweet, caramelized, and fragrant within the crust, giving this pizza a unique, savory flavor.

Makes one large pizza | WINTER • SPRING

TO MAKE THE CRUST

1 In a small saucepan, using a candy thermometer, warm ⅓ cup plus 1 tablespoon of the almond milk to 110°F (43°C), or lukewarm to the touch. Remove the pan from the heat and whisk in the sugar and yeast. Let it sit for 10 minutes or until foamy.

2 In a small bowl, mix the remaining 3 tablespoons of almond milk with the chia or flax meal. Let the mixture sit for 10 minutes to gel.

3 In a food processor, combine the flour, tapioca starch or arrowroot, salt, and oil; pulse several times to combine. Add the chia or flax gel and the yeasty mixture, then process to form a runny dough. Add the onion and pulse until it is well incorporated. The dough will be very wet and runny.

4 Line a rimmed baking sheet with parchment paper and grease the parchment lightly with oil.

5 Spoon the dough onto the prepared baking sheet, spreading and shaping it into a large pizza crust with an even thickness. Let the dough rise at room temperature for 30 minutes until it doubles in size. Preheat the oven to 375°F (190°C).

FOR THE CRUST

⅓ cup plus 4 tablespoons almond milk, divided

½ teaspoon coconut sugar

1½ teaspoons active dry yeast

1½ tablespoons chia or flax meal

¾ cup (96 g) gluten-free flour, such as quinoa, buckwheat, brown rice, etc.

½ cup (60 g) tapioca starch or arrowroot powder

¾ teaspoon sea salt

2 tablespoons neutral coconut oil, at room temperature, or olive oil

1 medium yellow onion, shredded or sliced

ingredients continue

FOR THE TOPPINGS

2 tablespoons melted neutral coconut oil or olive oil, plus more for drizzling the chard leaves

1 large or 2 small fennel bulbs, thinly sliced

1 large leek, white and pale green parts only, sliced

Sea salt

1 large bunch Swiss chard, leaves and stems separated, stems diced into small pieces and leaves roughly chopped

1 tablespoon balsamic vinegar

Freshly ground black pepper

1 garlic clove, minced

Pinch of red pepper flakes

Horseradish Cream (page 301), for serving

TO PREPARE THE TOPPINGS AND BAKE THE PIZZA

1 While the dough is rising, warm the oil in a large sauté pan over medium-high heat. Add the fennel and sauté for 5 minutes. Add the leek, season with salt to taste, and continue to sauté for another 7 minutes. Add the chard stems and cook for another 5 minutes or until all the vegetables are soft. At the last minute, add the balsamic vinegar and mix until it is completely absorbed. Finish with a grind of black pepper, remove the pan from the heat, and set it aside.

2 Place the chard leaves in a large bowl. Add the garlic, red pepper flakes, a pinch of salt, and a drizzle of oil, and mix well with your hands. Set aside.

3 When the dough is done rising, transfer it to the oven and bake for 15 minutes until the crust is dry and pre-cooked. Remove the crust from the oven and raise the oven temperature to 400°F (200°C).

4 Spread the sautéed vegetables over the crust and pile the chard leaves on top. Transfer the pizza to the oven and bake for 15 to 20 minutes or until the edges of the crust are slightly golden and the chard leaves are wilted.

5 Remove the pizza from the oven and let it cool slightly. Garnish with Horseradish Cream; slice and serve immediately.

FRITTERS AND VEGGIE BURGERS

IT JUST TAKES a few compatible ingredients and a binder to make convenient, flavorful burgers and fritters that can be enjoyed in an infinite number of ways. This chapter has a veggie burger recipe for every season, each packed with vegetables available at a given time of the year and able to stand on its own in terms of enticing flavor and nourishment. There are also fritters—lacy, crispy, and golden-edged—offered as an elegant option for completing a meal.

218
Coconut Black Rice and Edamame Veggie Burgers

221
Zucchini Fritters

223
Summer Corn and Greens Fritters

226
Beet and Zucchini Veggie Burgers

229
Cauliflower Fritters

230
Sweet Potato, Millet, and Black Bean Veggie Burgers with Kale Slaw

233
Mushroom and Parsnip Fritters

236
Oven-Baked Potato Latkes

239
Mung Bean and Barley Veggie Burgers

COCONUT BLACK RICE AND EDAMAME VEGGIE BURGER

I like to let my veggie burgers take on a flavor and life of their own, without worrying about imitating meat. I will include beans or legumes to satisfy the protein quota, but when it comes to the rest of the ingredients, I let the season and what's on hand guide me as much as possible.

This is a uniquely flavored veggie burger and one of my all-time favorites. With a base of kaffir lime–flavored coconut black rice, and studded with brilliant green edamame, this burger is full of all the vibrant color and flavor one craves in the spring—rich, zesty, and a bit tropical. Kaffir lime leaves are magical—intoxicating in aroma, fruity, limey, and overall very refreshing. I've seen kaffir lime leaves sold fresh or frozen in many Asian and Indian markets, but in case you cannot find them, simply omit them from the recipe.

Makes 8 to 9 burgers | SPRING

FOR THE RICE

1 cup forbidden black rice

1¾ cups canned unsweetened Thai coconut milk

Handful of kaffir lime leaves, bruised with a knife (optional)

Pinch of salt

FOR THE BURGERS

2 cups shelled edamame, shelled fava beans, or green peas

1 cup raw pistachios or pumpkin seeds

1 teaspoon cumin seeds

1 teaspoon coriander seeds

½ teaspoon black mustard seeds

¼ cup chia or flax meal

3 (45 g) soft Medjool dates, pitted and mashed with a fork

2 tablespoons sesame tahini

1 shallot, minced

3 garlic cloves, minced

Zest and juice of 1 lime

1 small red chili, seeded and minced or ½ teaspoon red pepper flakes

Large handful of fresh mint leaves, chopped

Sea salt

8 or 9 burger buns or wraps, for serving

Cilantro Tahini Sauce (page 303), for serving

TO PREPARE THE RICE

Combine all the ingredients in a small saucepan and bring the mixture to a boil over medium-high heat. Lower the heat and simmer, covered, for 30 minutes until the rice is tender and the liquid is absorbed. Remove the pan from the heat and set it aside to cool.

TO MAKE THE VEGGIE BURGERS

1 Bring a large pot of well-salted water to a boil. Fill a large bowl with ice water and set it nearby. If you're using edamame, drop them into the boiling water and blanch for 3 to 4 minutes, then immediately drain and transfer them to the ice water to stop the cooking. If you're using fresh fava beans, blanch them for 1 to 2 minutes in the boiling water, then drain and transfer them to the ice water bath; when they are completely chilled, squeeze each bean out of its outer skin and discard the skins. If you're using peas, blanch them for 30 seconds in the boiling water, then drain and transfer them to the ice bath. When the beans are chilled

through, drain them well in a colander.

2 Grind the pistachios or pumpkin seeds into a coarse meal in a food processor.

3 Grind the cumin, coriander, and mustard seeds in a mortar and pestle or in a designated coffee grinder.

4 In a large bowl, partially mash the edamame, fava beans, or peas with a potato masher or fork, leaving some bigger pieces and whole beans here and there.

5 Preheat the oven to 475°F (250°C). Line a rimmed baking sheet with parchment paper.

6 Add 2 cups of the cooked rice, the ground pistachios or pumpkin seeds, ground spices, chia or flax meal, dates, tahini, shallot, garlic, lime zest and juice, chili or red pepper flakes, mint, and sea salt to the bowl with the mashed edamame, favas, or peas. You will have leftover coconut rice, which is delicious on its own and can be served warm as a side. Store it refrigerated in an airtight glass container. Mix everything together thoroughly with your hands. Form the mixture into 8 or 9 burger patties, and place them on the prepared baking sheet. Transfer the burgers to the oven and bake for 15 minutes until toasted and firm.

7 Remove the burgers from the oven and let them cool slightly, then serve them in the burger buns or wraps of your choice with Cilantro Tahini Sauce and Asparagus Fries (page 242). Leftover burgers can be stored in an airtight container in the refrigerator for up to 3 days.

ZUCCHINI FRITTERS

Zucchini is the perfect candidate for making vegetable fritters. Its tender, neutral flesh becomes pleasantly sweet when fried or baked. I try to avoid frying whenever possible, and these oven-baked fritters are just as golden on the outside and soft on the inside as their fried counterparts. (Pictured on page 216.)

Makes about 12 fritters | SPRING • SUMMER

4 small or 3 medium zucchini (1½ pounds / 680 g total), shredded

Sea salt

1½ teaspoons melted neutral coconut oil or olive oil, plus more for oiling the parchment paper

½ medium yellow onion, chopped

1 large garlic clove, minced

1 large egg

Freshly ground black pepper

Handful of fresh mint, dill, or parsley, chopped (optional)

⅓ cup chia or flax meal

¼ cup crumbled or finely diced feta cheese (optional)

Tzatziki Sauce (see page 96), Avocado Mayo (page 299), Apple-Miso Mayo (page 300), Cashew Cream Sauce of your choice (pages 301 to 302), or plain yogurt with fresh herbs, for serving

1 Place the shredded zucchini in a colander over a bowl, sprinkle with a couple pinches of salt, toss well, and set it aside to release its liquid for about 10 minutes.

2 Preheat the oven to 400°F (200°C). Line a large rimmed baking sheet with parchment paper and brush it lightly with oil.

3 After 10 minutes, squeeze the zucchini, one small handful at a time, to get rid of as much liquid as possible. Place the squeezed zucchini in a medium bowl, add the onion, garlic, egg, black pepper to taste, and chopped fresh herbs. Stir to combine. Add the chia or flax meal and mix thoroughly using your hands. Fold in the feta, if using. Let the mixture sit for 15 minutes, allowing the chia or flax to gel.

4 Form the fritters using a ¼-cup measure and arrange them on the prepared baking sheet. Flatten each fritter with the back of a spoon and brush them with the oil. Transfer the baking sheet to the oven and bake for 15 minutes, then flip the fritters. You may want to remove the baking sheet from the oven and wait a couple of minutes before flipping for easier handling; the fritters will become firmer with a short rest. Bake the fritters for another 15 minutes, until golden on both sides.

5 Remove the fritters from the oven and serve them warm with the sauce of your choice.

SUMMER CORN AND GREENS FRITTERS

This is a quick and tasty way of incorporating a bunch of dark leafy greens into your meal. I've made many versions of these fritters using different greens, such as kale, Swiss chard, and collards, and all are equally delicious. The pockets of fresh summer corn provide a beautiful sweetness and crunch.

Makes about 10 fritters | SUMMER

2 bunches (2 pounds / 1 kg) kale, stems removed and reserved for another use (such as Odds and Ends Vegetable Broth, page 313)

Sea salt

2 tablespoons neutral coconut oil, at room temperature, divided, plus more for oiling the parchment paper

1 large yellow onion, chopped

Kernels from 1 ear of corn, or ½ cup thawed frozen corn kernels

Freshly ground black pepper

½ cup chia or flax meal

Horseradish Cream (page 301), Chipotle Cream (page 301), or Avocado Mayo (page 299), for serving

1 Place the kale leaves in a large pot and cover them with purified water. Add a pinch or two of salt and bring the water to a boil over medium-high heat. Lower the heat to a strong simmer and cook partially covered for 15 minutes. Drain the kale and rinse it with cold water to stop the cooking. Optionally, save the cooking water to use in soups and stews; you can freeze it in an airtight container for up to 1 month.

2 Meanwhile, warm 1 tablespoon of the oil in a medium saucepan over medium heat. Add the onion and a pinch of salt, and sauté for 10 minutes, until the onion is translucent. Add the corn and sauté for another 3 minutes. Remove from the heat and set aside.

3 Squeeze the cooked kale leaves with your hands to remove any excess water. Place them in a food processor and pulse to break them down into small pieces with a few bigger chunks remaining. You may need to do this in batches, depending on the size of your food processor.

4 Preheat the oven to 375°F (190°C). Line a large rimmed baking sheet with parchment paper and brush it lightly with oil.

5 Place the chopped kale in a large bowl, add the remaining tablespoon of coconut oil, a pinch of salt, black pepper to taste, the sautéed onions and corn, and the chia or flax meal. Mix thoroughly with your hands. Let the mixture rest for 30 minutes to allow the chia or flax meal to gel.

6 Form the fritters using a ¼-cup measure and arrange them on the prepared baking sheet. Flatten each fritter with the back of a spoon. Transfer the baking sheet to the oven and bake for 15 minutes, then flip the fritters. You may want to remove the baking sheet from the oven and wait a couple of minutes before flipping for easier handling; the fritters will become firmer with a short rest. Bake the fritters for another 15 minutes, until golden on both sides.

7 Remove the fritters from the oven and serve them warm with the sauce of your choice.

BEET AND ZUCCHINI VEGGIE BURGERS

A stunning, light veggie burger option for the summer, these are fluffy from zucchini, with substance from beet, lentils, and chia. As with all veggie burgers in this chapter, no bread crumbs, eggs, or cheese are required.

Makes 6 burgers | SUMMER

1 tablespoon neutral coconut oil

1 medium onion, chopped

1 medium carrot, peeled if not organic and shredded

1 small chili, seeded and finely chopped (optional)

Sea salt

1 small red beet, cooked and shredded

1 cup cooked green or French lentils (see page 70 for cooking instructions)

Juice of ½ lemon

Freshly ground black pepper

1 small zucchini, shredded

2 to 3 garlic cloves, minced

⅓ cup chia or flax meal

6 burger buns or wraps, for serving

Avocado Mayo (page 299) or Apple-Miso Mayo (page 300), for serving

Tomato slices, lettuce, red onion, and sprouts or microgreens, for serving

1 Melt the oil in a medium sauté pan over medium heat. Add the onion, carrot, chili, if using, and a big pinch of salt, and sauté for 5 to 7 minutes, until the onion is translucent. Add the shredded beet, lentils, lemon juice, and black pepper to taste. Stir to combine and cook for about 3 minutes, until most of the liquid is evaporated. Taste for salt and adjust if needed. Transfer the mixture to a large bowl and let it cool slightly.

2 Add the zucchini and garlic to the bowl and mix to combine, then add the chia or flax meal and stir to mix thoroughly. Let the mixture rest for 15 minutes to allow the chia or flax to gel.

3 Preheat the oven to 475°F (250°C). Line a rimmed baking sheet with parchment paper.

4 Form 6 patties using a ½-cup measure, and arrange them on the prepared baking sheet. Transfer the baking sheet to the oven and bake for 15 to 20 minutes until toasted in appearance.

5 Remove the patties from the oven and let them cool slightly before serving; the burgers will firm up when cooled.

6 Serve the patties in the buns or wraps if you like, with the mayo of your choice, tomato slices, lettuce, red onion, and sprouts or microgreens. Leftover burgers can be stored in an airtight container in the refrigerator for up to 3 days.

CAULIFLOWER FRITTERS

These cauliflower fritters are baked, not fried, requiring less effort on the cook's part, with no compromise on flavor. Full of that sweet and earthy roasted cauliflower flavor, crispy on the outside, soft on the inside, with a studding of seeds and wisps of greens, these little fritters can make any fall lunch or dinner into a happy affair.

Makes 12 to 14 fritters | FALL

- 1½ teaspoons melted neutral coconut oil, plus more for brushing the parchment
- 1 small or ½ large head cauliflower, chopped into small florets
- 1 medium carrot, peeled if not organic and shredded
- 2 cups chopped fresh spinach
- Sea salt and freshly ground black pepper
- 2 tablespoons toasted sesame seeds or nigella seeds
- ⅓ cup chia or flax meal
- 1 egg
- ¼ cup crumbled or finely diced feta cheese (optional)
- Avocado Mayo (page 299), Carrot Top Chimichurri (page 315), or plain yogurt, for serving

1 Preheat the oven to 400°F (200°C). Line a rimmed baking sheet with parchment paper and brush it lightly with coconut oil.

2 Place the cauliflower florets in a food processor and pulse to chop them into rice-size pieces. Take care not to chop the cauliflower too much; some pieces will be bigger than others, and that's fine. You should have about 2½ to 3 cups riced cauliflower.

3 Transfer the cauliflower to a large bowl. Add the carrot, spinach, salt and pepper to taste, sesame or nigella seeds, chia or flax meal, and egg. Mix thoroughly, first with a spoon to break up the egg and then with your hands. Fold in the feta, if using. Let the mixture rest for 15 minutes to allow the chia or flax to gel.

4 Form the fritters using a ¼-cup measure and arrange them on the prepared baking sheet. Flatten each fritter with the back of a spoon and brush them with the 1½ teaspoons of melted coconut oil. Transfer the baking sheet to the oven and bake for 15 minutes, then flip the fritters. You may want to remove the baking sheet from the oven and wait a couple of minutes before flipping for easier handling; the fritters will become firmer with a short rest. Bake the fritters for another 10 minutes, until crispy on both sides. Flip the fritters again and place them back in the oven, letting them get crispy for another 5 minutes.

5 Remove the fritters from the oven and let them cool slightly, then serve them alongside a green salad with the sauce of your choice.

SWEET POTATO, MILLET, AND BLACK BEAN VEGGIE BURGERS WITH KALE SLAW

There is no denying that these burgers are perfect for autumn—with their stunning color, reminiscent of fall foliage, and their hearty collection of ingredients, including orange roots, black beans, chickpeas, rosemary, thyme, and dark, leafy kale.

Makes 12 burgers | FALL • WINTER

¼ cup millet, washed and soaked in purified water overnight

Sea salt

1 cup cooked or canned black beans

1 medium carrot, peeled if not organic and grated

1 large garlic clove, minced

½ cup walnuts

1 medium sweet potato, peeled and roughly chopped

1 cup cooked or canned chickpeas

1 tablespoon neutral coconut oil

1½ teaspoons cumin seeds

½ teaspoon red pepper flakes

About 1 tablespoon chopped fresh rosemary (optional)

About 1 tablespoon chopped fresh thyme (optional)

1 medium yellow onion, chopped

2 to 3 kale leaves, stems removed, leaves thinly sliced

Freshly ground black pepper

Juice of ½ lemon

½ cup chia or flax meal

12 burger buns or wraps, for serving

Smoky Sun-Dried Tomato Cream (page 302), for serving

Kale Slaw (recipe follows), for serving

1 Drain and rinse the millet. Combine it with ½ cup of purified water and a pinch of salt in a small pot. Bring the pot to a boil over high heat, then reduce the heat to low, cover the pot, and simmer for 20 minutes or until the water is absorbed. Remove the pot from the heat and let it sit for 10 minutes, then fluff the millet with a fork and allow it to cool.

2 Place the black beans in a large mixing bowl and briefly mash them with a fork, leaving most of them whole. Add the millet, grated carrot, and garlic.

3 Pulse the walnuts in a food processor to chop them into small to medium pieces, then add them to the bowl with the black bean mixture.

4 Add the sweet potato to the food processor and pulse to chop it into small pieces. Add the chickpeas and pulse to combine. Add the mixture to the bowl.

5 Melt the oil in a medium sauté pan over medium heat. Add the cumin, red pepper flakes, rosemary, and thyme, if using, and stir everything around for 1 minute. Add the onion and a pinch of salt, and sauté for 2 minutes. Add the kale leaves and black pepper to taste, and sauté for another 3 minutes or until the kale is wilted.

6 Add the sautéed mixture to the bowl, along with the lemon juice and chia or flax meal. Add salt and pepper to taste and mix thoroughly with your hands. Let the

mixture rest for 15 to 20 minutes to allow the chia or flax meal to gel.

7 Preheat the oven to 475°F (245°C). Line a rimmed baking sheet with parchment paper.

8 Form the burger patties using a ½-cup measure and arrange them on the prepared baking sheet. Transfer the patties to the oven and bake for 15 to 20 minutes, until they look toasty and browned.

9 Remove the patties from the oven and let them cool slightly; the burgers will firm up once cooled.

10 Serve the patties on buns or in the wraps of your choice with the Sun-Dried Tomato Cream and Kale Slaw. Leftovers can be stored in an airtight container in the refrigerator for up to 3 days.

Kale Slaw

Makes 4 cups | FALL • WINTER

½ small red onion, thinly sliced

Juice of 1 lemon, divided

2 to 3 large kale leaves, stems removed, leaves chopped into bite-size pieces

Sea salt

Freshly ground black pepper

Olive oil, for drizzling

1 Pour half of the lemon juice over the onion slices in a medium bowl. Toss to coat and set aside.

2 Place the kale in another medium mixing bowl, drizzle the rest of the lemon juice over it, sprinkle with salt and pepper to taste, and lightly drizzle with olive oil. Massage the kale with your hands for a couple minutes, until the leaves are slightly wilted.

3 Drain the onions and add them to kale. Toss and serve.

MUSHROOM AND PARSNIP FRITTERS

These fritters might be different than the fritters you are used to. I got the idea from the delicious and fluffy potato, flour, and egg cakes I grew up eating in Russia, called *kartofelniki*. Parsnips take on the role of potatoes here—similarly starchy and soft in texture, but with their own distinct, mildly sweet, and earthy flavor. A studding of mushrooms adds some bite and substance, making these pillowy cakes an excellent contender for a savory breakfast, lunch, or side dish.

Makes 14 small fritters | FALL • WINTER

1 pound (454 g) parsnips, peeled and sliced

3 green onions, white and light green parts, thinly sliced

1½ teaspoons tamari

3 tablespoons neutral coconut oil, divided

1 teaspoon smoked Spanish paprika

Sea salt

Leaves from 3 fresh thyme sprigs

1 large yellow onion, chopped

1 pound (454 g) crimini mushrooms, sliced

Freshly ground black pepper

¼ cup (45 g) plus 2 tablespoons brown rice flour, divided, plus more if needed for rolling out the fritters

Avocado Mayo (page 299), Tahini Sauce of your choice (pages 303 to 304), or plain Greek yogurt, for serving

1 Arrange the parsnip slices in a steaming basket and place it over a pot with boiling water. Cover and steam for 10 to 15 minutes or until they are tender. Transfer them to a medium bowl and mash with a potato masher. Add the green onions, tamari, 1 tablespoon of coconut oil, the paprika and a small pinch of salt. Mix until well combined.

2 Melt the remaining 2 tablespoons of coconut oil in a large sauté pan over medium heat. Add the thyme, onion, and a pinch of salt. Sauté for 10 to 12 minutes, until the onion is slightly golden. Add the mushrooms, season to taste with salt and pepper, and sauté until the mushrooms are lightly browned, about 8 minutes. Add the onion-mushroom mixture to the parsnip mash and mix to incorporate. Wipe the pan clean with a paper towel and keep it out for frying the fritters. Add ¼ cup brown rice flour to the vegetable mixture and mix it thoroughly.

3 Sprinkle your work surface with 2 tablespoons of the brown rice flour. Scoop 2 tablespoons of the fritter mixture onto the flour and gently roll it into a sphere with the palm of your hand, coating it with the flour. Flatten the sphere and shape it into a small cake with your hands. Place the formed fritter on a large plate or cutting board. Repeat until all the fritter mixture is used up.

4 Heat up the wiped-out sauté pan over medium heat. Working in batches, cook the fritters without oil for 4 to 5 minutes on each side, until golden brown. Add a little oil if they begin to stick to the pan.

5 Serve the fritters with the sauce of your choice. Leftover fritters can be stored in an airtight container in the refrigerator for up to 4 days.

OVEN-BAKED POTATO LATKES

Potato latkes are one of my biggest weaknesses—I grew up on those crispy, golden cakes, and was commonly the first one at the kitchen table whenever my mother fried up a portion. As much as I love to eat them, frying latkes is something I've always dreaded because of the lengthy stove time, splashing hot oil, and smoke. Coming up with this oven-baked latke recipe was a revelation; now I'm able to indulge my frequent cravings without hours spent at the stove. And even better, the cakes come out of the oven just as lacy and golden as they would from the frying pan.

Note: The amount of latkes you end up with depends on the type of shredder you use. I use a food processor with a shredding attachment, which produces more volume than a regular box grater.

Makes about 8 to 12 latkes | WINTER

4 tablespoons melted neutral coconut oil or olive oil, plus more for brushing the parchment paper

1½ pounds (680 g) potatoes, shredded

Juice of ½ lemon

1 teaspoon sea salt

½ medium yellow onion, finely chopped

1 garlic clove, minced

Freshly ground black pepper

¼ cup plus 1 tablespoon chia or flax meal

Cashew Cream Sauce of your choice (pages 301 to 302), Avocado Mayo (page 299), Apple-Miso Mayo (page 300), or plain yogurt, for serving

Chopped fresh dill and/or parsley, for serving (optional)

1 Preheat the oven to 375°F (190°C). Line a rimmed baking sheet with parchment paper and brush it lightly with oil.

2 Place the shredded potatoes in a colander over a large bowl; squeeze the lemon juice over top and sprinkle with the salt. Toss to coat and let the potatoes sit for 10 minutes to drain.

3 After 10 minutes, squeeze the potatoes with your hands, one little portion at a time, to get rid of as much liquid as possible. Place the potatoes in a medium bowl. Add the onion, garlic, black pepper to taste, and the chia or flax meal; mix thoroughly with your hands. Let the mixture sit for 15 minutes to allow the chia or flax to gel.

4 Form the latkes using a ¼-cup measure and arrange them on the prepared baking sheet. Flatten each latke with a spoon to get thinner, crispier results, and brush them with 2 tablespoons of the oil. Transfer the latkes to the oven and bake for 20 minutes, then carefully flip them, brush the other side with the remaining 2 tablespoons of oil, and bake for another 20 minutes, until golden on both sides.

5 Remove the latkes from the oven and serve them warm with the sauce of your choice and some chopped fresh dill and/or parsley, if desired.

MUNG BEAN AND BARLEY VEGGIE BURGERS

These wholesome veggie burgers are perfect for winter, made with protein-rich mung beans, hearty barley grain, nuts, herbs, and spices—all considered for their warmth and kindness to the body.

Note: To cook mung beans, soak 1 cup of dried beans in purified water overnight. Drain and rinse the beans and combine them with about 4 cups of purified water in a medium pot. Bring to a boil over high heat, reduce the heat to a simmer and cook, partially covered, for 10 to 15 minutes, until tender, then add salt. 1 cup of dried mung beans yields about 3 cups of cooked beans.

Makes 9 large burgers | WINTER

1 tablespoon neutral coconut oil

1 large yellow onion, chopped

½ teaspoon red pepper flakes

Leaves from a few fresh thyme sprigs

Leaves from a few fresh oregano sprigs (optional)

4 packed cups roughly chopped kale leaves

½ pound (227 g) crimini mushrooms, sliced

Sea salt and freshly ground black pepper

1 tablespoon tomato paste

1 teaspoon sweet Hungarian paprika

2 cups cooked pearl barley (see page 110 and reserve the cooking water to make Silky Barley Water, page 112)

2 cups cooked mung beans (see note)

¼ cup chia or flax meal

5 garlic cloves, minced

1 tablespoon brown rice vinegar or apple cider vinegar

1 tablespoon balsamic vinegar

1 cup toasted walnuts or pecans, ground into coarse crumbs

Bburger buns or collard green wraps, for serving

Cashew Cream Sauce of your choice (pages 301 to 302) or Avocado Mayo (page 299), for serving

1 Melt the oil in a large sauté pan over medium heat. Add the onion, red pepper flakes, and herbs and sauté for 5 to 7 minutes, until translucent. Add the kale and stir until it is wilted, about 2 minutes. Add the mushrooms and salt and pepper to taste, and cook until the liquid evaporates and the mushrooms begin to brown, 8 to 10 minutes. Add the tomato paste and paprika, and mix to incorporate. Remove from the heat.

2 Preheat the oven to 400°F (200°C). Line a rimmed baking sheet with parchment paper.

3 Combine the barley, mung beans, mushroom sauté, chia or flax meal, garlic, and both vinegars in a food processor; pulse to combine into a chunky mixture. Transfer the mixture to a large bowl, add the ground nuts, and mix well with a spoon.

4 Scoop out a heaping ½ cup of the mixture and use your hands to form it into a burger patty. Repeat with the remaining burger mixture and place the patties on the prepared baking sheet. Transfer them to the oven and bake for 20 minutes until toasted in appearance.

5 Remove the patties from the oven and let them cool slightly. Serve in buns or wraps of choice. Accompany the burgers with your sauce of choice, fresh greens, and Pickled Turnips (page 258).

JUST VEGGIES

242
Asparagus Fries

244
Mildly Pickled Spring Vegetables

247
Marinated Tomatoes

248
Marinated Eggplant

251
Beet Sauté

252
Honey-Miso Delicata Squash

254
Roasted Parsnips and Pears with Za'atar

257
Steamed and Marinated Beets and Celery Root

258
Pickled Turnips

261
Braised Cabbage

I REMEMBER EATING a ruby red tomato that I picked off the vine in my mother's garden, so ripe that it was bursting at its seams. I did nothing more than wash it, slice it, and give it a sprinkling of salt and pepper, but from the very first bite, its flavor was transformative. Everything came together perfectly at that moment—I caught the tomato at the peak of its season, it had been well cared for and grew in good soil, and I was eating outdoors with plenty of sun and fresh summer air. I had never imagined that a memory of a single tomato could be etched so deep into my mind after so many years, but I still reminisce about that moment.

Most seasonal vegetables and fruit only need a simple nudge to reach their highest potential. This chapter will present you with a few useful techniques—marinating, pickling, braising, stewing, glazing, and roasting—to create sides and small plates of just vegetables. Sometimes that's all you need to complete the perfect meal.

ASPARAGUS FRIES

This is a well-loved recipe in my kitchen, to which I return frequently in the spring, when asparagus is at its most vibrant. A crispy coating of nuts, seeds, spices, and nutritional yeast—the vegan answer to cheese—coats the tender asparagus spears. It's an excellent (and addictive) side when freshly roasted, sort of like nutritious green fries, and the leftovers are delicious on a salad or inside a sandwich.

Choose asparagus spears of medium thickness—if they're too thin, the fries won't hold their shape.

Serves 4 | SPRING

4 tablespoons freshly squeezed lemon juice

2 tablespoons purified water

2 tablespoons chia or flax meal

½ cup ground raw pumpkin seeds, pistachios, or other nuts of choice

¼ cup sesame seeds

½ cup nutritional yeast

2 teaspoons garlic powder

1 teaspoon salt, plus more for sprinkling

1 teaspoon coconut sugar

1½ teaspoons cumin seeds, freshly ground

¼ teaspoon red pepper flakes

1 bunch asparagus, about 25 to 30 spears, tough ends removed and saved for Odds and Ends Vegetable Broth (page 313) or discarded

1 In a shallow dish, whisk together the lemon juice, water, and chia or flax meal. Set the mixture aside for 10 minutes to allow the chia or flax to gel.

2 In a large bowl or zip-top bag, combine the ground nuts or seeds, sesame seeds, nutritional yeast, garlic powder, salt, coconut sugar, ground cumin, and red pepper flakes; mix well or seal the bag and shake to combine thoroughly. Pour about 1/3 cup of this mixture onto a large plate.

3 Preheat the oven to 395°F (200°C). Line a rimmed baking sheet with parchment paper.

4 Dip the asparagus, one spear at a time, into the lemon-chia mixture, then transfer it to the plate with the dry coating. Using a fork, generously cover each spear with the mixture to coat. Avoid touching the asparagus and the coating with your hands as much as possible, in order to keep the coating as dry as possible and on the asparagus.

5 Carefully transfer the coated asparagus spears to the prepared baking sheet. Continue adding more of the coating mixture to the plate as it gets used up. Transfer the coated asparagus spears to the oven and bake them for 15 to 20 minutes, until the coating is dry and golden.

6 Remove the asparagus fries from the oven and serve immediately. The leftovers will get soggy when refrigerated, but the flavor will stay delicious for 2 to 3 days.

FOR THE PICKLES

3½ pounds (1½ kg) mixed spring vegetables, such as radishes, snow peas, sugar snaps, zucchini, salad turnips, asparagus, etc.

5 cups purified water

½ cup apple cider vinegar

2½ tablespoons sea salt

3 whole cloves

½ teaspoon coriander seeds

2 to 3 bay leaves

A few black peppercorns

½ teaspoon coconut sugar (optional)

3 to 4 garlic cloves, sliced

Handful of fresh dill, roughly chopped

Handful of fresh cilantro leaves (optional)

Pinch of red pepper flakes

MILDLY PICKLED SPRING VEGETABLES

I grew up with pickling and preserving as part of my culture. Food was rarely abundant in the Soviet Union, unless you grew it yourself and took care of preserving your harvest for the infertile, colder months. There was always a friendly competition going on between families during preserving season, over who had the crunchiest pickles, the juiciest preserved tomatoes, the sweetest marinated bell peppers, and so on. It was considered important not to use vinegar in the process, instead building up flavor with the best fresh vegetables, plenty of aromatic herbs and spices, and, of course, the perfect ratio and technique. I learned a few tips along the way: including horseradish leaves in the jar help make pickles crunchy, and nothing can give your preserves better flavor than fresh currant bush leaves. If you are lucky to have a garden and grow either of those gems, don't hesitate to throw them into the pickling mix.

When the first young and tender cucumbers arrived in the spring, it was customary to give them the quick-pickle treatment overnight. These crisp and addictive spring pickles are a variation on that theme. Much like my mother did, I use a minimal amount of vinegar in this recipe to avoid overpowering the other aromatics. (Pictured on page 240.)

Makes 1 large jar | SPRING • SUMMER

1 Slice the radishes in half, remove the strings from the peas, slice the zucchini into thick rounds, cut the salad turnips into wedges, and trim and cut the asparagus spears into 1½-inch-thick pieces.

2 Combine all the vegetables in a large, heatproof bowl. Pour the water over the vegetables, making sure the vegetables are completely submerged. Drain the vegetables in a colander set over a medium pot—this will be your water for the marinade. If you have more or less water than the recipe calls for, adjust the amount of vinegar, salt, and spices according to the proportions provided in the ingredient list—they don't have to be exact.

3 Add the apple cider vinegar, salt, cloves, coriander, bay leaves, black peppercorns, and coconut sugar, if using, to the water. Bring the mixture to a boil over medium heat, lower the heat to a simmer, and cook uncovered for 3 minutes. Remove the pan from the heat, cover it with a lid, and let it sit for 10 minutes.

4 Return the vegetables to the heatproof bowl. Add the garlic, dill, cilantro, if using, and red pepper flakes to the bowl with the vegetables. Pour the marinade over the vegetables. Submerge the vegetables in the marinade using a plate and some sort of weight—a jar filled with water works well. Let the vegetables marinate at room temperature for 24 hours.

5 Remove the weight and the plate from the bowl. The vegetables are ready and should be crunchy and taste like pickles. Transfer the pickles to an airtight container and refrigerate them for up to 1 week. Make sure the pickles are covered with brine when storing; this will make them last longer.

MARINATED TOMATOES

The best way to enjoy a perfectly ripe summer tomato is on its own, with a light sprinkle of sea salt and black pepper and a drizzle of olive oil. If you are lucky enough to have a lot of ripe tomatoes that need to be used up, this recipe is ideal. The spicy, aromatic marinade is full of fresh herbs and garlic, making the tomatoes a perfect accompaniment to any summer spread. I've seen them disappear with impressive speed at a potluck.

Serves 8 to 10 | SUMMER

FOR THE MARINADE

¼ cup olive oil

¼ cup apple cider vinegar

1 tablespoon coconut sugar or other granulated sugar

1 tablespoon sea salt

FOR THE TOMATOES

2 red bell peppers, seeded and roughly chopped

1 jalapeño, seeded and roughly chopped

Cloves from 1 head garlic, peeled and roughly chopped

2 pounds (1 kg) ripe summer tomatoes, quartered or cut into 8 wedges, if large

About 1 cup finely chopped fresh dill and parsley

1 Whisk together all the marinade ingredients in a medium bowl until well combined; set aside.

2 Combine the bell peppers, jalapeño, and garlic in a food processor; pulse to chop the mixture into small pieces.

3 In a glass or ceramic dish, arrange the ingredients in layers—first the tomato slices, then the chopped pepper mixture, and finally the herbs. Pour the marinade over top, cover the dish, and let it sit at room temperature for 1 hour. Transfer the dish to the refrigerator and chill for at least 8 hours and up to 5 days before serving. The taste will improve considerably after a day or two of marinating. For best flavor, take the tomatoes out of the refrigerator and let them warm up to room temperature before serving.

MARINATED EGGPLANT

My love for marinated vegetable sides stems from growing up on the cusine of the Northern Caucasus region of Russia, known for brighter flavors and a heavier use of herbs and spices than that of traditional Russian cuisine. This dish is inspired by those regions, and I cannot say enough about how powerfully flavored eggplant becomes when it is left to develop in a well-proportioned mixture of oil, garlic, vinegar, and herbs. This little side is one of the first things friends ask me to make for any food-centric gathering we might have. Place it on top of green salads, include it as a side for anything grilled, or put a few slices on a sandwich—any way you use this eggplant, it is a versatile flavor bomb.

Serves 4 to 6 | SUMMER • FALL

2 medium eggplants

2 tablespoons sea salt

2 tablespoons melted neutral coconut oil

Freshly ground black pepper

1 tablespoon coconut sugar or brown sugar

4 garlic cloves, minced

2 tablespoons apple cider vinegar

2 teaspoons chili sauce (Sriracha)

2 tablespoons chopped fresh parsley

3 tablespoons olive oil

1 Preheat the oven to 400°F (200°C). Line a rimmed baking sheet with parchment paper.

2 Cut each eggplant in half lengthwise, then cut each half into ½-inch-thick (13-mm) slices. Place the sliced eggplant in a colander set over a large bowl. Sprinkle with the salt, toss to coat, and let the eggplant drain at room temperature for 20 to 30 minutes. Quickly rinse the salt off of the eggplant slices and squeeze out any excess liquid with your hands.

3 Place the eggplant in a medium bowl, drizzle with the coconut oil and season with a grind of black pepper; toss to coat. Arrange the eggplant in a single layer on the prepared baking sheet. Transfer the eggplant to the oven and roast for 20 minutes, then flip the slices and roast for another 15 minutes until soft and golden. Remove the eggplant from the oven.

4 Meanwhile, combine the the sugar, garlic, vinegar, chili sauce, parsley, and the olive oil in a large bowl. Add the roasted eggplant slices to the bowl and toss to coat.

5 Transfer the marinated eggplant to an airtight container or cover the bowl tightly with plastic wrap. Refrigerate for 24 hours before serving. Enjoy within 5 days.

BEET SAUTÉ

This is a quick and simple sauté of beets, carrots, onion and peppers. Use it as an elegant add-in to any meal for extra color and flavor, or enjoy on its own, atop a tartine. Any of the fritters (see chapter 7), the Mung Bean and Barley Veggie Burgers (page 239), or Sweet Potato, Millet, and Black Bean Veggie Burgers (page 230) will make a great pairing for this sauté.

Serves 4 | SUMMER • FALL

- 3 medium red beets, baked, boiled, or steamed until fully cooked
- 3 tablespoons neutral coconut oil or other vegetable oil
- 2 small or 1 large carrot, peeled and grated
- 1 large yellow onion, diced
- 1 red bell pepper, seeded and diced
- 2½ tablespoons tomato paste
- ½ small chili, seeded and finely chopped
- 1 tablespoon freshly squeezed lemon juice
- Sea salt and freshly ground black pepper

1 Peel and grate the cooked beets; set them aside.

2 Warm the oil in a medium sauté pan over medium heat, add the carrots and onion, and sauté for 2 to 3 minutes. Add the bell pepper, sauté for 2 to 3 more minutes, then stir in the tomato paste; mix thoroughly. Add the shredded beet, chili, lemon juice, and salt and pepper to taste. Stir to combine and reduce the heat to low. Cover and cook for about 10 minutes or until all of the vegetables are soft. Check periodically and add 1 to 2 tablespoons of water if the mixture becomes too dry.

3 Remove the pan from the heat. Serve the vegetables hot or cold, as an addition to any meal, on a sandwich or tartine, or as an accompaniment to any grains, beans, or salad. Store leftovers in an airtight container in the refrigerator for up to 1 week.

HONEY-MISO DELICATA SQUASH

I thought I knew everything about the possibilities of cooking squash, and then I tried this stovetop method of flash-frying thin rings of delicata squash in a pan, then glazing them in a thick, garlicky sauce of honey, miso, vinegar, and tamari. The result amazes me every time with its abundance of various flavors, from umami to sour to sweet. It is worth seeking out delicata squash for this recipe, as its skin is soft enough to eat and its shape makes for perfectly portioned rings.

Serves 4 | FALL • WINTER

1½ teaspoons brown rice vinegar or freshly squeezed lime juice

1½ tablespoons freshly squeezed lime juice, divided

1 teaspoon chili sauce (Sriracha)

1½ teaspoons tamari or shoyu soy sauce

1 tablespoon unpasteurized white miso paste

1½ teaspoons honey

2 tablespoons neutral coconut oil, divided

1 medium delicata squash, seeded and sliced into about ½-inch-thick rings

1 teaspoon sesame oil

3 large garlic cloves, thinly sliced

1 tablespoon toasted sesame seeds

1 tablespoon finely chopped fresh basil or green onion, optional

1 Whisk together the brown rice vinegar, 1 tablespoon of the lime juice, the Sriracha, and the tamari in a small bowl; set aside.

2 In another small bowl, whisk together the miso paste, honey, and the remaining ½ tablespoon of lime juice; set aside.

3 Line a large plate with paper towels. In a large frying pan, warm 1 tablespoon of the coconut oil over medium heat. Add half of the delicata squash in a single layer and cook for about 3 minutes, until golden. Flip the squash pieces and cook them on the other side for about 2 minutes, until golden. Transfer the cooked squash to the paper towel–lined plate. Add the remaining tablespoon of coconut oil to the pan and repeat the process with the remaining squash.

4 Reduce the heat to low and add the sesame oil to the pan. Add the garlic and sauté for 30 seconds or until fragrant. Add the brown rice vinegar mixture to the pan, increase the heat to medium-high, and bring the mixture to a strong boil. Cook for 1 to 2 minutes until the sauce thickens and become syrupy. Remove the pan from the heat.

5 Add the miso mixture to the pan and stir until smooth. Add the cooked squash and gently toss to coat each piece with the glaze. Transfer the squash to a platter, sprinkle with the sesame seeds and basil or green onion, if using. Serve right away with rice or any other grain of choice.

ROASTED PARSNIPS AND PEARS WITH ZA'ATAR

This simple and elegant starter or side displays a good-looking combination of winter fruit and humble root vegetables. The sweetness of caramelized parsnip and juicy pear is brought forward by tangy tahini sauce and aromatic za'atar. Za'atar is an incredibly savory, Middle Eastern spice blend of sesame seeds, sumac, and dried herbs, which can be used to spice up many vegetable dishes, sauces. and breads. Serve this as a starter to Leek and Mushroom Barley Risotto (page 168), Bukhara Farro Pilaf (page 175), Spelt Fettuccine with Melted Rainbow Chard (page 210), or Leek, Fennel, and Chard Pizza with Gluten-Free Onion Crust (page 213).

Serves 4 to 6 | FALL • WINTER

1½ pounds (680 g) parsnips

1 large red onion

1 tablespoon melted neutral coconut oil or olive oil

Sea salt and freshly ground black pepper

2 ripe pears, cored and sliced

Tahini Sauce of your choice (pages 303 to 304)

2 tablespoons za'atar spice blend

2 tablespoons finely chopped fresh parsley (optional)

1 Preheat the oven to 400°F (200°C). Line a rimmed baking sheet with parchment paper.

2 Peel the parsnips and cut them into long strips. Peel and cut the onion into 8 wedges. Place the parsnips and onion on the prepared baking sheet, drizzle with the oil, and sprinkle with salt and pepper to taste. Toss to coat and arrange the vegetables in a single layer. Transfer the baking sheet to the oven and roast for 15 minutes. Flip the parsnip strips and onion wedges, and roast for 10 to 15 more minutes or until the vegetables are soft, caramelized, and golden brown in places. Remove the baking sheet from the oven.

3 Arrange the parsnips, onion, and pears on a serving plate. Drizzle with some Tahini Sauce, sprinkle with the za'atar and parsley, if using, and serve.

STEAMED AND MARINATED BEETS AND CELERY ROOT

A very special treatment for two modest root vegetables. My aim was to come up with the healthiest possible preparation—the vegetables are steamed and then marinated in a light but fragrant mixture of spices, herbs, garlic, and a minimal amount of oil. The result is as nourishing as it is flavorful. Serve these beets and celery root as a side dish, on salads, or inside sandwiches.

Serves 4 to 6 | FALL • WINTER

3 to 4 small red or golden beets, quartered

1 large celery root, about 1½ pounds (680 g), sliced into wedges

1½ teaspoons cumin seeds

1 teaspoon coriander seeds

2 teaspoons sea salt

1 teaspoon sweet Hungarian paprika

2 tablespoons olive oil

4 garlic cloves, minced

Juice of 1 lemon

2 tablespoons finely chopped fresh dill

2 tablespoons finely chopped fresh parsley

1 Arrange the beets in the lower level and celery root in the upper level of a two-level bamboo steamer. If you are using a different type of steamer, you can steam the vegetables together or separately (red beets will color the celery root if you steam the two vegetables together). Steam for 20 to 25 minutes or until the vegetables are soft when pricked with a fork.

2 Heat a small frying pan over medium heat. Add the cumin and coriander seeds and toast them for 2 to 3 minutes, until fragrant. Remove the pan from the heat and grind the spices in a mortar and pestle.

3 Combine the ground spices, salt, paprika, olive oil, garlic, and lemon juice in a small bowl.

4 When the vegetables are finished steaming, let them cool until they are safe to touch, then peel them, transfer them to a shallow dish, and add the herbs. Pour the marinade over top and toss to coat. Cover the vegetables and let them marinate at room temperature for 1 to 3 hours before serving. Keep any leftovers in an airtight container in the refrigerator for up to 5 days.

PICKLED TURNIPS

These electric-pink pickled turnips are inspired by traditional Lebanese pickles, which are often included in the well-loved falafel sandwich. Ready within a quick week, they are great on salads, tartines, and sandwiches, or served as a side at an outdoor grilling party or potluck.

MAKES 1 LARGE JAR | FALL • WINTER

1½ cups purified water, divided

2½ tablespoons sea salt

1½ pounds (680 g) turnips, peeled and sliced into sticks

1 small red beet, peeled and sliced

2 bay leaves

1 garlic clove, thinly sliced

1 teaspoon coriander seeds

½ teaspoon black peppercorns

A few sprigs of fresh dill

Dash of red pepper flakes

½ cup apple cider vinegar

1 In a small saucepan, heat ½ cup of the water and add the salt. Stir just until the salt is dissolved, then remove the pan from the heat and set it aside to cool.

2 Place the turnips, beet, bay leaf, garlic, coriander seeds, black peppercorns, dill, and pepper flakes in a large, clean glass jar with a tight-fitting lid.

3 Add the vinegar and the remaining 1 cup of water to the salty water, and pour the brine over the vegetables. Seal the jar and let the vegetables pickle at room temperature for 1 week. Refrigerate until you're ready to serve, and use the pickles within 1 month.

BRAISED CABBAGE

There is a tiny Ethiopian food stand at our local farmers' market, where we like to buy lunch after we finish shopping. They serve a delicious plate of mustardy lentils and braised cabbage, paired with the spongy teff bread, *injera*, which is traditionally used in place of utensils to absorb all the flavors of the spicy sides. I've recreated all the components of this lunch at home, and this braised cabbage came out on top—I come back to it quite often, especially during the colder seasons. Ample wedges of cabbage slowly stew in their own juices and broth with rings of carrot, onion, and pepper, transforming into some of the most tender, buttery, and flavorful cabbage I've ever tasted.

Serves 6 to 8 | WINTER

3 tablespoons ghee or neutral coconut oil, plus more for oiling the baking dish

1 medium head green cabbage, cut into 8 wedges

2 medium carrots, peeled and sliced

1 large onion, sliced

¼ cup vegetable broth or purified water

Sea salt and freshly ground black pepper

Pinch of red pepper flakes

1 teaspoon ground turmeric (optional)

1 Preheat the oven to 325°F (160°C). Grease a 9 x 13-inch (23 x 33-cm) baking dish lightly with the ghee or coconut oil.

2 Arrange the cabbage wedges snugly in the prepared baking dish, and scatter the carrots and onion over top and in between the wedges. Drizzle the ghee or coconut oil and broth or water over the cabbage, season with salt and pepper to taste, and sprinkle with the red pepper flakes and turmeric, if using.

3 Cover the baking dish with foil, transfer it to the oven, and braise the cabbage and vegetables for 1 hour. Remove the dish from the oven and carefully flip the cabbage wedges. Braise for 1 more hour or until tender.

4 Increase the oven temperature to 400°F (200°C). Remove the baking dish from the oven and take off the foil, then return the dish to the oven and roast for another 15 to 20 minutes, until the cabbage is golden brown.

5 Remove the cabbage from the oven and serve hot.

SWEETS FOR EVERY SEASON

THESE ARE SOME OF MY FAVORITE RECIPES that I've developed while on my continuous quest for lighter sweets full of nutritious ingredients. Most of the recipes are built around the ripeness of jammy seasonal fruit (and some vegetables), complemented by herbs and spices and containing very little sugar.

264
Pineapple Tart

267
Mango Cashew Cream Pudding with Vanilla and Lime

268
Cold Semolina Slice with Blackberry Compote

271
Key Lime Pie

274
Cherry Skillet Cobbler

277
Raw Peach Crumble

278
Upside-Down Plum Cake with Autumn Herbs

281
Apple and Walnut Galettes

283
Cranberry Pear Crumble Bars

287
Sweet Potato Chocolate Brownies

288
Sweet Potato Caramel Pecan Pie

290
Meyer Lemon Pots de Crème

293
Chocolate and Orange Bundt Cake

PINEAPPLE TART

This simple fruit tart showcases the sweetness of caramelized, roasted pineapple, with a minimal amount of added sugar. A drizzle of lime juice and zest rounds out the bright, tropical flavors in this light fruit dessert.

Makes one 9-inch tart | SPRING • SUMMER

FOR THE CRUST

1½ cups (150 g) sprouted spelt flour or whole spelt flour

¼ teaspoon sea salt

½ cup neutral coconut oil, chilled, plus more at room temperature for oiling the pan

4 to 5 tablespoons iced purified water

FOR THE FILLING

1 medium ripe pineapple, peeled, cored, and thinly sliced

1 tablespoon coconut sugar

1 tablespoon freshly squeezed lime juice

Zest of 1 lime

TO MAKE THE CRUST

1 Combine the flour and salt in a food processor. Cut the chilled coconut oil into small pieces and add them to the flour. Pulse until the mixture resembles sand. Add 4 tablespoons of the ice water and pulse to combine. Test the mixture by pressing it between your fingers; it should stick together. If it seems too dry, add more water, 1 tablespoon at a time, until the dough sticks together between your fingers.

2 Grease a 9-inch tart pan with the soft coconut oil. Add the dough and press it into the bottom of the pan to form an even crust, starting in the middle and working up the sides. Prick the dough with a fork several times, then transfer it to the refrigerator and chill for 1 hour.

3 Preheat the oven to 350°F (180°C).

4 Cover the crust with a piece of parchment paper and weight it down with baking beans or other pie weights. Place the tart pan on a rimmed baking sheet and transfer it to the oven. Blind bake for 20 minutes. Remove the crust from the oven and set it aside to cool.

TO ASSEMBLE AND BAKE THE TART

1 Arrange the pineapple slices in a circular pattern inside the cooled crust, filling it tightly. Sprinkle with the coconut sugar.

2 Transfer the tart to the oven and bake for 35 to 40 minutes, until the crust is golden and the pineapple is soft and caramelized. Remove the tart from the oven, brush it with the lime juice, and sprinkle with the lime zest when still hot. Let the tart cool before unmolding and slicing.

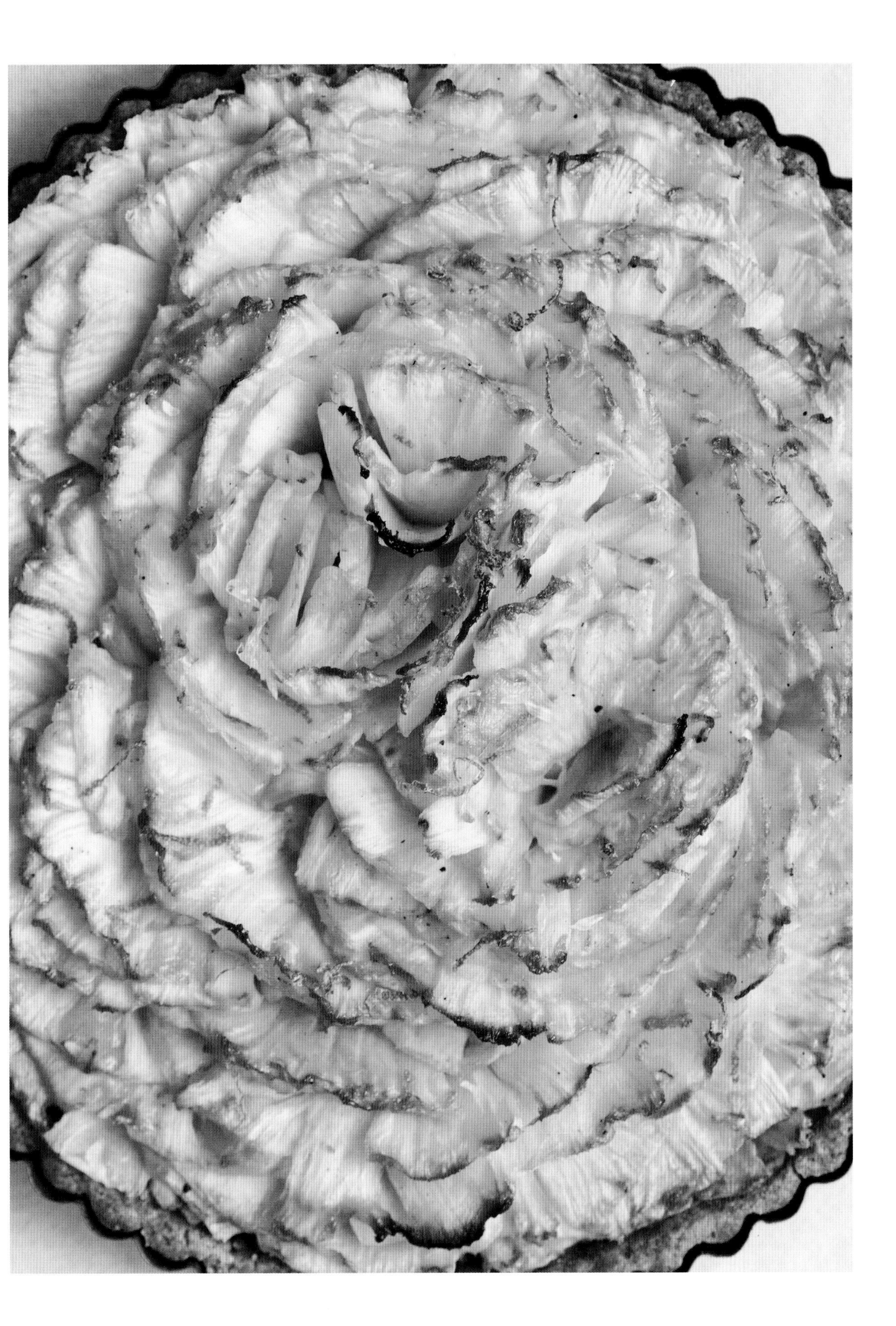

MANGO CASHEW CREAM PUDDING WITH VANILLA AND LIME

Sometime in the late winter and early spring, vibrantly yellow mangoes start making their way to our produce isles, treating us to a much-needed taste of the tropical sun after a long winter. To celebrate mango season, I like to make this smooth, vanilla-scented cashew cream, with swirls and layers of juicy mango, lime, and chia purée. It can even be eaten as a more indulgent breakfast, if you feel so inclined.

Makes 6 small or 4 generous portions | SPRING • SUMMER

Zest of 1 lime

5 tablespoons freshly squeezed lime juice

3 tablespoons chia seeds, divided

2 ripe Champagne or Ataulfo mangoes

2 tablespoons plus ¼ cup pure maple syrup, divided

1 cup raw cashews, soaked in purified water for 4 hours

½ cup almond milk, preferably homemade (page 298)

1 teaspoon vanilla extract

¼ cup plus 2 tablespoons melted neutral coconut oil

1 Combine the lime zest and juice with 2 tablespoons of the chia seeds in a medium bowl. Stir until well combined and let the mixture thicken at room temperature while you prepare the rest of the ingredients.

2 Peel the mangoes and slice the flesh off the pits. Reserve half of one mango and cut it into small cubes; set aside

3 Place the rest of the mango flesh into a blender, add 2 tablespoons of the maple syrup, and purée until smooth. Pour the purée into the bowl with the chia gel, add the reserved mango cubes, and stir to combine. Rinse the blender.

4 Drain and rinse the cashews, add them to the blender along with the almond milk, the remaining ¼ cup of maple syrup, the remaining tablespoon of chia seeds, and the vanilla extract. Blend on high until smooth, scraping down the sides of the blender if necessary. Add the coconut oil and blend on low until it is fully incorporated.

5 Spoon about 2 tablespoons of the cashew pudding into each individual serving bowl, followed by 1 heaping tablespoon of the mango purée. Continue to scoop both mixtures in layers until all the pudding and purée is used up. Optionally, make a swirl on top with a fork.

6 Cover the puddings and chill them completely in the refrigerator. Serve cold within 3 days.

COLD SEMOLINA SLICE WITH BLACKBERRY COMPOTE

Cold semolina or farina pudding is a simple, affordable dessert, and one that my paternal grandmother served often. As a child, I visited my grandparents every Friday after school, and after a customary lunch of dumpling soup and chilled kasha with milk, a plate with a cold semolina slice and fruit kissel (a sort of fruit pudding) was a required sweet finish to the meal. I absolutely loved it as a kid—the creamy, mild, milky semolina pudding pairs beautifully with sweet, fruity compote. This dessert can also be eaten for breakfast, especially if you use the more nutritious whole-grain semolina (which won't be quite as smooth). Make the compote with any berries you crave or have on hand.

Makes one 8-inch pudding | SUMMER

FOR THE BLACKBERRY COMPOTE

3 heaping cups fresh or frozen and thawed blackberries

Juice of ½ lemon

3 tablespoons pure maple syrup

1½ teaspoons arrowroot powder

Zest from 1 lemon (optional)

FOR THE SEMOLINA PUDDING

4 cups almond milk

2 tablespoons pure maple syrup, or more if desired

Pinch of sea salt

¾ cup (140 g) semolina

1 tablespoon vanilla extract

2 tablespoons ghee or neutral coconut oil, plus more for oiling the pie dish

TO MAKE THE BLACKBERRY COMPOTE

1 Combine the blackberries, lemon juice, and maple syrup in a small saucepan and bring the mixture to a gentle boil over medium heat. Reduce the heat to low and simmer uncovered for 1 to 2 minutes until jammy.

2 In the meantime, combine the arrowroot powder with ½ tablespoon of purified water in a small bowl; whisk to combine. Pour this mixture over the simmering blackberries and mix it in until the compote thickens slightly. Remove the pan from the heat and set it aside to cool. The compote will keep in an airtight container in the refrigerator for up to 5 days.

TO MAKE THE SEMOLINA PUDDING

1 Combine the milk, maple syrup, and salt in a medium saucepan and bring the mixture to a boil over medium heat. Slowly pour in the semolina, whisking constantly to prevent clumping. Reduce the heat to a simmer and cook for 5 minutes, whisking frequently, or until the pudding thickens.

2 Remove the pan from the heat, add the vanilla extract and ghee or coconut oil, and mix to combine. Cover the pan and set it aside to cool to room temperature.

3 Grease an 8-inch pie dish with ghee or coconut oil. Whip the semolina with an electric mixer for

about 5 minutes, until very creamy, fluffy, and bubbly. Pour the pudding into the prepared pie dish and even out the surface. Cover the dish with plastic wrap and refrigerate the pudding for about 2 hours or until it has set. Alternatively, pour the pudding into well-oiled ramekins for individual-size portions.

4 Slice the set pudding and serve it topped with blackberry compote and lemon zest, if using. If you used ramekins for individual portions, invert them onto plates or serve them as is, topped with the compote and lemon zest.

KEY LIME PIE

Although my version of key lime pie doesn't include condensed milk or eggs, it is completely identical to the original in both flavor and texture—no one will ever know that it is vegan. Whipped aquafaba contributes pleasant fluffiness to the filling, and the graham cracker crust is a snap to prepare.

Makes one 9-inch pie | SUMMER

FOR THE CRUST

6 tablespoons ghee or neutral coconut oil, at room temperature or melted, plus more for oiling the pan

11 ounces (315 g) organic graham crackers

FOR THE FILLING

1 (13.5-ounce) can unsweetened Thai coconut milk

⅓ cup (70 g) unrefined raw granulated sugar

1 tablespoon neutral coconut oil

1 teaspoon vanilla extract

1½ cups aquafaba (liquid reserved from cooked or canned beans, see page 9)

¾ cup raw cashews, soaked in purified water for 2 to 4 hours

½ cup plus 2 tablespoons, plus 1 teaspoon freshly squeezed lime juice, divided

Handful of baby spinach leaves, for color

¼ cup (31 g) powdered unrefined raw sugar

TO MAKE THE CRUST

1 Preheat the oven to 350°F (180°C). Grease a 9-inch pie pan with ghee or coconut oil.

2 Grind the graham crackers into fine crumbs in a food processor. You should have about 2 cups of ground crackers. Add the ghee or oil and pulse to combine.

3 Press the graham mixture into the bottom and up the sides of the prepared pie pan, forming an even crust.

4 Transfer the pie pan to the oven and bake for 12 minutes, until golden brown at the edges. Remove the pie pan from the oven and set it aside to cool.

TO MAKE THE FILLING

1 Combine the coconut milk and granulated sugar in a medium saucepan over medium heat. Bring the mixture to a steady but not too vigorous boil, and cook for 20 minutes, stirring frequently, or until the mixture reduces to a little over a cup. Remove the pan from the heat and whisk in the coconut oil and vanilla extract. Cover and let the mixture cool completely to room temperature.

2 At the same time, pour the aquafaba in another medium saucepan. Bring it to a steady, but not too vigorous boil over medium heat. Cook to reduce to ½ cup for about 30 minutes. Remove the pan from the heat, cover, and let cool completely to room temperature. Both steps can be done the night before; just leave the condensed milk and reduced aquafaba in the refrigerator overnight.

3 Drain and rinse the cashews. Place them in an upright blender (high-speed works best here) along with the ½ cup plus 2 tablespoons lime juice

and spinach leaves; and blend until smooth. If you're working with a regular, non high-speed blender, strain the blended mixture through a fine-mesh sieve for the smoothest texture, then return it to the blender.

4 Add the cooled condensed coconut milk mixture to the blender; blend until well combined and smooth. Pour the mixture into a medium bowl and set aside.

5 Pour the aquafaba into a medium bowl and whip it with an electric hand mixer on high speed. After a minute, without stopping the mixer, add the remaining 1 teaspoon of lime juice and begin to add the powdered sugar, 1 tablespoon at a time. Continue to beat the aquafaba until stiff peaks form, about 6 minutes.

6 Measure out 1 cup of the aquafaba fluff and quickly fold it into the pie filling mixture. Pour the filling into the crust, cover the pie pan, and refrigerate until firm, preferably overnight. Cover the bowl with the aquafaba fluff and refrigerate it as well.

7 When you're ready to serve the pie, take the remaining aquafaba fluff out of the refrigerator and, if deflated, re-whip it with an electric mixer until stiff peaks form. Slice the pie and serve it topped with the whipped aquafaba.

Note: Optionally, use the recipe for Gluten-Free Pie Crust on page 288. In this case, use a 7-inch spring form pan instead of a pie pan, cover the bottom with a circle of parchment paper, and oil the bottom and sides thoroughly. Press the dough against the bottom and about 2 inches up the sides of the pan. Don't worry about creating an even edge; this will create a rustic look. Otherwise, follow the pie recipe as is.

CHERRY SKILLET COBBLER

Making a cobbler is one of the easiest ways to embrace any given season's fruit in dessert form. In my household, we adore cherries and make the most of their brief season with this sumptuous dish. If it isn't cherry season, feel free to use whichever berries are readily available.

Serves 6 | SUMMER

FOR THE FILLING

1½ teaspoons neutral coconut oil, for greasing the pan

1½ pounds (680 g) fresh sweet cherries, pitted

2 tablespoons coconut sugar

1 tablespoon arrowroot powder (optional)

1 teaspoon vanilla extract (optional)

FOR THE CRUMBLE TOPPING

1 cup (120 g) rolled oats

¾ cup (75 g) almond flour

¼ cup raw almonds, chopped

1 teaspoon baking powder

Pinch of sea salt

¼ cup pure maple syrup

¼ cup neutral coconut oil, chilled

TO MAKE THE FILLING

1 Preheat the oven to 375°F (190°C). Grease a 9- to 10-inch cast iron skillet with the coconut oil.

2 Place the cherries in a large bowl, add the sugar, arrowroot powder, and vanilla, if using, and stir to combine. Spoon this mixture into the skillet in an even layer.

TO MAKE THE TOPPING AND BAKE THE CRUMBLE

1 Combine the oats, almond flour, chopped almonds, baking powder, and salt in a large bowl; toss to combine. Add the maple syrup and stir to incorporate.

2 Cut the chilled coconut oil into small pieces and add them to the mixture. Mix everything together with your hands, pressing the mixture between your fingers to incorporate the coconut oil into the crumble.

3 Sprinkle the crumble on top of the cherries, and transfer the skillet to the oven. Bake for 30 minutes, until the topping is golden, then cover the skillet with a piece of parchment paper and bake for another 10 minutes until the filling is jammy and bubbly. Remove the skillet from the oven and let it cool slightly. Serve it as is or with a scoop of ice cream on the side.

RAW PEACH CRUMBLE

Raw food recipes are ideal for summertime, when it's simply too hot to turn on the oven. When peaches are at the peak of their juicy ripeness, this simple crumble of dates, nuts, and spices turn them into the perfect summer dessert in a matter of minutes.

Serves 2 to 4 | SUMMER

3 (45 g) large, soft Medjool dates, pitted

¼ cup raw pecans or walnuts

½ teaspoon neutral coconut oil

Small pinch of sea salt

A pinch each of ground cinnamon, nutmeg, and ginger (optional)

4 to 5 ripe peaches or nectarines, pitted and sliced

1 In a food processor, combine the dates, pecans or walnuts, coconut oil, salt, and spices, if using. Pulse until the mixture is chopped into a chunky crumble.

2 Arrange the sliced peaches or nectarines in a serving dish, in a pattern if you like, and top with the crumble. Serve as is or with a scoop of vanilla ice cream.

UPSIDE-DOWN PLUM CAKE WITH AUTUMN HERBS

Upside-down fruit cakes, with their stunning appearance, have been known to trick unaware parties with the seeming complexity of their preparation. In reality, they are some of the easiest cakes to make, requiring not much else than good fruit, a basic cake batter, and one quick flip when they come out of the oven.

This upside-down cake owes its simplicity to the sweetness of late summer plums and the unique, piney qualities of rosemary and sage—ingredients that don't require too much else to perform beautifully. The simple, crumbly cake dough, dotted with more herbs, envelops the jammy, roasted plum halves.

Makes one 7-inch round cake | SUMMER • FALL

⅓ cup melted neutral coconut oil, plus more for oiling the pan

⅓ cup (70 g) plus 1 tablespoon coconut sugar, divided

1 to 2 tablespoons chopped fresh sage

1 tablespoon chopped fresh rosemary

4 to 6 ripe plums, halved and pitted

1 cup (100 g) sprouted spelt flour or whole spelt flour

½ cup (50 g) finely ground almonds (almond meal) or ½ cup (50 g) more spelt flour

1 teaspoon baking powder

½ teaspoon baking soda

Pinch of sea salt

1 cup warm purified water

1½ teaspoons freshly squeezed lemon juice or apple cider vinegar

1 teaspoon vanilla extract

1 Preheat the oven to 350°F (180°F). Grease a 7-inch spring form pan with coconut oil.

2 Sprinkle the bottom of the prepared pan with about ½ tablespoon of the coconut sugar and one third of the herbs. Arrange the plums snugly at the bottom of the pan, cut-side down. Sprinkle with the other ½ tablespoon of the coconut sugar.

3 Combine the flour, almond meal, the rest of the herbs, the baking powder, baking soda, salt, and the remaining ⅓ cup of sugar in a bowl. Add the water, coconut oil, lemon juice, and vanilla extract. Mix to combine and pour the batter over the plums. Carefully lift and drop the pan a couple of times to eliminate air bubbles.

4 Transfer the pan to the oven and bake for 50 to 55 minutes or until a toothpick inserted into the center comes out clean. Remove the cake from the oven and let it cool to room temperature.

5 Once the cake is cool, carefully invert it onto a plate. Unmold the form and remove the bottom. Slice and serve.

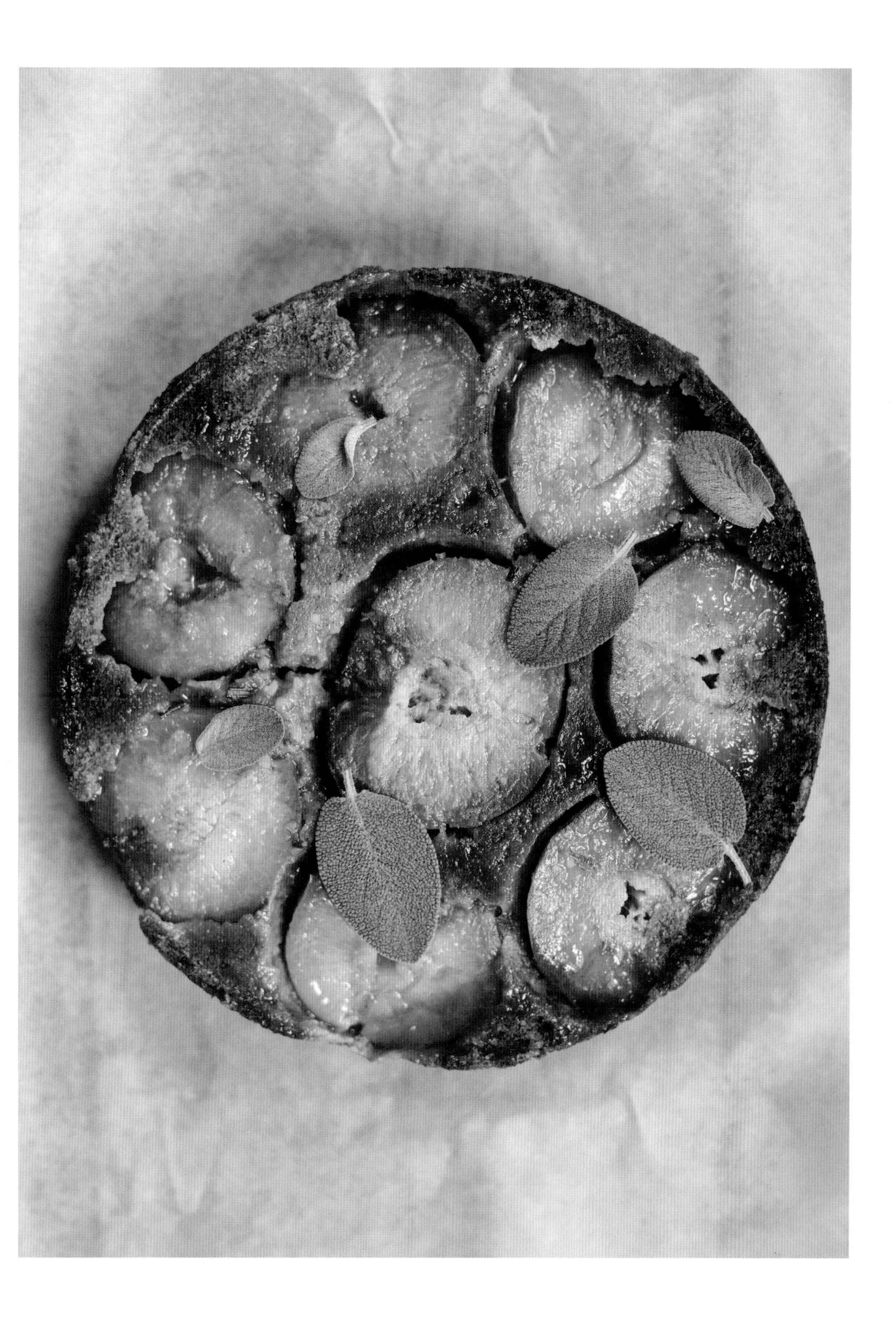

APPLE AND WALNUT GALETTES

Galette is that rustic, free-form pastry shape that is perfect for whatever seasonal fruit you have on hand. With galettes, the messier the folds of your edges, the better, and the more fruit juice that oozes out onto your baking sheet, the merrier. This recipe is meant to highlight the fall harvest of new apples with a sprinkling of walnuts and poppy seeds, but it can also be used as a guide to making a galette with any fruit or berry that is in season.

Makes two 7-inch galettes | FALL • WINTER

FOR THE DOUGH

1½ cups (150 g) sprouted spelt flour or whole spelt flour, plus more for rolling the dough

1½ teaspoons coconut sugar

Pinch of sea salt

3 tablespoons melted neutral coconut oil or ghee

½ cup plus 2 tablespoons hot purified water

FOR THE FILLING

6 tablespoons coconut sugar

Seeds from 6 cardamom pods, ground

1 teaspoon ground cinnamon

½ teaspoon ground nutmeg

½ cup raw walnuts, chopped

4 tablespoons poppy seeds, plus more for sprinkling on top

1 tablespoon melted neutral coconut oil or ghee

3 to 4 small apples, cored and thinly sliced

TO MAKE THE DOUGH

1 Place the flour in a medium mixing bowl, add the sugar and salt, and mix with a fork to combine. Make a well in the center of the flour mixture, and pour the oil into it. Slowly pour the hot water over the oil, stirring with a fork and slowly incorporating the flour into the liquid. When all the flour has been incorporated, turn the dough out onto a floured work surface and knead it with your hands until smooth. Add more water, 1 teaspoon at a time, if the dough appears too dry. That being said, give the flour a chance to absorb all the water first; most likely you won't need any more.

2 Divide the dough in half. Flatten each piece into a round disc, wrap them in plastic wrap, and let them rest for 30 minutes at room temperature.

TO MAKE THE FILLING AND BAKE THE GALETTE

1 Preheat the oven to 400°F (200°C). Line a large rimmed baking sheet with parchment paper.

2 Combine the coconut sugar, cardamom, cinnamon, and nutmeg in a small bowl. Combine the walnuts and the poppy seeds in another bowl.

3 Roll out the dough on a floured work surface, one portion at a time, into ⅛-inch-thick circular sheets, about 9 inches in diameter. Place one sheet of dough on the prepared baking sheet, keeping it to one side to make room for the second galette.

recipe continues

4 Brush the dough with melted coconut oil and sprinkle with 1 tablespoon of the coconut sugar–spice mixture. Arrange half of the apple slices in a spiral, leaving a 2-inch border of dough all around. Sprinkle with 2 more tablespoons of the sugar and spice mixture and half of the walnut-poppy mixture. Fold over the 2-inch edges, working circularly, one section at a time, until the galette has a rustic, folded border. Brush the edges with melted coconut oil and sprinkle with more poppy seeds. Repeat this process with the second portion of dough and the remaining filling ingredients. Drizzle any leftover melted oil over the filling of both galettes.

5 Transfer the baking sheet to the oven and bake the galettes for 45 minutes, until they are golden on top. Remove the galettes from the oven, let them cool slightly, then slice and serve.

CRANBERRY PEAR CRUMBLE BARS

These crumble bars are my tried and true dessert recipe for autumn or winter holiday potlucks—guaranteed to impress guests with their festive flavors. When baked, chopped pears melt into a heavenly, sweet layer on top of a simple dough base, studded with tart, bubbling pockets of cranberries and topped with a messy crumble of nuts, oats, and spices. They are the ultimate crowd pleaser.

Makes around 18 bars | FALL • WINTER

TO MAKE THE DOUGH

1 Preheat the oven to 350°F (180°C). Line a 9 x 11-inch (23 x 28 cm) baking dish with parchment paper, extending it up the sides of the dish.

2 Place the banana, coconut oil, and coconut sugar in a food processor and purée until smooth. Add the flours, baking powder, baking soda, salt, and two thirds of the ground cardamom; process until everything is incorporated. With the motor still running, pour the water through the feed tube and process until well combined. Add the ginger and vinegar and pulse to incorporate. Alternatively, you can mix all the dough ingredients by hand. First mash the banana with a fork, then keep mixing according to the order above. Push the dough into the prepared baking dish and distribute evently with a spoon.

TO PREPARE THE FRUIT

Combine the cranberries and pears with the coconut sugar, cinnamon, and nutmeg in a medium bowl. Distribute the fruit mixture evenly on top of the dough in the baking pan.

recipe continues

Note: You can use either 2 cups of oat flour or 2 cups of spelt flour in place of the combination of oat flour and almond flour in this recipe.

FOR THE DOUGH

1 large, very ripe banana

½ cup (110 ml) neutral coconut oil, at room temperature

⅓ cup (70 g) coconut sugar

1 cup (125 g) rolled oats, ground into flour, or 1 cup (100 g) whole spelt flour or sprouted spelt flour

1 cup (100 g) almond flour or meal

1 teaspoon baking powder

½ teaspoon baking soda

Pinch of sea salt

Seeds from 12 green cardamom pods, freshly ground, divided

1 cup purified water

2 tablespoons finely chopped fresh ginger

1 tablespoon apple cider vinegar

FOR THE FRUIT

2 cups fresh cranberries

2 ripe pears, cored and chopped into bite-size cubes

¼ cup (35 g) coconut sugar

1 teaspoon ground cinnamon

¼ teaspoon ground nutmeg

FOR THE CRUMBLE

½ cup rolled oats

½ cup raw pecans, walnuts, or almonds, chopped

1 tablespoon coconut sugar

½ teaspoon ground cinnamon

Pinch of sea salt

3 tablespoons neutral coconut oil, chilled, cut into small pieces

TO MAKE THE CRUMBLE TOPPING AND BAKE THE BARS

1 In the same bowl you used for the fruit, combine the oats, nuts, sugar, cinnamon, salt, and remaining ground cardamom; mix well. Add the oil to the bowl and use your fingers to work it into the other ingredients, until everything is well combined. Sprinkle the topping evenly over the fruit.

2 Transfer the baking dish to the oven and bake for 45 to 50 minutes, until the cranberries are bubbling through the topping and the crumble is golden in color. Remove the pan from the oven and let it cool, then use the parchment paper to lift the cake out of the pan and onto a cutting board. Slice it into bars and serve warm or at room temperature. Store the bars at room temperature if consumed within 1 day or refrigerated in an airtight container for up to 3 days.

SWEET POTATO CHOCOLATE BROWNIES

Much like cashews, sweet potatoes are another darling of the vegan dessert world. They contribute a moist and rich texture to baked goods with a mildly sweet, neutral flavor, plus the added bonus of wholesomeness and nutrition. These chocolatey brownies are the perfect sweet pick-me-up—simple in preparation and decadent in flavor, but with much lighter ingredients than their traditional counterparts. They are great at room temperature but even better cold, and will keep well in the refrigerator for 5 days.

Makes 12 large or 24 small brownies | FALL • WINTER

1 cup (200 g) chopped dark chocolate or dark chocolate chips

1½ cups raw hazelnuts

½ cup (50 g) almond flour

3 tablespoons unsweetened cocoa powder, plus more for dusting the brownies

Pinch of sea salt

9 to 10 (140 g) large, soft Medjool dates, pitted

1 medium sweet potato, baked, peeled, and roughly chopped (see page 288)

¼ cup almond butter

1 Preheat the oven to 350°F (180°C). Line an 8-inch square baking dish with parchment paper, extending the paper up the sides. Place the chocolate in the freezer.

2 Spread the hazelnuts on a baking tray and toast them in the oven for 10 minutes. Remove them from the oven and let them cool, then rub them in a clean kitchen towel to remove the skins. Reserve a few whole nuts for garnishing the brownies, and place the rest of the nuts in a food processor; grind into a meal. Make sure you don't overprocess. Transfer to a large mixing bowl and set them aside.

3 Place the chilled chocolate in the food processor and grind into the smallest pieces possible. Transfer to the bowl with the ground hazelnuts and add the almond flour, cocoa powder, and salt. Stir to mix evenly.

4 Combine the dates, sweet potato chunks, and almond butter in the food processor and purée until smooth. Spoon this mixture into the bowl with the ground hazelnuts and chocolate; stir to combine thoroughly.

5 Spoon the batter into the prepared baking dish and even out the top with a spoon. Transfer the dish to the oven and bake for 25 to 30 minutes, until the top of the brownie is firm to the touch.

6 Remove the pan from the oven and let it cool to room temperature, then transfer the brownie to a cutting board, using the parchment paper to lift it out of the pan. Dust the brownie with cocoa powder. Chop the reserved whole hazelnuts and sprinkle them on top, if desired. Slice the brownie into bars.

SWEET POTATO CARAMEL PECAN PIE

Sweet potato caramel is a favorite trick that I have had up my sleeve for years. Roasted sweet potato, when combined with dates and seed or nut butter, becomes incredibly similar in flavor to caramel, making it a beautiful filling for pecan pie. This pie is as impressive in flavor as it is in appearance. (Pictured on page 262.)

Makes one 9-inch pie | FALL • WINTER

FOR THE CRUST

1 tablespoon chia meal

2 to 4 tablespoons iced purified water, divided

½ cup neutral coconut oil, chilled, plus more at room temperature for oiling the pan

½ cup (70 g) buckwheat or quinoa flour

½ cup (50 g) almond flour

¼ cup (30 g) tapioca flour

2 tablespoons coconut sugar

Pinch of sea salt

FOR THE FILLING

1 medium (about 7-ounces / 200-g) sweet potato

9 to 10 (140 g) large, soft Medjool dates, pitted

1 heaping cup pecan halves

1 tablespoon pure maple syrup

Seeds from 8 cardamom pods, freshly ground, divided

Sea salt

½ cup sesame tahini

⅓ cup almond butter

4 tablespoons neutral coconut oil, at room temperature

TO MAKE THE CRUST

1 In a small bowl, mix together the chia meal and 1 tablespoon of the cold water. Cover the bowl and place it in the refrigerator for a few minutes.

2 Prepare a 9-inch tart pan, preferably with a removable bottom, by oiling it generously with the softened coconut oil.

3 In a food processor, combine the buckwheat or quinoa flour, almond flour, tapioca flour, coconut sugar, and salt; pulse to mix. Add the chilled chia paste and pulse to incorporate. Cut the chilled coconut oil into cubes, add them to the food processor, and keep pulsing until the mixture resembles sand.

4 Add 2 tablespoons of the cold water, and process until incorporated. Test the mixture by pressing it between your fingers; it should stick together. If not, add more water, 1 tablespoon at a time, until the dough sticks together between your fingers.

5 Press the dough into the prepared tart pan, starting in the middle and working up the sides to create an even crust. Prick the dough with a fork several times; cover and refrigerate for 30 minutes.

6 Meanwhile, preheat the oven to 350°F (180°C). After the dough has chilled for 30 minutes, cover it with parchment paper, weight it down with baking beans, and place it on a rimmed baking sheet. Transfer the pan and baking sheet to the oven and blind bake for 20 minutes, then remove the weights and parchment paper and bake for another 15 minutes or until it is golden at the edges. Remove the crust from the oven and set it aside to cool.

TO MAKE THE PIE

1 Increase the oven temperature to 400°F (200°C). Prick the sweet potato with a fork several times and place it naked on the rack, baking for about 40 minutes, or until it is soft throughout. Remove the sweet potato from the oven, let it cool, then peel it and cut it into chunks. This step can be done the day before.

2 Place the dates in a medium bowl. Cover them with boiling water and let them soak while you toast the nuts.

3 Lower the oven temperature to 350°F (180°C). Line a rimmed baking sheet with parchment paper.

4 Place the nuts on the prepared baking sheet, drizzle them with maple syrup, and sprinkle with half of the freshly ground cardamom and a pinch of salt. Transfer the nuts to the oven and toast them for 10 minutes or until golden. Remove the baking sheet from the oven and set it aside to cool.

5 Drain the dates and place them in a food processor along with the sweet potato, tahini, almond butter, coconut oil, the remaining cardamom, and a pinch of salt. Process until the mixture is well combined and smooth.

6 Spoon the filling into the crust and even it out with a spoon. Arrange the pecans on top, lightly pressing them into the filling.

7 Place the pie in the freezer for about 30 minutes or until firm. Remove the pie from the tart form; slice and serve. Cover the pie and store it in the refrigerator for up to 4 to 5 days or in the freezer for up to 1 month—the pie will never become completely frozen, just firm, and it will melt in your mouth. Remove the pie from the freezer right before serving.

MEYER LEMON POTS DE CRÈME

In the cold depths of winter, nature provides us with a much-needed twinkle of brightness in the form of citrus fruit. Meyer lemons, a crossbreed between regular lemons and mandarin oranges, have a distinct, aromatic sweetness.

Mousse-like desserts are wonderful for a graceful and light finish to a meal. Here, the custardy consistency is achieved with the help of agar-agar, a neutral sea vegetable–based thickener. The result is an airy, zesty, and mildly sweetened pot de crème.

Note: If you are using regular, non-Meyer lemons for this dessert, I strongly recommend using organic ones. I've noticed that non-organic lemons tend to have less flavor and are typically more sour than their organic counterparts. Also, their zest and juice may give a bitter note to the finished product, especially in a delicate dessert such as these pots de crème, which rely mostly on the quality of the lemons for their flavor.

Serves 6 | FALL • WINTER

3 cups almond milk, homemade preferably (page 298), divided

¼ cup plus 1 tablespoon pure maple syrup

Small pinch of sea salt

¼ teaspoon ground turmeric

1½ tablespoons agar-agar flakes

1 cup freshly squeezed Meyer lemon juice

4 teaspoons arrowroot powder

1 teaspoon vanilla extract (optional)

Zest of 2 Meyer lemons, divided

1 Combine the almond milk, maple syrup, salt, turmeric, and agar-agar flakes in a medium saucepan. Bring the mixture to a boil over medium heat, whisking frequently, then lower the heat to a slow simmer and cook, partially covered, for 5 minutes, whisking periodically, or until the agar-agar flakes have completely dissolved.

2 Meanwhile, combine the lemon juice and arrowroot powder in a small bowl. Add this mixture to the saucepan with the simmering milk. Whisk to incorporate and simmer for about 1 minute, until the mixture thickens slightly.

3 Pour the mixture into a blender and add the vanilla extract, if using. Blend until the mixture is smooth and airy, about 20 seconds. Taste and add more maple syrup, if needed. Add half of the lemon zest and pulse a few times to incorporate.

4 Distribute the mixture among individual serving cups or bowls and sprinkle with the remaining lemon zest. Cover with plastic wrap and refrigerate until completely set; serve cold. They will keep well in the refrigerator for up to 3 days.

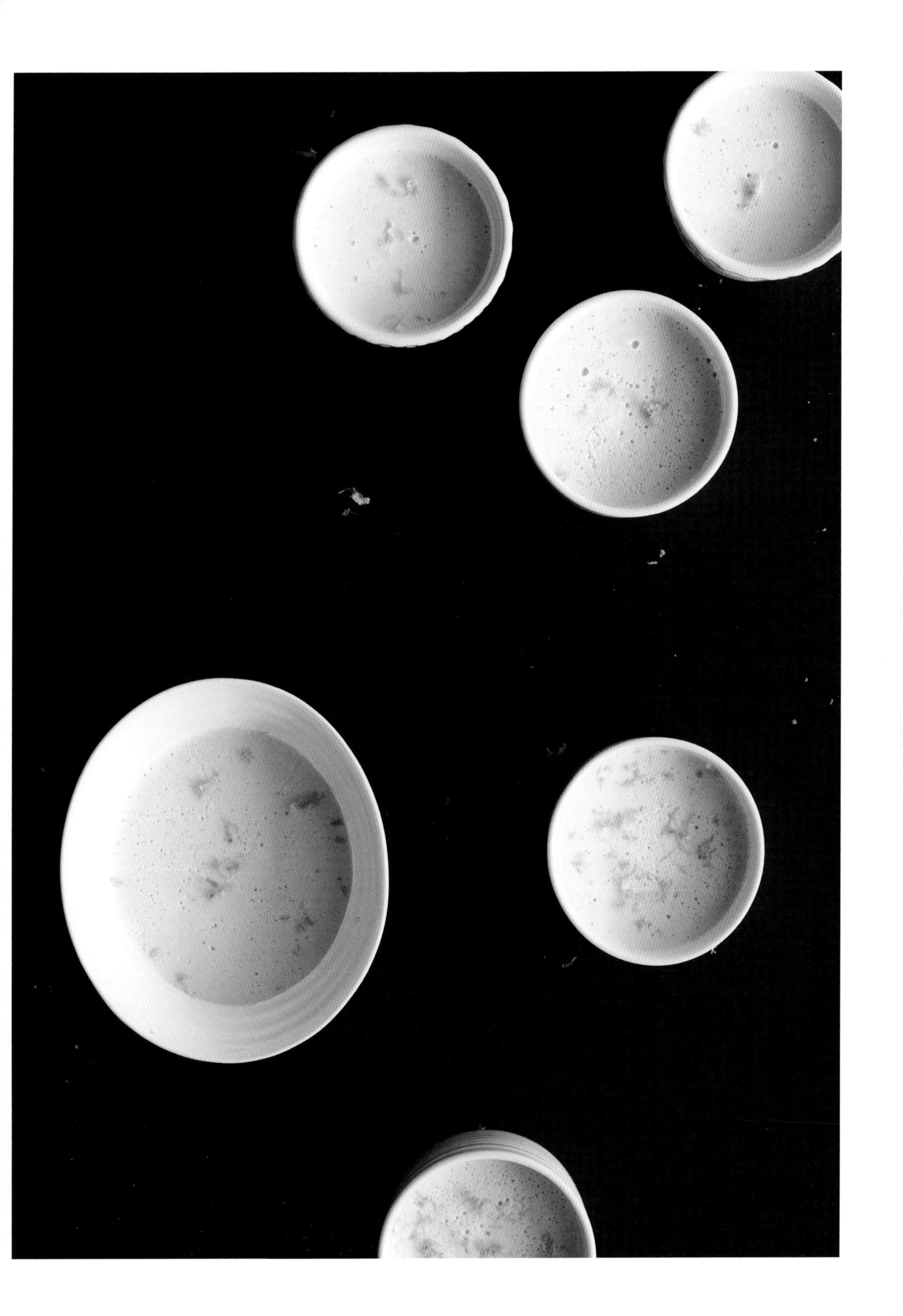

CHOCOLATE AND ORANGE BUNDT CAKE

Since chocolate and orange is one of the most heavenly dessert combinations, I've enhanced my go-to gluten-free and vegan chocolate cake recipe with the welcome addition of aromatic orange. Here, the decadent, moist cake combines beautifully with zesty notes of citrus and rich sweetness from dates, with no other added sweetener.

Makes one 10-inch Bundt cake | WINTER

FOR THE CAKE

1 cup soft Medjool dates, pitted

2 tablespoons neutral coconut oil, at room temperature, plus more for oiling the Bundt pan

1 cup (180 g) brown rice flour or other gluten-free flour, such as quinoa, garbanzo, buckwheat, etc.

½ cup (50 g) almond flour or more of the gluten-free flour

½ cup unsweetened cocoa powder

1 teaspoon baking soda

1 teaspoon baking powder

Pinch of sea salt

Zest of 1 to 2 organic oranges

1 cup freshly squeezed orange juice

⅓ cup unsweetened apple sauce

1 tablespoon balsamic vinegar

FOR THE CHOCOLATE SAUCE

¼ cup (45 g) finely chopped dark chocolate

1 teaspoon neutral coconut oil

Zest of 1 organic orange

Handful of raw shelled pistachios, chopped (optional)

TO MAKE THE CAKE

1 Soak the dates in hot purified water for 10 minutes.

2 Preheat the oven to 375° F (190° C). Grease a Bundt pan with coconut oil.

3 Combine the flours, cocoa powder, baking soda, baking powder, salt, and orange zest in a large bowl; mix thoroughly.

4 Reserve ½ cup of the date soaking water and add it to a blender along with the dates and orange juice; blend until smooth. Add the applesauce, oil, and balsamic vinegar, and pulse to combine. Pour the date mixture into the bowl with the dry ingredients and stir just until everything is incorporated.

5 Pour the batter into the prepared Bundt pan, transfer it to the oven, and bake for 55 to 60 minutes, until a toothpick inserted into the center comes out clean. Remove the cake from the oven and let it cool for at least 20 minutes, then invert the cake onto a plate or cake stand.

TO MAKE THE SAUCE AND SERVE THE CAKE

Melt the chocolate in a double boiler, add the coconut oil, and stir to combine. Pour the glaze over the cake and garnish with the orange zest and pistachios, if using. Slice and serve.

BASICS AND SAUCES

THESE BASIC RECIPES are great ammunition for intuitive, flavor-forward cooking—from multicolored tahini sauces to cashew creams, revolutionary vegan mayo to the most savory and piquant romesco. I think of them as the cornerstones of my cooking; with these basics and sauces at the ready, it's easy to create layers of vibrant flavors in everyday meals. These staples make appearances in other recipes throughout the book, but they are also wonderful starting points for creating your own inspired meals.

296
Cooking Beans

297
Simple Lemon-Marinated Beans or Lentils

298
Nut Milk

299
Avocado Mayo

300
Apple-Miso Mayo

301
Horseradish Cream

301
Chipotle Cream

302
Smoky Sun-Dried Tomato Cream

303
Cilantro Tahini Sauce

303
Turmeric Tahini Sauce

304
Beet Tahini Sauce

304
Tahini Miso Sauce

307
Romesco

308
Spring Roll Dipping Sauce

308
Universal Tomato Sauce

310
Multigrain Spiced Bread Loaf

313
Odds and Ends Vegetable Broth

314
Quick-Pickled Onions

315
Carrot Top Chimichurri

COOKING BEANS

Chances are you've heard that all dried beans, grains, nuts, and seeds contain phytic acid in their bran and hulls, which preserves them but also prevents many important nutrients from being absorbed in the human body. Therefore, it's important to soak your beans prior to cooking, as soaking neutralizes the phytic acid and activates the germination process, making more nutrients and digestive enzymes available to you. To help break down the phytic acid even more efficiently, especially during shorter soaking times, I like to add a splash of acidic liquid, such as lemon juice or vinegar, to the beans' soaking water. I also like to add kombu to the beans' cooking water for its beneficial minerals, flavor, and its ability to tenderize the beans, making them easier to digest.

Makes about 3 cups

1 cup dried beans, sorted, washed, and soaked in purified water overnight

2 garlic cloves, crushed

2 bay leaves

1- to 2-inch piece kombu (optional)

Sea salt

1 Drain and rinse the beans. In a medium pot, combine the beans, garlic, bay leaves, and kombu, if using. Add enough purified water to cover the beans by about 4 inches.

2 Bring the mixture to a boil over high heat and use a slotted spoon to skim off any foam that forms on the surface. Reduce the heat to a simmer and cook, partially covered, for 30 minutes. Check periodically, making sure that the water is still simmering; adjust the heat if needed. Taste a few of the beans—if they are all soft and creamy inside, add salt to taste and let the beans simmer for another 7 minutes. If they are not all tender, continue cooking for another 10 minutes and check again. Depending on the freshness of the beans, the cooking process can take from 30 minutes to several hours. Drain the beans and discard the kombu and bay leaves. Use the beans immediately or let them cool and then store them in an airtight container for up to 5 days.

SIMPLE LEMON-MARINATED BEANS OR LENTILS

It's great to have this simple salad handy in the refrigerator. Make it on the weekend to have for the week—add it to greens for an easy salad, mix it with sliced cucumbers and tomatoes, or spoon it on top of grain bowls.

Serves 2 to 4

- 3 cups cooked beans or lentils (one type or mixed; see page 296)
- 3 to 5 garlic cloves, minced
- About ¼ cup finely chopped fresh dill
- About ¼ cup finely chopped fresh parsley
- Juice of 1 large or 2 small lemons
- 2 tablespoons olive oil
- Sea salt and freshly ground black pepper

1 In a large bowl, combine the beans (preferably freshly cooked and still warm) with the garlic, dill, parsley, lemon juice, olive oil, and salt and pepper to taste. Toss well until everything is evenly incorporated.

2 Enjoy the salad right away, or, preferably, cover the bowl and refrigerate it for a couple hours or overnight before serving. Store the salad in an airtight container in the refrigerator for up to 5 days. Preferably, bring it to room temperature before serving.

NUT MILK

I promise that once you make your own nut milk, you will not want to go back to the store-bought variety. No pre-made nut milk out on the market is as fresh, creamy, bright white, and delicious as the homemade kind. Making nut milk at home also gives you control over the ingredients, while many store-bought plant milks contain stabilizers and other unwanted additives. I use nut milk almost every day for a variety of things, including smoothies, desserts, lattes, and even some savory dishes.

Most of the time, I prefer to use almonds, as they yield the most neutral, creamy milk. However, you can use any nut or seed in this recipe (if using cashews, there is no need to strain them). Feel free to add flavorings or sweeteners to your nut milk: cinnamon, vanilla, cardamom, dates, and a small pinch of salt are all delicious additions to a basic nut milk.

When I make almond milk for nut milk–based desserts—such as Meyer Lemon Pots de Crème (page 290), Mango Cashew Cream Pudding with Vanilla and Lime (page 267), or Cold Semolina Slice with Blackberry Compote (page 268)—I use a 1:3 ratio of almonds to water, so the end result is thicker, creamier, and more flavorful.

I like to slip the skins off the almonds when making milk for a dessert where color matters. The skins pop off easily after soaking the nuts overnight.

Makes 3 to 4 cups

1 cup raw almonds or other nuts or seeds, soaked in purified water overnight

3 to 4 cups purified water

1 Drain and rinse the almonds. Place them in a blender with the water and blend until completely smooth.

2 Working with 1 cup at a time, pour the nut mixture through a nut milk bag or a fine-mesh sieve lined with several layers of cheesecloth into a large bowl. Lift the nut bag or cheesecloth, gathering up the edges and slowly squeezing out the nut milk, getting as much liquid out as possible. Empty the nut pulp out of the nut bag or cheesecloth and pour the strained milk into a bottle. Continue this process with the rest of the unstrained milk.

3 Store the nut milk in a sealed bottle in the refrigerator for up to 3 days.

AVOCADO MAYO

This incredibly simple and flavorful condiment gets its creamy texture and mayonnaise-like flavor from avocados. It's very versatile and can be served on sandwiches, spooned over grain bowls, or used as a salad dressing.

Makes about 2 cups

2 ripe but firm avocados, pitted and peeled

Juice of 1 lemon

2 tablespoons olive oil

2 tablespoons Dijon mustard

Sea salt and freshly ground black pepper

1 In a medium bowl, mash the avocados with a fork. Add the lemon juice, olive oil, mustard, and salt and pepper to taste; mix thoroughly until smooth.

2 For the best color and flavor, use the mayo within 1 day. However, if you don't mind a little discoloration, you can keep it in an airtight container in the refrigerator for up to 3 days.

APPLE-MISO MAYO

I'm going to let go of any modesty and say that this recipe is quite revolutionary—amazingly close in flavor to mayonnaise but more robust, with creamy, stewed apples and savory miso as its base. Use this as you would classic mayo—on sandwiches and in salads.

Makes about 1½ cups

2 medium apples, peeled, cored, and chopped

1 tablespoon apple cider vinegar

1 teaspoon coconut sugar or other sugar of choice

About 3 tablespoons purified water, plus more if needed

2 teaspoons Dijon mustard

2 teaspoons unpasteurized miso paste

⅛ teaspoon chili sauce (Sriracha)

1½ teaspoons freshly squeezed lemon or lime juice

Freshly ground black pepper

⅓ cup (85 ml) plus 1 tablespoon olive oil

Sea salt (optional)

1 Combine the apples, apple cider vinegar, sugar, and water in a medium saucepan over medium-high heat. Bring the mixture to a boil, reduce the heat to a slow simmer, and cook, covered, until the apples are completely soft, about 15 minutes. Check the apples periodically and add a splash of water if the liquid evaporates.

2 Combine the cooked apples, mustard, miso paste, Sriracha, lemon or lime juice, and black pepper to taste in a blender or food processor. Blend until smooth. With the blender still running on low, slowly pour in the olive oil in small portions, making sure each portion is fully whipped before adding the next one.

3 Taste for salt and adjust if needed. Transfer the mayo to an airtight container and store it in the refrigerator for up to 1 week.

CASHEW CREAMS

Cashew cream is an incredibly versatile, plant-based vehicle for adding zing to many meals. There are infinite ways to flavor cashew creams; here are a few of my favorites.

Horseradish Cream

(Pictured on page 294.)

Makes about 1½ cups

- 1 cup raw cashews, soaked in purified water for 2 to 4 hours
- ½ cup purified water
- 1½ tablespoons shredded horseradish root, or as desired
- 1 tablespoon plus 1 teaspoon tamari
- 1 tablespoon Dijon mustard
- 1 small garlic clove, peeled
- 1 tablespoon freshly squeezed lemon juice

1 Drain and rinse the cashews, then transfer them to a blender and add the rest of the ingredients. Blend until smooth.

2 Store the cashew cream in an airtight container in the refrigerator for up to 1 week.

Chipotle Cream

Makes about 1½ cups

- 1 cup raw cashews, soaked in purified water for 2 to 4 hours
- ½ cup purified water
- ½ chipotle pepper in adobo sauce or 1 teaspoon chipotle powder, plus more if desired
- 1 tablespoon plus 1 teaspoon tamari
- 1 tablespoon Dijon mustard
- 1 small garlic clove, peeled
- 1 tablespoon freshly squeezed lemon juice

1 Drain and rinse the cashews, then transfer them to a blender and add the rest of the ingredients. Blend until smooth.

2 Store the cashew cream in an airtight container in the refrigerator for up to 1 week.

Smoky Sun-Dried Tomato Cream

Makes about 1½ cups

1 cup raw cashews, soaked in purified water for 2 to 4 hours

½ cup purified water

1 tablespoon smoked Spanish paprika

2 sun-dried tomatoes preserved in oil

1 tablespoon plus 1 teaspoon tamari

1 tablespoon Dijon mustard

1 small garlic clove, peeled

1 tablespoon freshly squeezed lemon juice

1 Drain and rinse the cashews, then transfer them to a blender and add the rest of the ingredients. Blend until smooth.

2 Store the cashew cream in an airtight container in the refrigerator for up to 1 week.

TAHINI SAUCES

Creamy, savory tahini creates the perfect base for delicious, plant-based sauces that can elevate any meal. Here are a few of my favorites, as stunning in color as they are in flavor.

Cilantro Tahini Sauce

Makes ¾ to 1 cup

¼ cup sesame tahini

¼ cup purified water

Juice of 1 lemon

1 small garlic clove, roughly chopped

1 cup fresh cilantro leaves, roughly chopped

Pinch of sea salt

1 Combine all the ingredients in a blender and blend until smooth.

2 Store the tahini sauce in an airtight container in the refrigerator for up to 5 days.

Turmeric Tahini Sauce

Makes about ¾ cup

¼ cup sesame tahini

¼ cup purified water

Juice of 1 lemon

1 teaspoon pure maple syrup or honey

½ teaspoon ground turmeric

Pinch of sea salt

Small pinch of red pepper flakes

1 Combine all the ingredients in a blender and blend until smooth.

2 Store the tahini sauce in an airtight container in the refrigerator for up to 1 week.

Beet Tahini Sauce

Makes about 1 cup

¼ cup sesame tahini

¼ cup purified water

Juice of 1 lemon

¼ small red beet, cooked and roughly chopped

1 small garlic clove, chopped

Pinch of sea salt

1 Combine all the ingredients in a blender and blend until smooth.

2 Store the tahini sauce in an airtight container in the refrigerator for up to 5 days.

Tahini Miso Sauce

Makes about ⅔ cup

1 tablespoon sesame tahini

1 tablespoon unpasteurized miso paste

4 tablespoons freshly squeezed lemon juice

3 tablespoons olive oil

1 teaspoon chili sauce (Sriracha)

1 teaspoon pure maple syrup (optional)

1 Mix together the tahini and miso paste in a small bowl until smooth. Add the rest of the ingredients and stir into a smooth sauce.

2 Store the tahini sauce in an airtight container in the refrigerator for up to 1 week.

ROMESCO

Discovering romesco was life-changing for me. Originally from the Catalonia region of Spain, this sauce has an amazingly savory piquancy, and if you're anything like me, you will want to slather it on everything once you prepare a batch.

Makes about 3 cups

1 large or 2 small red bell peppers, seeded and cut into large chunks

2 medium tomatoes, cut in half

4 tablespoons melted neutral coconut oil or olive oil, divided

Sea salt and freshly ground black pepper

½ cup raw almonds, soaked in purified water overnight, drained and rinsed

1 chili, seeded and sliced

Cloves from 1 head garlic, sliced

1 tablespoon red wine vinegar

1 teaspoon smoked Spanish paprika (optional)

1 tablespoon olive oil

About 2 tablespoons chopped fresh parsley (optional)

1 Preheat the oven to 425°F (218°C). Line a shallow baking dish with parchment paper.

2 Place the bell peppers and tomatoes in the prepared baking dish, drizzle with 1 tablespoon of the coconut oil, and stir to coat. Spread out the vegetables in a single layer, flipping the tomatoes so they are cut-side down. Sprinkle with salt and black pepper to taste and transfer the baking dish to the oven. Roast for 20 minutes or until the peppers are completely cooked through and soft.

3 Warm the remaining 3 tablespoons of coconut oil in a medium saucepan over medium heat. Add the chili and sauté for about 2 minutes, until it is soft and golden in places. Use a slotted spoon to transfer the chili to a plate, leaving the chili oil in the pan.

4 Reduce the heat to medium low. Add the almonds, garlic slices, and a pinch of salt to the pan and sauté for 3 to 4 minutes, until the garlic is golden. Remove the pan from the heat.

5 Remove the skin from the roasted tomato halves (it should come right off). In a food processor, combine the bell pepper, tomatoes and their juices, chili, almond-garlic mixture, the oil from the pan, the red wine vinegar, and the smoked paprika, if using. Blend until the mixture reaches your desired texture—you can make romesco smooth or chunky, depending on your preference.

6 Add the tablespoon of olive oil and parsley, if using. Pulse to combine. Taste for salt and pepper and adjust if needed. Store the romesco in an airtight container in the refrigerator for up to 1 week.

SPRING ROLL DIPPING SAUCE

(Pictured on page 294.)

Makes about ½ cup

4 tablespoons almond butter

1½ tablespoons tamari

1½ tablespoons pure maple syrup

4 tablespoons freshly squeezed lemon juice

½ teaspoon chili sauce (Sriracha)

1 In a bowl, whisk together all the ingredients until smooth.

2 Store the sauce in an airtight container in the refrigerator for up to 5 days.

UNIVERSAL TOMATO SAUCE

Makes about 2 cups

1½ teaspoons olive oil

1 to 2 garlic cloves, minced

½ teaspoon dried oregano

1 pound (454 g) tomatoes, diced

½ teaspoon coconut sugar or other sugar of choice

Pinch of red pepper flakes

Sea salt and freshly ground black pepper

1 Warm the olive oil in a deep pan over medium-low heat. Add the garlic and oregano, let the garlic sweat for about 1 minute, then increase the heat to medium. Add the tomatoes, sugar, red pepper flakes, and salt and pepper to taste. Bring the mixture to a boil, stirring occasionally, then reduce the heat to medium-low and simmer for 90 minutes. Remove the pan from the heat.

2 Let the sauce cool to room temperature, then transfer it to an airtight container and store it in the refrigerator for up to 5 days.

MULTIGRAIN SPICED BREAD LOAF

Here is my go-to bread recipe, packed with nutrient-rich whole grains and aromatic spices. This bread falls into the category of soda bread, which rises with the help of baking soda instead of yeast, and is therefore significantly lower maintenance. It is a versatile loaf that will make a great accompaniment to any meal.

Makes 1 loaf

Neutral coconut oil or other vegetable oil, for oiling the pan

2 cups (200 g) sprouted spelt flour or whole spelt flour

½ cup (100 g) whole rye flour

¼ cup (40 g) corn grits

¼ cup (45 g) steel cut oats

¼ cup mixed chopped nuts and seeds, such as walnuts, pecans, hazelnuts, sunflower seeds, pumpkin seeds, sesame seeds, and poppy seeds, plus more for garnish

¼ cup (35 g) coconut sugar

1 teaspoon salt

1 teaspoon baking soda

1 tablespoon coriander seeds

Seeds from 5 cardamom pods, freshly ground

½ teaspoon ground cinnamon

1⅓ cups plain kefir or yogurt

1 Preheat the oven to 400°F (200°C). Thoroughly grease a loaf pan with coconut oil.

2 Combine the spelt and rye flours, corn grits, steel cut oats, nuts and seeds, sugar, salt, baking soda, coriander, cardamom, and cinnamon in a large bowl. Make a well in the center and pour in the kefir or yogurt. Using a fork, gradually incorporate the flour mixture into the kefir in a circular motion. You should end up with a very soft but not too sticky dough. Turn the dough out onto a well-floured work surface and gently roll it around to coat it in flour—do not knead the dough.

3 Place the dough in the prepared loaf pan, and lift and drop the pan several times to get the dough to shape evenly. Sprinkle the top of the dough with nuts and seeds of choice, and use a small, sharp knife to cut a few crosswise slits in the top of the loaf.

4 Transfer the loaf to the oven and bake for 40 to 45 minutes, until the crust is golden. To test if the bread is ready, tap the base of the loaf—it should make a hollow sound. Store the loaf at room temperature for 2 days or refrigerated in an airtight container for up to 5 days.

ODDS AND ENDS VEGETABLE BROTH

I've developed a habit of making this broth almost weekly out of leftover vegetable ends, stems, stalks, and whatnot, and I always have a few ziplock bags of it in my freezer. I wouldn't know how to get by without it. For instance, my little daughter Paloma's favorite emergency meal, nutritious teff polenta (page 75), is done within twenty minutes if I have a supply of flavorful vegetable broth on hand. If you eat a lot of vegetables, you shouldn't ever worry about buying broth or collecting whole vegetables to make one—you likely go through plenty of veggie scraps to take care of it.

Week's worth of vegetable scraps (roughly chopped stems of green leafy vegetables, broccoli, cauliflower, and herbs; tops from fennel, turnips, and leeks; tough ends of asparagus; etc.)

1 yellow onion, cut in half

4 garlic cloves, crushed

3 bay leaves

1 carrot (optional)

1 teaspoon black peppercorns (optional)

1 teaspoon coriander seeds (optional)

Sea salt

Juice of 1 lemon (optional)

1 Place the vegetable scraps in a large soup pot. Add the onion, garlic, bay leaves, carrot, black peppercorns, and coriander seeds, if using. Pour in enough purified water to cover the vegetables completely, or as much as the pot can hold. Salt the water generously and bring it to a boil over medium-high heat. Reduce the heat to a simmer and cook, partially covered, for 20 minutes, until all the vegetables are soft. Add the lemon juice, if using, and remove the pot from the heat.

2 Cover the pot and let the broth cool to room temperature. For the best flavor, refrigerate the broth overnight before you strain it. Strain the broth through a fine-mesh sieve into a large airtight container. Store the broth in the refrigerator for up to 5 days or in the freezer for up to 1 month.

QUICK-PICKLED ONIONS

These onions take just minutes to prepare, and they have the power to turn any ordinary salad or grain bowl into a bright meal with their sharp, zingy flavor.

Makes about one 16-ounce jar

½ cup brown rice vinegar or apple cider vinegar

1 cup warm purified water

1½ teaspoons sea salt

1 teaspoon coconut sugar or other sugar of choice

1 medium red onion, thinly sliced

1 bay leaf (optional)

1 to 2 sprigs fresh rosemary (optional)

1 Combine the vinegar, water, salt, and sugar in a large glass jar or other nonreactive, airtight container. Stir to dissolve the salt and sugar. Add the onion slices, bay leaf, and rosemary, if using, seal the jar, and shake gently to mix.

2 Let the onion marinate at room temperature for at least 1 hour; the onion will become more flavorful as more time passes. Store the pickled onion in an airtight container in the refrigerator for up to 2 weeks; for best flavor, enjoy them during the first week.

CARROT TOP CHIMICHURRI

I have yet to meet anyone able to resist freshly made chimichurri. This garlicky Argentinian sauce is traditionally made with parsley and served with meat, but it can elevate many vegetarian dishes just as well. It also solves my dilemma of how to use lush carrot tops that often come with market carrots—carrot top chimichurri is almost identical in flavor to the original. That being said, if you do not have carrot tops, the classic way is to make it with parsley. (Pictured on page 294.)

Makes 1 to 1½ cups

3 packed cups torn carrot top greens (most hard stems removed)

4 garlic cloves, chopped

2 tablespoons red wine vinegar

1 teaspoon sea salt

¼ teaspoon red pepper flakes

Freshly ground black pepper

½ cup olive oil

1 In a food processor, combine the carrot tops, garlic, red wine vinegar, salt, red pepper flakes, and black pepper to taste; pulse into a chunky purée. With the motor running, slowly pour the olive oil through the feed tube until it is well incorporated.

2 Transfer the chimichurri to a clean glass jar with a lid, and keep it in the refrigerator for up to 5 days.

ACKNOWLEDGMENTS

To our family, Paloma and Ernie, for your unwavering support, incredible patience, endless encouragement, and healthy appetite throughout the whole process of creating this book.

To Kevin, for all your help, honesty and eagerness in tasting every dish, keen design eye, and countless trips to the market.

To our dear friends Masha and Zhenya for your generosity, humor, taking on all the leftovers, and babysitting.

To our editor, Juree Sondker, and everyone at Roost Books for this opportunity, and for all your expertise while working on this project. We couldn't have found a better home for our books.

To our agent, Alison Fargis, for your insight and patience, and for guiding us through this whole process once again. We feel so lucky and honored to work with you.

To all Golubka Kitchen readers, for trying our recipes, for your support and thoughtful feedback throughout the years, and for believing in the power of plants. This book wouldn't be possible without you.

PREFERRED BRANDS

Grains

Alter Eco
Bob's Red Mill
Lotus Foods

Heirloom Beans

Rancho Gordo

Canned Beans (BPA-free can, beans cooked with kombu)

Eden Foods

Neutral-Flavored Coconut Oil

La Tourangelle
Nutiva
Traders Joe's

Brown Rice Vinegar

Eden Foods

Miso

Miso Master
South River

Tamari

San-J

Nuts, Seeds, and Nut Butters

Blue Mountain Organics
Nuts.com

Sea Vegetables

Eden Foods

Dried Edible Flowers, Herbs, and Spices

mountainroseherbs.com

Flours

Arrowhead Mills
Blue Mountain Organics
Bob's Red Mill
To Your Health Sprouted Flour Company

100% Buckwheat Soba Noodles and Other Whole-Grain Noodles

Eden Foods

Sprouted Burger Buns, Bread, and Tortillas

Ezekiel Bread

Chocolate and Chocolate Chips

Enjoy Life
Taza

Upright Blenders

Blendtec
Vitamix

Food Processor

Cuisinart

Julienne Peeler

Zyliss Y Peeler

INDEX

agar-agar
- as pantry item, 12
- Meyer Lemon Pots de Crème, 290

almonds
- almond butter, 11
- almond flour, 14
- almond milk, 298
- as pantry item, 12
- *See also* nuts, nut butters

apple cider vinegar, unpasteurized, 10

apples
- Apple and Walnut Galettes, 281–82
- Apple-Miso Mayo, 300
- Teff and Apple Pancakes, 36

aquafaba
- about, 9
- Blueberry Buckwheat Pancakes, 29
- Key Lime Pie, 271–73
- Teff and Apple Pancakes, 36

arame, 12

arborio rice, 8

arrowroot powder, 14

asparagus
- Asparagus and Leek Pancakes, 25
- Asparagus Fries, 242
- Cauliflower Riceless Risotto with Spinach and Corn, 157
- Spring Bowl, 44

avocados
- Avocado Mayo, 299
- Collard Wraps with Chickpea-Avocado Mash, Roasted Carrots, and Spicy Cranberry Relish, 104–6
- Golden Beet and Pomelo Winter Panzanella, 83
- Grilled Pineapple and Avocado Salad, 51
- Naked Taco Bowl, 62
- Pickled Turnip, Avocado, Barley, and Black Rice Sushi Rolls, 110–12
- Roasted Yam and Collard Green Enchiladas, 101–3
- Smoky Cauliflower and Black Bean Hummus Burritos, 99–100
- Spring Bowl, 44
- Superfood Summer Porridge, 30

balsamic vinegar, 11

bamboo steamer, 16

barberries, in Bukhara Farro Pilaf, 175–76

barley
- Barley and Chia Seed Porridge with Candied Kumquats, 39
- cooking, 110
- Leek and Mushroom Barley Risotto, 168–70
- Mung Bean and Barley Veggie Burgers, 239
- as pantry item, 8
- Pickled Turnip, Avocado, Barley, and Black Rice Sushi Rolls, 110–12
- Silky Barley Water with Ginger and Citrus, 112

beans
- Coconut Black Rice and Edamame Veggie Burger, 218–20
- cooking, 296
- Curried Bean and Brussels Sprout Stew with Roasted Kabocha Squash, 133–34
- Heirloom Beans, Fennel, and Citrus Salad, 78
- Mung Bean and Barley Veggie Burgers, 239
- Naked Taco Bowl, 62
- as pantry items, 9
- Simple Lemon-Marinated Beans or Lentils, 297

Smoky Cauliflower and Black Bean Hummus Burritos, 99–100
Sweet Potato, Millet, and Black Bean Veggie Burgers with Kale Slaw, 230–32
Tomato and Eggplant Green Mung Dal, 125–26
White Bean and Sweet Potato Dumplings, 201–4
beets
Beet and Zucchini Veggie Burgers, 226
Beet Sauté, 251
Beet Tahini Sauce, 304
Borscht, 141–42
Buckwheat Risotto with Roasted Beets, 158
Golden Beet and Pomelo Winter Panzanella, 83
Steamed and Marinated Beets and Celery Root, 257
Steamed Chioggia Beet and Pear Salad, 80
blackberries in Cold Semolina Slice with Blackberry Compote, 268–70
blueberries in Blueberry Buckwheat Pancakes, 29
bowls, single-meal, 44, 59, 62, 65, 73
bread
Golden Beet and Pomelo Winter Panzanella, 83
Multigrain Spiced Bread Loaf, 310
Peach and Tomato Panzanella, 55
Spring Panzanella with Radishes and Peas, 46
Squash and Pomegranate Panzanella with Autumn Herbs, 69
broccoli
Blistered Tomato and Green Bean Fettuccine in Smoky Sauce, 185
Broccoli Stem Riceless Risotto, 155–56
Creamy Coconut Lentils with Broccoli, 119
Brussels sprouts
Curried Bean and Brussels Sprout Stew with Roasted Kabocha Squash, 133–34
Lentil, Pomegranate, and Brussels Sprout Salad, 70
Rutabega and Brussels Sprout Riceless Risotto, 165–67
buckwheat
Blueberry Buckwheat Pancakes, 29
Buckwheat Risotto with Roasted Beets, 158
as pantry item, 9, 14
Spring Bowl, 44

cabbage
Borscht, 141–42
Braised Cabbage, 261
freezing, 91
Late Autumn/Winter Bowl, 73–74
Naked Taco Bowl, 62
Spring Cabbage Rolls, 91–92
Summer Rolls with Savory Cabbage and Sugar Snaps, 88
carrots
Beet and Zucchini Veggie Burgers, 226
Beet Sauté, 251
Borscht, 141–42
Braised Cabbage, 261
Bukhara Farro Pilaf, 175–76
Carrot Top Chimichurri, 315
Cauliflower Fritters, 229
Chilled Thai Coconut Soup with Zucchini and Carrot Noodles, 120–22
Collard Wraps with Chickpea-Avocado Mash, Roasted Carrots, and Spicy Cranberry Relish, 104–6
Couscous Stuffed Collard Greens in Coconut Curry Sauce, 107–9
Creamy Coconut Lentils with Broccoli, 119
Kitchari Winter Stew, 145
Late Autumn/Winter Bowl, 73–74
Lentil Tomato Stew with Turnips and Collard Greens, 130
Portobello Bolognese Pasta, 209
Roasted Root Vegetable Oven Risotto, 171–72
Summer Bowl, 59
Sweet Potato, Millet, and Black Bean Veggie Burgers with Kale Slaw, 230–32
cashews
as pantry item, 12
making milk from, 298
cast iron skillet, 15, 26, 35, 161, 175, 185, 188, 200, 274
cauliflower
Cauliflower Fritters, 229
Cauliflower Riceless Risotto with Spinach and Corn, 157
Smoky Cauliflower and Black Bean Hummus Burritos, 99–100
Warm Salad of Roasted Cauliflower, Grapes, and Forbidden Black Rice, 66
celery root
Celery Root Miso Soup, 136

celery root (*continued*)
Steamed and Marinated Beets and Celery Root, 257
chard
Creamy Steel Cut Oats with Rainbow Chard and Pine Nuts, 40
Leek, Fennel, and Chard Pizza with Gluten-Free Onion Crust, 213–14
Spelt Fettuccine with Melted Rainbow Chard, 210
cherries in Cherry Skillet Cobbler, 274
chia seeds/meal, 12
chickpeas
Chickpea and Kohlrabi Salad Wraps, 93–94
Collard Wraps with Chickpea-Avocado Mash, Roasted Carrots, and Spicy Cranberry Relish, 104–6
Healing Squash and Chickpea Soup, 139–40
Late Summer/Early Fall Bowl, 65
Lemony Teff Polenta with Tahini, Leeks, and Chickpeas, 75–77
A Soup of Odds and Ends, 146
Steamed Chioggia Beet and Pear Salad, 80
Sweet Potato, Millet, and Black Bean Veggie Burgers with Kale Slaw, 230–32
chili sauces, 11
chimichurri
Carrot Top Chimichurri, 315
Spaghetti Squash Noodles with Eggplant-Lentil Meatballs, 192–94
chipotle
Chipotle Cream, 301
Naked Taco Bowl, 62
White Bean and Sweet Potato Dumplings, 201–4
chocolate
Chocolate and Orange Bundt Cake, 293
Sweet Potato Chocolate Brownies, 287
citrus juicers, 17
cloves in Watermelon Rind Marmalade, 58
coconut milk
Buckwheat Risotto with Roasted Beets, 158
Cauliflower Riceless Risotto with Spinach and Corn, 157
Chilled Thai Coconut Soup with Zucchini and Carrot Noodles, 120–22
Coconut Black Rice and Edamame Veggie Burger, 218–20
Couscous-Stuffed Collard Greens in Coconut Curry Sauce, 107–9
Creamy Coconut Lentils with Broccoli, 119
Curried Bean and Brussels Sprout Stew with Roasted Kabocha Squash, 133–34
Key Lime Pie, 271–73
Rutabega and Brussels Sprout Riceless Risotto, 165–67
Tropical Cru, 61
coconut oil, unrefined extra-virgin, 10
coconut sugar, 13
coffee grinder, 16
collard greens
Chickpea and Kohlrabi Salad Wraps, 93–94
Collard Wraps with Chickpea-Avocado Mash, Roasted Carrots, and Spicy Cranberry Relish, 104–6
Couscous-Stuffed Collard Greens in Coconut Curry Sauce, 107–9
Lentil Tomato Stew with Turnips and Collard Greens, 130
Roasted Yam and Collard Green Enchiladas, 101–3
corn
Cauliflower Riceless Risotto with Spinach and Corn, 157
corn grits, 9
Naked Taco Bowl, 62
Polenta Crust Pizza with Romesco and Tomatoes, 188
Summer Bowl, 59
Summer Corn and Greens Fritters, 223–24
Tropical Cru, 61
cranberries
Collard Wraps with Chickpea-Avocado Mash, Roasted Carrots, and Spicy Cranberry Relish, 106
Cranberry Pear Crumble Bars, 283–84
cucumbers
Chickpea and Kohlrabi Salad Wraps, 93–94
Cucumber Noodles with Melon Spheres and Herb Vinaigrette, 187
Peach and Tomato Panzanella, 55
Roasted Portobello and Eggplant Gyros, 96–97
Smooth Vegetable Gazpacho with Watermelon Chunks, 123
Strawberry, Spinach, and Edamame Salad, 49
Summer Bowl, 59

Tropical Cru, 61
curry powder
Couscous-Stuffed Collard Greens in Coconut Curry Sauce, 107–9
Curried Bean and Brussels Sprout Stew with Roasted Kabocha Squash, 133–34

dates
Chocolate and Orange Bundt Cake, 293
as pantry item, 13
Raw Peach Crumble, 276
Sweet Potato Caramel Pecan Pie, 288–89
dill
Borscht, 141–42
Chickpea and Kohlrabi Salad Wraps, 93–94
Mildly Pickled Spring Vegetables, 244–45
Roasted Portobello and Eggplant Gyros, 96–97
Simple Lemon-Marinated Beans or Lentils, 297
Spring Panzanella with Radishes and Peas, 46
Steamed and Marinated Beets and Celery Root, 257
dressing, salad. *See* vinaigrettes

edamame (soy)
Coconut Black Rice and Edamame Veggie Burger, 218–20
Strawberry, Spinach, and Edamame Salad, 49
eggplants
Late Summer/Early Fall Bowl, 65
Marinated Eggplant, 248
Roasted Eggplant and Bell Pepper Pizza with Gluten-Free Sweet Potato Crust, 199–200
Roasted Portobello and Eggplant Gyros, 96–97
Spaghetti Squash Noodles with Eggplant-Lentil Meatballs, 192–94
Summer Paella, 161
Tomato and Eggplant Green Mung Dal, 125–26
eggs, pastured, 15
equipment needs, 15–17

farro
Bukhara Farro Pilaf, 175–76
Late Summer/Early Fall Bowl, 65
as pantry item, 8
fats, 10
fava beans
Broccoli Stem Riceless Risotto, 155–56
Spring Vegetable Black Rice Pilaf, 152
fennel
Heirloom Beans, Fennel, and Citrus Salad, 78
Leek, Fennel, and Chard Pizza with Gluten-Free Onion Crust, 213–14
Summer Paella, 161
Tipsy Watermelon, Fennel, and Arugula Salad, 56
fiddleheads
Broccoli Stem Riceless Risotto, 155–56
Spring Vegetable Black Rice Pilaf, 152
figs
Early Fall Soba Noodles with Broiled Figs, Kabocha Squash, and Kale, 191
Fig and Grape Oven Pancake, 35
flours, 14
food processor/blender, 15
forbidden black rice. *See* rice, forbidden black
freekeh
as pantry item, 8
Summer Bowl, 59

galette dough, 281
garlic, 7
ghee, 10
ginger, 7
goat's milk cheese, 15
grains, 8–9
grapefruit
Heirloom Bean, Fennel, and Citrus Salad, 78
Silky Barley Water with Ginger and Citrus, 112
grapes
Concord, about, 34
Fig and Grape Oven Pancake, 35
Rosemary Concord Grape Compote, 34
Warm Salad of Roasted Cauliflower, Grapes, and Forbidden Black Rice, 66
green beans
Blistered Tomato and Green Bean Fettuccine in Smoky Sauce, 185
Summer Bowl, 59
Summer Paella, 161

hemp hearts in Superfood Summer Porridge, 30
honey
Honey-Miso Delicata Squash, 252
as pantry item, 13
Superfood Summer Porridge, 30
hummus, black bean, 99

jalapeño
Grilled Pineapple and Avocado Salad, 51
Smoky Cauliflower and Black Bean Hummus Burritos, 99–100

jalapeño (*continued*)
- Strawberry, Spinach, and Edamame Salad, 49

jicama, in Tropical Cru, 61

kaffir lime leaves
- Chilled Thai Coconut Soup with Zucchini and Carrot Noodles, 120–22
- Coconut Black Rice and Edamame Veggie Burger, 218–20
- as pantry item, 13

kale
- Daikon Radish Pad Thai, 206
- Early Fall Soba Noodles with Broiled Figs, Kabocha Squash, and Kale, 191
- Healing Squash and Chickpea Soup, 139–40
- Kale Slaw, 232
- Late Summer/Early Fall Bowl, 65
- Mung Bean and Barley Veggie Burgers, 239
- Red Rice and Lacinato Kale Risotto, 162–64
- Summer Corn and Greens Fritters, 223–24
- Sweet Potato, Millet, and Black Bean Veggie Burgers with Kale Slaw, 230–32

kohlrabi in Chickpea and Kohlrabi Salad Wraps, 93–94

kombu
- Healing Squash and Chickpea Soup, 139–40
- as pantry item, 12
- Spaghetti Squash Ramen with Marinated Tempeh, 127–28
- when cooking beans, 296

kombucha in Tipsy Watermelon, Fennel, and Arugula Salad, 56

kumquats
- Barley and Chia Seed Porridge with Candied Kumquats, 39
- substitutes for, 39

leeks
- Asparagus and Leek Pancakes, 25
- Leek, Fennel, and Chard Pizza with Gluten-Free Onion Crust, 213–14
- Leek and Mushroom Barley Risotto, 168–70
- Lemony Teff Polenta with Tahini, Leeks, and Chickpeas, 75–77
- Spring Vegetable Black Rice Pilaf, 152

lemongrass
- Chilled Thai Coconut Soup with Zucchini and Carrot Noodles, 120–22
- Healing Squash and Chickpea Soup, 139–40
- as pantry item, 13

lemons
- Healing Squash and Chickpea Soup, 139–40
- Lemony Teff Polenta with Tahini, Leeks, and Chickpeas, 75–77
- Meyer Lemon Pots de Crème, 290
- as pantry items, 7
- Simple Lemon-Marinated Beans or Lentils, 297

lentils
- Beet and Zucchini Veggie Burgers, 226
- Creamy Coconut Lentils with Broccoli, 119
- Late Autumn/Winter Bowl, 73–74
- Lentil, Pomegranate, and Brussels Sprout Salad, 70
- Lentil Tomato Stew with Turnips and Collard Greens, 130
- as pantry item, 9
- Simple Lemon-Marinated Beans or Lentils, 297
- Spaghetti Squash Noodles with Eggplant-Lentil Meatballs, 192–94
- Spring Cabbage Rolls with Mushrooms, Lentils, Rice, and Tomato Sauce, 91–92
- Tomato and Eggplant Green Mung Dal, 125–26

limes
- Key Lime Pie, 271–73
- Mango Cashew Cream Pudding with Vanilla and Lime, 267
- as pantry items, 7

mangoes
- Mango Cashew Cream Pudding with Vanilla and Lime, 267
- Tropical Cru, 61

maple syrup, 13

melons in Cucumber Noodles with Melon Spheres and Herb Vinaigrette, 187

mesh strainers, 16

microplane zesters, 17

milk bags, nylon or cotton, 17

millet
- Coriander Millet Porridge with Rosemary Concord Grape Compote, 33–34
- Millet Polenta with Spring Vegetables and Greens, 52–53
- as pantry item, 9
- Sweet Potato, Millet, and Black Bean Veggie Burgers with Kale Slaw, 230–32

miso
- Apple-Miso Mayo, 300

Celery Root Miso Soup, 136
Honey-Miso Delicata Squash, 252
as pantry item, 11
Tahini Miso Sauce, 304
mortars and pestles, 16
mung beans
cooking, 239
Kitchari Winter Stew, 145
Mung Bean and Barley Veggie Burgers, 239
Tomato and Eggplant Green Mung Dal, 125–26
mushrooms
Chilled Thai Coconut Soup with Zucchini and Carrot Noodles, 120–22
as pantry item, 13
Late Autumn/Winter Bowl, 73–74
Leek and Mushroom Barley Risotto, 168–70
Mung Bean and Barley Veggie Burgers, 239
Mushroom and Parsnip Fritters, 233
Portobello Bolognese Pasta, 209
Roasted Portobello and Eggplant Gyros, 96–97
Spaghetti Squash Ramen with Marinated Tempeh, 127–28
Spring Cabbage Rolls with Mushrooms, Lentils, Rice, and Tomato Sauce, 91–92
mustard, 11

nettles in Broccoli Stem Riceless Risotto, 155–56
nori
as pantry item, 12
Pickled Turnip, Avocado, Barley, and Black Rice Sushi Rolls, 110–12
nuts, nut butters, 12

oats, oatmeal
Cherry Skillet Cobbler, 274
Cranberry Pear Crumble Bars, 283–84
Creamy Steel Cut Oats with Rainbow Chard and Pine Nuts, 40
as pantry item, 8–9, 14
Superfood Summer Porridge, 30
olive oil, extra-virgin, 10
olives
Chickpea and Kohlrabi Salad Wraps, 93–94
Golden Beet and Pomelo Winter Panzanella, 83
Marinated Roasted Bell Pepper Kamut Spiral Pasta, 195–97
Summer Bowl, 59
onions, 7
oranges
Chocolate and Orange Bundt Cake, 293
Heirloom Beans, Fennel, and Citrus Salad, 78

pantry items, basic, listing of, 7–11
panzanellas. *See* bread
papaya, in Tropical Cru, 61
paprika, 8
parsley in Carrot Top Chimichurri, 315
parsnips
Mushroom and Parsnip Fritters, 233
Roasted Parsnips and Pears with Za'atar, 254
peaches
Peach and Tomato Panzanella, 55
Raw Peach Crumble, 276
Teff and Apple Pancakes, 36
pears
Cranberry Pear Crumble Bars, 283–84
Roasted Parsnips and Pears with Za'atar, 254
Steamed Chioggia Beet and Pear Salad, 80
peas
Broccoli Stem Riceless Risotto, 155–56
Chickpea and Kohlrabi Salad Wraps, 93–94
Coconut Black Rice and Edamame Veggie Burgers, 218
Mildly Pickled Spring Vegetables, 244–45
Millet Polenta with Spring Vegetables and Greens, 52–53
Spring Bowl, 44
Spring Panzanella with Radishes and Peas, 46
Spring Vegetable Black Rice Pilaf, 152
Spring Vegetable Chowder, 116
Summer Rolls with Savory Cabbage and Sugar Snaps, 88
pepper grinder, 16
peppers, bell
Beet Sauté, 251
Borscht, 141–42
Marinated Roasted Bell Pepper Kamut Spiral Pasta, 195–97
Marinated Tomatoes, 247
Summer Paella, 161
Roasted Eggplant and Bell Pepper Pizza with Gluten-Free Sweet Potato Crust, 199–200
Romesco, 307
persimmon in Squash and Pomegranate Panzanella with Autumn Herbs, 69

pineapples
Grilled Pineapple and Avocado Salsa, 51
Pineapple Tart, 264
pistachios
Asparagus Fries, 242
Coconut Black Rice and Edamame Veggie Burger, 218
Superfood Summer Porridge, 30
Squash, and Kale, 191
plums
Teff and Apple Pancakes, 36
Upside-Down Plum Cake with Autumn Herbs, 278
pomegranates
Lentil, Pomegranate, and Brussels Sprout Salad, 70
Rutabega and Brussels Sprout Riceless Risotto, 165–67
Squash and Pomegranate Panzanella with Autumn Herbs, 69
pomelo in Golden Beet and Pomelo Winter Panzanella, 83
potatoes
Borscht, 141–42
Kitchari Winter Stew, 145
Oven-Baked Potato Latkes, 236
Spring Vegetable Chowder, 116
prunes in Portobello Bolognese Pasta, 209
pumpkin in Bukhara Farro Pilaf, 175–76

quinoa
as pantry item, 9, 14
Late Autumn/Winter Bowl, 73–74

radishes
Daikon Radish Pad Thai, 206
Mildly Pickled Spring Vegetables, 244–45
Roasted Radish Flatbread, 182–84
Spring Bowl, 44
Spring Panzanella with Radishes and Peas, 46
raisins
Bukhara Farro Pilaf, 175–76
Steamed Chioggia Beet and Pear Salad, 80
Superfood Summer Porridge, 30
ramps
Broccoli Stem Riceless Risotto, 155–56
Spring Vegetable Black Rice Pilaf, 152
red wine vinegar, 11
rhubarb
Stewed Rhubarb Amaranth Porridge, 22
Strawberry and Rhubarb Oven Pancake, 26
rice
Arborio, 8, 161, 171–72
brown rice flour, 14
brown rice vinegar, 10
Coconut Black Rice and Edamame Veggie Burger, 218–20
Curried Bean and Brussels Sprout Stew with Roasted Kabocha Squash, 133–34
forbidden black, 8, 66, 110, 152, 218
Kitchari Winter Stew, 145
as pantry item, 8
Pickled Turnip, Avocado, Barley, and Black Rice Sushi Rolls, 110–12
Red Rice and Lacinato Kale Risotto, 162–64
Spring Cabbage Rolls with Mushrooms, Lentils, Rice, and Tomato Sauce, 91–92
Spring Vegetable Black Rice Pilaf, 152
Warm Salad of Roasted Cauliflower, Grapes, and Forbidden Black Rice, 66
rosemary
Rosemary Concord Grape Compote, 34
Squash and Pomegranate Panzanella with Autumn Herbs, 69
Sweet Potato, Millet, and Black Bean Veggie Burgers with Kale Slaw, 230–32
Upside-Down Plum Cake with Autumn Herbs, 278
rutabaga in Rutabaga and Brussels Sprout Riceless Risotto, 165–67

saffron, in Bukhara Farro Pilaf, 175–76
sage
Early Fall Soba Noodles with Broiled Figs, Kabocha Squash, and Kale, 191
Squash and Pomegranate Panzanella with Autumn Herbs, 69
Upside-Down Plum Cake with Autumn Herbs, 278
sangria in Tipsy Watermelon, Fennel, and Arugula Salad, 56
sea salt, 11
seasonal cooking, 3, 5–6
seasonings, basic, listing of, 11
sea vegetables, 12
seeds, seed butters
making milk from, 298
as pantry items, 12
sesame oil, toasted, 10
sheep's milk cheese, unpasteurized, 15
shiitake mushrooms, dried. *See* mushrooms

soda bread, 310
spaghetti squash. *See* squash, spaghetti
spelt, sprouted or whole
- Asparagus and Leek Pancakes, 25
- Basic Sprouted or Whole Spelt Eggless Pasta, 180
- Cranberry Pear Crumble Bars, 283–84
- as pantry item, 14
- Multigrain Spiced Bread Loaf,
- Pineapple Tart, 264
- Roasted Radish Flatbread, 182–84
- Spelt Fettuccine with Melted Rainbow Chard, 210
- Sprouted or Whole Spelt Tortillas, 87
- Strawberry and Rhubarb Oven Pancake, 26
- Upside-Down Plum Cake with Autumn Herbs, 278
- White Bean and Sweet Potato Dumplings, 201–4

spice grinders, 16
spices, 7–8
spinach
- Cauliflower Riceless Risotto with Spinach and Corn, 157
- Marinated Roasted Bell Pepper Kamut Spiral Pasta, 195–97
- Spring Vegetable Black Rice Pilaf, 152
- Spring Vegetable Chowder, 116
- Strawberry, Spinach, and Edamame Salad, 49
- White Bean and Sweet Potato Dumplings, 201–4

squash, spaghetti
- Spaghetti Squash Noodles with Eggplant-Lentil Meatballs, 192–94
- Spaghetti Squash Ramen with Marinated Tempeh, 127–28

squash, winter
- Curried Bean and Brussels Sprout Stew with Roasted Kabocha Squash, 133–34
- Early Fall Soba Noodles with Broiled Figs, Kabocha Squash, and Kale, 191
- Healing Squash and Chickpea Soup, 139–40
- Honey-Miso Delicata Squash, 252
- Late Autumn/Winter Bowl, 73–74
- Lentil, Pomegranate, and Brussels Sprout Salad, 70

Squash and Pomegranate Panzanella with Autumn Herbs, 69
Sriracha sauce, 11
staples, basic, listing of, 11
stews
- Creamy Coconut Lentils with Broccoli, 119
- Curried Bean and Brussels Sprout Stew with Roasted Kabocha Squash, 133–34
- Kitchari Winter Stew, 145
- Lentil Tomato Stew with Turnips and Collard Greens, 130

stoves/ovens, gas vs. electric, 17
strawberries
- Stewed Rhubarb Amaranth Porridge, 22
- Strawberry, Spinach, and Edamame Salad, 49
- Strawberry and Rhubarb Oven Pancake, 26

sweeteners, 13
sweet potatoes
- Late Autumn/Winter Bowl, 73–74
- Naked Taco Bowl, 62
- Roasted Eggplant and Bell Pepper Pizza with Gluten-Free Sweet Potato Crust, 199–200
- Roasted Root Vegetable Oven Risotto, 171–72
- Roasted Yam and Collard Green Enchiladas, 101–3
- Sweet Potato, Millet, and Black Bean Veggie Burgers with Kale Slaw, 230–32
- Sweet Potato Caramel Pecan Pie, 288–89
- Sweet Potato Chocolate Brownies, 287
- White Bean and Sweet Potato Dumplings, 201–4

tahini
- Beet Tahini Sauce, 304
- Cilantro Tahini Sauce, 303
- as pantry item, 11
- Lemony Teff Polenta with Tahini, Leeks, and Chickpeas, 75–77
- Sweet Potato Caramel Pecan Pie, 288–89
- Tahini Miso Sauce, 304
- Tahini Sauces, 303
- Turmeric Tahini Sauce, 303
- Warm Salad of Roasted Cauliflower, Grapes, and Forbidden Black Rice, 66

tamari, 11
tamarind paste in Daikon Radish Pad Thai, 206
tapioca, 14

teff flour
Lemony Teff Polenta with Tahini, Leeks, and Chickpeas, 75–77
as pantry item, 9
Teff and Apple Pancakes, 36
tomatoes
Blistered Tomato and Green Bean Fettuccine in Smoky Sauce, 185
Borscht, 141–42
Late Summer/Early Fall Bowl, 62
Lentil Tomato Stew with Turnips and Collard Greens, 130
Marinated Tomatoes, 247
Naked Taco Bowl, 62
on panzanellas, 46
Peach and Tomato Panzanella, 55
Polenta Crust Pizza with Romesco and Tomatoes, 188
Portobello Bolognese Pasta, 209
Roasted Portobello and Eggplant Gyros, 96–97
Roasted Yam and Collard Green Enchiladas, 101–3
Smoky Sun-Dried Tomato Cream, 302
Smooth Vegetable Gazpacho with Watermelon Chunks, 123
Spring Cabbage Rolls with Mushrooms, Lentils, Rice, and Tomato Sauce, 91–92
Summer Bowl, 59
Summer Paella, 161
Tomato and Eggplant Green Mung Dal, 125–26
Universal Tomato Sauce, 308
tortillas, homemade, 87
turmeric
Bukhara and Farro Pilaf, 175–76
Coriander Millet Porridge with Rosemary Concord Grape Compote, 33–34
Kitchari Winter Stew, 145
Healing Squash and Chickpea Soup, 139–40
Tomato and Eggplant Green Mung Dal, 125–26
Turmeric Tahini Sauce, 303
turnips
Chickpea and Kohlrabi Salad Wraps, 93–94
Lentil Tomato Stew with Turnips and Collard Greens, 130
Pickled Turnip, Avocado, Barley, and Black Rice Sushi Rolls, 110–12
Pickled Turnips, 258
A Soup of Odds and Ends, 146
tzatziki sauce, 96

vanilla
Mango Cashew Cream Pudding with Vanilla and Lime, 267
Stewed Rhubarb Amaranth Porridge, 22
vegetable peelers, 17
vegetable scraps
Odds and Ends Vegetable Broth, 313
A Soup of Odds and Ends, 146
vinaigrettes, 46, 55, 69, 187
vinegar, types of, 10–11

wakame, 12
watermelon
Cucumber Noodles with Melon Spheres and Herb Vinaigrette, 187
Smooth Vegetable Gazpacho with Watermelon Chunks, 123
Tipsy Watermelon, Fennel, and Arugula Salad, 56
Watermelon Rind Marmalade, 58

yams. *See* sweet potatoes

za'atar spice blend
about, 254
Roasted Parsnips and Pears with Za'atar, 254
Roasted Portobello and Eggplant Gyros, 96–97
zucchini
Beet and Zucchini Veggie Burgers, 226
Blueberry Buckwheat Pancakes, 29
Chilled Thai Coconut Soup with Zucchini and Carrot Noodles, 120–22
Zucchini Fritters, 221